The Contemporary Circus

Art of the Spectacular

Ernest Albrecht

THE SCARECROW PRESS, INC.
Lanham, Maryland • Toronto • Plymouth, UK
2006

SCARECROW PRESS, INC.

Published in the United States of America
by Scarecrow Press, Inc.
A wholly owned subsidary of
The Rowman & Littlefield Publishing Group, Inc.
4501 Forbes Boulevard, Suite 200, Lanham, Maryland 20706
www.scarecrowpress.com

Estover Road
Plymouth PL6 7PY
United Kingdom

British Library Cataloguing in Publication Information Available

Library of Congress Cataloging-in-Publication Data

Albrecht, Ernest J., 1937–
    The contemporary circus : art of the spectacular / Ernest Albrecht.
        p. cm.
    Includes bibliographical references and index.
    ISBN-13: 978-0-8108-5734-6 (pbk. : alk. paper)
    ISBN-10: 0-8108-5734-0 (pbk. : alk. paper)
    1. Circus. I. Title.
GV1801.A43 2006
791.3—dc22   2006020841

∞™ The paper used in this publication meets the minimum requirements of
American National Standard for Information Sciences—Permanence of Paper
for Printed Library Materials, ANSI/NISO Z39.48-1992.
Manufactured in the United States of America.

For Christopher, Eric, Lily, and Olivia

Contents

Acknowledgments

$\mathcal{A}$ work of this kind would have made no sense and could not have been completed without the unstinting cooperation of the many circus artists who graciously and generously gave of their time to talk with me at length, often on several occasions, to explain their artistic visions, their working habits, and their creative process—all of which were such vital and inspiring parts of their work as artists of the circus. I am filled with gratitude for the kindness and friendship many of these people, whose names are listed at the end of the bibliography, have bestowed on me.

I would not, however, have come to appreciate the artistry that goes into creating any circus had it not been for the friendship of Miles White, who was the costume designer for the Ringling Bros. and Barnum & Bailey Circus for more than a dozen years. His enthusiasm for sharing with me the treasures of his design sketches first started me on the road that led to writing this book.

My approach to many of the people whose words are recorded herein was through the press agents and public relations directors of the various circuses for whom they worked. I would particularly like to thank Phil Thurston and Joel Dein of the Big Apple Circus, who afforded me unfettered access to the people who were the creative forces behind this unique and exciting example of the New American Circus, which, incidentally, happens to be the title of the book that was the precursor to this study.

Since this study has covered the span of eight years, I have dealt with several people associated with Ringling Bros. and Barnum & Bailey, principally Barbara Pflughaupt and her associate, Jeff Lovari, who always managed to take my requests for interviews, get them approved, and make them happen, often with the assistance of Rodney Huey. More recently I have had the pleasure of working with Darin Johnson.

Of course, many of these interviews required the approval and cooperation of the people who ran these organizations, namely Kenneth Feld of Feld Entertainment and Paul Binder and Michael Christensen of the Big Apple Circus, all of whom also submitted to lengthy and numerous interviews with the same grace and openness as the other artists of their organizations.

My associations with Cirque du Soleil have similarly been long, fruitful, and rewarding. My thanks here go to Mario D'Amico, vice president of marketing, and the many members of the Cirque staff, including Brigitte Belanger, Chantal Cote, Nedjma Belbahri, and Marianne Dodelet. In the very beginning of this project it was Jean David who provided extraordinary access to many of the artists of Cirque du Soleil. And near the end of the process, Ann Paladie reviewed the portion of the text relative to Cirque and ensured its accuracy and timeliness.

I am especially indebted to Maike Schulz and Paul Gutheil for their photographic contributions not only to this project but to *Spectacle* magazine, whose examination of the art of circus has run parallel to this study. Their images have always made the artistry of the circus come alive long after the performances ended. I would also like to thank Robert Sugarman, Stewart McGill, and Timothy Jecko, who contributed articles to the magazine that they allowed me to use again here.

This work was much facilitated by the sabbatical leave I was granted by Middlesex County College during my tenure there, and the library staff of the college never flinched from providing me hard copies of sources I had discovered.

During the lengthy process during which this work came into being, I was fortunate to have the support and encouragement of my good friends Hovey Burgess and Dominque Jando, whose brains I picked quite shamelessly at times.

My colleague at Middlesex County College, Albert Nicolai, provided the final reading before the text was handed over to Renée Camus of Scarecrow Press, and I am grateful to both for their enthusiasm and insights, and their dedication to making this project a reality.

Finally I would like to thank my family—my wife, Pearl, and my sons, Christopher and Eric—for tolerating the fanaticism that is so much a part of being a circus fan, for that is, after all, what drove this project through the years. I have enjoyed every minute of the adventure, and I hope they and you, my readers, will enjoy the end result as much.

Introduction

The Circus as an Art Form

$\mathcal{I}$n 1974 Alexis Gruss and his *Cirque National à l'ancienne* reintroduced western audiences to the sanctity of the single ring and the possibilities of the circus as an art form. This is the circus that inspired both Paul Binder of the Big Apple Circus and Guy Caron of Cirque du Soleil, and it was the first to feature many of the elements that came to be the hallmarks of the contemporary circus.

The Grusses' annual productions are still performed by no more than twelve people, nine of whom are members of Alexis's immediate family. Everyone pitches in wherever needed, whether making crepes in the reception tent before the performance, ushering, or moving props. Yet there is never the sense of anyone having to rush from one chore to the next or having arrived at his moment in the spotlight even slightly winded. Here is the ensemble work that has come to be one of the hallmarks of the contemporary circus, presented in a style that is both joyous and graceful, suggesting in its supreme effortlessness that circus is a natural extension of mankind's love of challenge taken to the level of art.

The Gruss circus also invokes and honors the equestrian spirit of the originators of the art form that came to be known as *circus*, and Alexis Gruss is himself nothing less than its high priest, imperviously serene, elegant, and in control, reacting to his horses as if they were precocious children.

The other eye-opening aspect of the Gruss performance is its ten-piece orchestra. What is so remarkable about it, apart from the sound they are able to produce, is the degree to which the orchestra and music are integrated into the overall performance. Each of the male members of the family joins the orchestra at various times during the performance on an assortment of instruments, and their accomplishments here are every bit as virtuosic as their exploits in the sawdust ring. Very often the musical interludes provide the transition from one ring display to another.

The family's women are hardly relegated to supporting roles. Gipsy, Alexis's wife, and their daughter, Maude, sometimes perform a novel tightwire act. Nathalie, Stéphan's wife, is a foot juggler, and all are expert horsewomen. Maude has presented the St. Petersburg Courier act handling no fewer than seventeen horses.

In addition to all the artistry seen in the various displays of skill, the physical trappings of the performance are extraordinarily tasteful, stylish, and elegant. Nary a sequin or spangle is to be seen on any costumes, which depend instead on fabric, drape, and detailing for their effect. Even the color palate is restrained, oftentimes echoing the colors of the horses.

No wonder Binder and Caron were so in awe of what they saw under the Gruss big top. There was nothing like it in the world of circus before 1974, and, one is tempted to say, it is still without peer despite recent equestrian-based productions like Althoff's Zauberwald in Germany, Theatre Cheval and Cavalia (both out of Canada), the UK's Equestrian Theatre, and France's Zingaro, all of which feature a wide variety of horsemanship in their productions.

Of these more recent equestrian extravaganzas, Zingaro produces the strongest evocation of the circus's equestrian heritage. Both of its productions to visit America and the communal, almost monastic existence of the troupe reminded noted circus historian Hovey Burgess of nothing less than his imagined view of the early equestrian circuses of Astley and Franconi.[1]

In America, the Big Apple Circus has managed to honor its original inspiration thanks to the equestrian base provided for many seasons by Binder's wife, Katja Schumann. Cirque du Soleil, founded in 1984, seven years after the Big Apple Circus, expanded the horizons of the contemporary circus by abandoning the circus's historic use of animal performers and making its human ensemble the centerpiece of its productions, with astonishingly brilliant acts of a size and complexity that were vanishing everywhere else. It further opened the new circus movement to hitherto unexplored possibilities with its determination to bring all the theatrical arts to bear on the creation of its performances. Under the guidance of its first director, Franco Dragone, and its artistic director Guy Caron, often in collaboration with Gilles Ste-Croix, Cirque du Soleil also brought the contemporary circus something else that was new: an intellectual component, with its heavily atmospheric, often surrealistic, imagistic performances.

The company's two greatest achievements to date have been its touring production, *Quidam*, and its resident, spectacular water-circus, *O*, both of which are thrilling examples of its sorties into the subterranean world of the subconscious and surreal. The world of *Quidam* is the darker of the two, and its characters are more detached from one another than they have been in any of the company's previous work. And yet, while the trappings of the physical production provided by Michel Crête and the costumes of Dominique Lemieux are quite striking, nothing provokes the imagination quite as thrillingly as the company acts that have been created specifically for each of these extraordinary journeys.

Looking back to the company's origins in the streets, for instance, *Quidam* raises the schoolyard game of jumping rope to the level of spectacle by continually compounding the difficulty, adding more and more ropes and an ever-increasing number of jumpers. Few circus companies in the world can present acts that are as big, complex, and beautifully put together as those seen in *Quidam*. The most thrilling of these is based on an ancient form of Italian acrobatics known as *banquine*, in which no fewer than fifteen acrobats demonstrate the flexibility of the human body in a gorgeously choreographed display that is literally breathtaking, not only for the amazing physical prowess of the performers (one tower rises to four high, the top mounter being propelled aloft without the aid of trampoline or teeterboard) but also for the beauty with which it is all accomplished. Here is a display worthy of any stage in any theatre in the world. It is equal parts brilliant dance and stunning acrobatics, enhanced by the lighting, the costumes, and perhaps most importantly the musical score. It should also be noted that in *Quidam*, the level and amount of dance incorporated into the performance have risen appreciably. Much of it is classically based and performed by exquisite dancers.

Because of the ambiguity of the imagery found in the productions of Cirque du Soleil, they have often been called obscure and impenetrable. In contrast there is certainly nothing ambiguous about the messages or the level of audience involvement engendered by another novel approach to circus witnessed in the performances of the African-American UniverSoul Circus.

There can be no more powerful example of what has been called "participatory celebration" than the electric excitement created by this audience, whipped up to a near frenzy by the ringmaster, Casual Cal Dupree. The audience cheers; they sing; they dance in the aisles; they shout, whistle, clap their hands, and stamp their feet. They are indisputably an essential and intrinsic part of the experience.

Dupree, part cheerleader, part revivalist, and part entertainer, is the show's main attraction. He guides the audience through the evening like a preacher shepherding his flock to salvation. He uses each of the acts as a parable to expound upon such issues as being a good father, being an obedient and respectful son or daughter, self-discipline, charity, cultural awareness, striving for excellence, and spiritual uplift in riffs that approach the operatic.

When the audience reacts with its cheers, Dupree exhorts them to further bursts of enthusiasm: "It's all right," he assures his wildly stimulated audience. "Have a good time." Do they ever!

But that is what the UniverSoul Circus is all about: prying its audience loose from its uptight inhibitions, its negative attitudes, and its failure to appreciate the beauty and wonder of its own accomplishments—thereby proving that there can be more to a circus than tricks.

In a very different venue, the three-ring arena, Ringling Bros. and Barnum & Bailey Circus has managed to walk a very delicate line, balancing the traditional with the contemporary. But that is not to say its creative people are uninterested in the one-ring format and other elements of the contemporary circus, as both its current Hometown Edition (or Gold Unit) and *Barnum's Kaleidoscape*, its first excursion into that genre, lavishly illustrate.

But the Ringling organization has also acquired a contemporary look and feel in its three-ring circuses. These represent an ongoing effort to make the arena circus more theatrical. Rather than following the lead of Cirque du Soleil into abstract symbolism, Ringling's creative staff has embraced a style of showmanship that has opted for an in-your-face, all-stops-out style of showmanship rivaling that of Broadway. Ringling Bros. and Barnum & Bailey's 133rd edition of The Greatest Show on Earth was so loaded with eye candy, so crammed full of high-energy excitement, that the circus, more than ever, became a nonstop feast of sensory stimulation.

A year later, the 134th edition took another step toward becoming its own form of musical theatre thanks to the addition of a female vocalist and an original score that was as melodic and jazzy as any Broadway show, its production numbers fully replacing the pageants that used to be called "spec." There is a subtle but important difference between the two forms, spec and production. The former relies on pageantry, floats, and a lavish array of gorgeously costumed characters. Production numbers, on the other hand, integrate all the theatrical elements and eliminate both the pageantry and the floats in favor of music, dance, scenic, and special effects. The pattern of movement is no longer confined to the inevitable counterclockwise march around the hippodrome. There is activity everywhere all the time, including the air as well as the track, often going in several directions at once, usually in counterpoint to the attractions that are simultaneously working in the rings.

While all of the contemporary circuses avidly acknowledge the effectiveness of combining circus with the theatrical arts, some have attempted to embrace the dramatic arts, incorporating narration into their productions. Circus Flora has managed to do this through several noteworthy productions, none more effectively than in its farewell to Flora, the elephant that gave the circus its name.

The show's narration of events, Circus Flora's unique feature, not only gave each act a context and a conclusion but always seemed more than welcome, given the charm of the story and the deftness of the tone and manner in which it was told by Cecil MacKinnon as YoYo the clown, mistress of ceremonies and revealer of the circus's inner mysteries. The acts were so nicely woven into the plot that it all moved along with a logic that seemed close to being inevitable.

If one were looking for a textbook example of how the circus and the dramatic arts can be successfully married, the search need go no further than the Midnight Circus and its production *All the World's a Stage*, in which no less a personage than old Will Shakespeare himself presided over the marriage.

All the World's a Stage was a brilliant conception that imagined what would happen if the Bard of Avon were suddenly to find himself surrounded by a circus. That such a meeting seemed perfectly logical was only the first of several *coups de theatre* that this amazingly deft production was able to pull off. Shakespeare appeared in the midst of a magician's classic transformation act, the one in which the magician stands on top of a trunk and a curtain is raised around him. When it is dropped, he has been transformed into a beautiful showgirl or a tiger. In this instance, it was Shakespeare who appeared in place of the magician, uninvited, unexpected, and decidedly unamused.

Thus began the real transformation, turning Shakespeare from a skeptic who looked at the circus about him rather suspiciously and asked, "Where are the words?" to a believer more than ready to take part in a charivari that ends the show on a level of triumph and celebration that could only be achieved when the audience has been made to identify with the characters to such a degree that they can participate fully in their victory.

So here is a theatrical circus that has all the best elements of drama: conflict, character development, and an exciting denouement, as well as the clowns, acrobats, and aerialists of the circus.

Another significant characteristic of the contemporary circus is its dependence on clowning to knit its productions into a unified whole, as we have seen with the Big Apple's Grandma, Ringling's Bello and David Larible, and Flora's Yo-Yo. Circus Oz, from Australia, takes that concept to its ultimate conclusion by turning everyone into a clown. Like many other new circuses, Circus Oz is certainly a show with an attitude, but happily that attitude is one of wild irreverence. Almost every act in its offerings has a satiric edge.

While everyone in the show has a specialty, all of them, including the three members of the band and even the rigger, take part in various ensemble pieces. That kind of interaction and their versatility have turned Circus Oz into an example of that much desired but seldom seen paragon, a true ensemble, found first in the Gruss family circus.

★ ★ ★

While the individual circuses of the contemporary circus movement share many of the characteristics already enumerated—the single ring, an equestrian foundation, a commitment to the theatrical and dramatic arts, the use of music, highlighting the preeminence of women, and the integration of the related performing arts like dance and acting as a means of enhancing the work of its performing artists and thereby achieving a greater degree of audience involvement—each is a unique combination of these elements, as personal as the work of the men and women who have collaborated to raise the circus to a level of artistic achievement equivalent to that of any of the performing arts, and whose work is as provocative and as stimulating as any of their fellow artists.

In order to appreciate this artistry fully, keep in mind the following divisions in this book. Part One highlights the various creative artists engaged in producing the contemporary circus and their approach to the collaborative effort that characterizes the contemporary circus. Part Two provides examples of how this collaboration has worked in specific instances and the dynamics that have shaped this collaboration in four distinct creations. The final part, Three, deals with the individual performing artists, describing how they have arrived at their own individual aesthetics, concluding with the training and nurturing of the artists of the future.

NOTE

1. Hovey Burgess. "Zingaro Gives a New Meaning to the Term 'Horse Opera.'" *Spectacle* (Winter 1998): 31.

I

THE CREATIVE TEAM

• 1 •

The Director and the Creative Process

$\mathcal{A}$s circus performances became more and more theatrical in the mid-1970s, circus directors came to be compared to their counterparts who work in the theatre. A more apt comparison, however, is with the film auteur. Like his cinematic counterpart, the circus director is as responsible for the content of a production as he is for its look and style. The directors of the contemporary circus are much more than traffic cops, moving people around and clocking the coming and goings in the ring. Ultimately, their work goes far beyond selecting the acts and arranging the order in which they are presented. The director is also responsible for discovering and selecting the images that the audience will see and experience.

Like the film auteur, the circus director directs the audience's attention and focus, but instead of choosing between close-ups, medium or long shots, the circus director controls what the audience sees through the lighting. It is the director who finally determines, in collaboration with the lighting designer, how light or dark the ring or arena will be, where the lighting will be focused, and what color it will be.

The circus director decides how the acts will enter or leave. Will they be discovered in a jump cut, as they so often are on the Ringling show, or introduced by a twist of the plot?

In the absence of a playwright or screen writer, the director often serves as author as well. He (or she, another innovation of the contemporary circus) often writes the script from which the performance proceeds. That script may range from little more than a schedule of acts to a full-blown exploration of a running theme. It may be carefully plotted out and recorded in some permanent or semipermanent form, or it may exist only in the director's imagination.

In all these ways, every circus performance is ultimately a unique expression of the director's view of the world. The performance ultimately tells us who or what each particular circus believes itself to be, at least as it is expressed by the individual director.

And, of course, since the various elements of the theatrical arts are now more fully invoked, the director's choices have become much more complex and extensive. Someone has to decide what the music, sound, costume, and design departments will contribute. That, too, is province of the director.

The work accomplished during the rehearsal period of the contemporary circus is akin to a film's editing process, which means that not only does the director edit the work of his technical collaborators, but that of the performing artists as well. Circus acts today must be willing to accept the fact that they are not going to be doing their act in the same way in every circus in which they appear. Increasingly, contractual demands require them to accept the costumes, staging, and music that best suit a director's production scheme.

The directors whose work we are about to examine here come to the circus from a variety of backgrounds, with a variety of sensibilities, and their visions of the circus differ markedly. They come from street and musical theatre, from dance and the classical stage. They have studied theatre and film in universities, and some have been tagging after circuses of every size and description since they were children.

They are all intent on exploring all the possibilities that circus production has to offer without the constraints of tradition and with a degree of adventure and creativity that has never before been seen in the circus.

★ ★ ★

The first step in the process of creating a new circus performance, according to Franco Dragone, who directed the first seven of Cirque du Soleil's productions, is to settle on a theme or a guiding inspiration. He then sets up a kind of colloquy between himself and his collaborators, whom he refers to as "conceptors." (This term is used by all the people at Cirque du Soleil. Its meaning, although not to be found in a dictionary of standard English, I think, is clear.) Dragone proposes the theme and a "debate" ensues as each conceptor attempts to respond to the director's provocation through his or her own medium.

"Sometimes the idea comes from the show. *O*, for instance, is a water show, and I wanted to explore that medium," he explains. So the designs his collaborators (or "conceptors") proposed reflected both the show's special location (a permanent theatre) and its medium (the water).

"There are two ways to approach a new idea," he says, adding to the explanation. "Either we use it [the unique element] somewhere and nowhere else, or we use it everywhere. I wanted to use it all together." And so in O the water is omnipresent.

Since the theme is the vital starting point, looking for a new theme, Dragone admits, can become a preoccupation, if not an obsession. He explains it thus: "Two things are happening in parallel. One is that we know we have to do a show. And the other is that the world moves on. I am like everyone else, preoccupied with what is happening in the world. I find something that I am concerned about in the world—something that interests me." From such thoughts a theme will eventually emerge.[1]

As simple and obvious as this kind of thinking may sound, too often circus artists tend to be self-absorbed, and they forget that they and the circus are part of the larger world, and their work in some way will reflect this participation.

Once Dragone has found an idea that interests him, he "chooses the technique to best express it." This could be the acrobatic structure of the show, for instance, or a new way of using traditional techniques. "We want to do something different each time," he insists.

"In *Alegria*, for instance, we wanted to change the floor, to make it more spectacular. So we invented the fast track." The floor, he offers by way of explanation, is always there, so he asked his collaborators to look at it to see what could be done with it that was new. The trick, if it may be called that, is to look behind the tradition and traditional techniques to see what there is that can be changed. "The solutions," he acknowledges, "come in stages" during the year-long rehearsal period that is more of an exploratory process than it is a repetition.[2]

As Dragone sees the creative process, it is his function to stimulate the conceptors. "At the first meeting I bring music, pictures, text. I write things." In this approach, he says, the internationally regarded theatrical director Peter Brook is his guide. At this point, there is only what Lyn Heward, Cirque du Soleil's retired president of the Creative Content Division, calls "the vague premonition."[3]

With some directors, like Franco Dragone, for instance, some vague premonitions are vaguer than others. Dragone will come in with inspirations or stimuli. But it is also possible to have a director like Guy Caron who arrives with a good idea of what he wants to accomplish from the moment he begins. The company's director of *Varekai*, Dominic Champagne, was, according to Heward, halfway between these two approaches.[4]

Since a circus performance is a form of visual art, the treatment of the theme or idea must first be visualized. In *Quidam*, the Belgium surrealist painter Delvaux provided the initial inspiration. His paintings are filled with people, but what Dragone saw in them was that there was always something sad or strange. The people seemed to have no connections to each other. "There are crowds," Dragone observed, "but you realize that nobody is watching anyone else. That is what I tried to stage."

Inspired by that memory, Dragone says, switching metaphors, "I am like a painter. I don't know what I want to do, or why; I just feel it. I give the artists the attitudes and create the ingredients [the context] of the tableau." Watching the performance ultimately, then, is like looking at a painting. The audience is free to make what it will of the director's arrangement of lights, sets, costumes, music, and performers.

During this period of creative gestation or fermentation, if you will, Dragone usually works very closely with two people: Dominique Lemieux, the costume designer, and Michel Crête, the scenic designer. There's a tremendous amount of mutual stimulation, because it's not a situation where one person comes up with the entire idea and then everyone else follows. It's the back and forth that is interesting. Even the director of the studio, where the performing artists are training, and the coaches and studio staff can stimulate various members within the creative team, as, for example, the scenic designer. "The coaches may come up with an idea for a light, airy act, for example, and that will give new food to the set designer who says, 'Okay we need this much space, and we want this much volume and this is the way we want this to be conceived.' It's really an exchange of collective creativity."[5]

A new phase of the collaborative process for each new production begins when the director informs the casting department of his requirements. The difference in manner of working between Guy Caron and Franco Dragone is evident in this area as well as most others. Dragone will pass an order to the casting department that says "I want this and this and this and this, and then he will come back sometime later and say, 'Okay what have you got for me?' Guy, on the other hand, is on their case every day."[6]

It should be apparent that it is inappropriate to use the term "rehearsal period" to describe the 13- to 24-month creative process through which a Cirque du Soleil production typically goes.[7] The performers are brought into the process approximately six months before they will begin work in the director's workshops, which represent the penultimate phase of the process. During this period of exploration, which the company has dubbed "research and development," they undergo extensive training to adjust to the technique chosen for the new show. This technique often takes the form of a specific style of dance. "In one show," Dragone says, "I wanted everyone to look like they were doing the tango, but without doing the tango. Or perhaps it might be *tai chi*. In *La Nouba* it was hip-hop." Whatever the technique, it is the unifying element that, in Dragone's words, "builds a troupe."

In these training sessions and workshops Dragone finds "the vocabulary of the show, how the actors will behave and move." As this is going on, "I navigate between all the aspects of the show," Dragone explains.[8]

During the initial research and development phase of production, care is taken to make sure the artists receive enough physical preparation and develop sufficient flexibility so that they will be able to meet the demands of the work load they will be subjected to in performance. This is the first step in the realization of what the conceptors have visualized for the performance.

The conceptors may come to the research and development department and say they would like to put a wall beside a trampoline, as they did, for instance, when developing *La Nouba*. This idea will then be tested through a series of experiments to see if such a concept is possible and if tricks can be found that are appealing, different, and sustainable. Thus a vocabulary is established for the conceptors, and it then becomes a matter of putting the "words" into the right place.

So in this context, the vocabulary, the words, are the tricks, the images. In working on *La Nouba*, Dragone was shown what could be done with a certain type of music in a particular environment and then he picked and chose what he wanted to put together. In this way the words become phrases, and the phrases are ultimately arranged into sentences by the director. There is no script, only ideas, and they are woven together to create a whole.[9]

Dragone visits these training sessions to observe and evaluate how the company and its technique are developing every four or five weeks. After six months he begins his workshops. At this point he is now working directly with the artists, including the musicians. "I find new food in the workshops," he says. "They [the actors] take it upon themselves to provide it. I cannot give it to them. I don't want to project a scenario onto them. It has to emerge."

This nurturing is explained by Witek Biegaj, who plays one of the quartet of *Les Cons*, "The Nuts," in *La Nouba*. "Franco worked with us mostly on our bodies," Biegaj explains. "He asked me to show him some movements about being stupid or dumb or crazy. Then he started to select certain movements and asked me to make them bigger or in a different way. The character developed out of the movement. He kept telling us we have to think like who we are: 'You need to have a craziness behind the eyes, something in your head.'" The director did not, however, tell them what to think. "That we had to develop in our heads for ourselves.

"Franco worked with us alone for a time, to help us find some way of working, of thinking and watching. We based our characters on his suggestions; then he chose from what we proposed. Always, he says, it has to come from us."

But more than mere witnesses, *Les Cons* perform a very important role in the development of the show's concept. "We're supposed to make the situations happen. We make the main character [the cleaning lady] fall in love with the prince. But this is information the audience doesn't need to have. It is just important that we understand." And, of course, it was Dragone who gave them this information to help them make what they do work for themselves, or as Biegaj put it, to help them find their "soul."[10]

This approach is confirmed by Steven Ragatz, who appeared in both *Mystère* and *Quidam* and went through the creative process of both productions. In the development and research phrase, he explains, the performers work their way through theatre games, improvisational exercises, and basic theatre techniques in an effort to develop a vocabulary that can be brought to the director in the next phase of the process.[11]

Here, the entire ensemble is gathered together into a large, open space. Various groups will be formed into tableau in which they are asked to demonstrate movements they have been working on in their training sessions. These workshop sessions are videotaped and studied by the conceptors later in the day.

Little, if any, specific direction is given any of the individual artists or groups at this time so as not to inhibit creativity. The director does not want anyone forming any preconceived notions of what he is after. Doing so may cause them to try to give him what he is looking for. The truth is that at this point, he does not know in any concrete or literal form what it is he is looking for. Now he has turned to the performers for further inspiration just as he had formerly looked to his fellow conceptors.

In preparing *Quidam*, Dragone asked the performers to try to move in a surrealistic manner, but he did not want a specific kind of surrealism. "He did not want us imitating Delvaux style."[12]

Ragatz believes the reasoning behind Dragone's approach is that "the people in the audience deserve the respect to be able to come to their own conclusions. He didn't want us to tie them down with literal images that leave no room for interpretation. This is the big difference between Cirque du Soleil and others who try to imitate it. Cirque is committed to the idea of not telling them everything. Others try to be too literal, and it is very flat."[13]

The characters that will eventually convey Dragone's image, Ragatz points out, are really based upon the artist's individual body types and shapes and the way individuals move. "All we have to define character is our physiques. And I have to credit Debbie Brown [choreographer] with being able to extract interesting movement vocabulary from people who are not dancers."

Ragatz recalls that developing the movement style for one of the character groups in *Mystère* involved a certain amount of physical pain, as well as anxiety. One of the acrobats proposed a movement in which he crossed the stage like a horse, the leading knee brought high while kicking the other leg out back. Dragone had everyone running around the stage in a circle over and over again doing "cheval" (as the movement came to be known) until he was satisfied that he had found what he was looking for.

Of course, it is only the director who sees the complete picture as it is forming. "Like a painter," Ragatz says, picking up on one of the company's favorite metaphors, "only the director is able to step back to look at what he has. We [the performers] can't do it. We only catch glimpses of it. So we have to trust the director's eye and judgment because we can never experience the performance from the audience's point of view. That's why the director is so important."[14]

Since the performers do not know what Dragone is looking for from them, the director's workshops are often fraught with anxiety for the artists who will play characters or *personnage* (the Cirque du Soleil term) as he asks them to demonstrate one attitude or another.[15] Ragatz puts it another way: "You do a lot of weird, silly stuff over and over."[16]

The problem for Dragone, as it is with almost everyone who attempts to stage a circus, is that 99 percent of the performers he has to work with are nonactors. "I'm an acrobat. I feel like an acrobat," Biegaj says by way of emphasizing the challenge he faces.[17] Thus the process is one of trial and error, experimentation and investigation for all concerned. It is not until several months have passed that the time will come to start editing and putting the elements together in what other artists would recognize as "rehearsals." These, too, are "guided by that obscure intuition" that began it all. Although this stage of a production's development comes quite late in the process, it is still only Dragone who knows for sure what it will end up being, and even he is not so sure. "It is impossible," he insists, "to know the rhythm of a show until you shake it. You need to be there, to shake it, and let it be insecure. When it happens you know."[18]

As late as one week before *La Nouba*'s first public performance no one had ever seen a complete show. At that point the company was seven months into the training and rehearsal period and there had been no run-throughs. The final performance still existed only in the director's imagination, in part because it is only at this point that the music is first put into the mix.

La Nouba played what amounted to previews for one month before the official media opening. During that time the production was continually evolving, even as it was playing public performances. A new act, the bicyclists, was added because Dragone wanted to break the rhythm of the show and provide an unexpected jolt. The most radical changes, however, took place with Benoit Jutras's score. Until the very last minute, it was very much a work in progress.[19]

For its production *Varekai*, which debuted in 2002, Cirque du Soleil put together a brand new creative team. Both Franco Dragone and Gilles Ste-Croix had opted to work on projects of their own for the time being, and for Cirque du Soleil, Lyn Heward explains, "It was important to us to be able to build resources, because there are a lot of demands for Cirque shows and Cirque entertainment projects in general, so we have begun building a new creative team.

"All of the members are not new. This team is really a fusion. We have a new director or, as we call him, *mitteur en scène.*" This role was entrusted to Dominic Champagne, a stage director who had done a great deal of work in films and television in Quebec. In addition, Andrew Watson assumed the role of director of creation, replacing Gilles Ste-Croix. Watson has an extensive background with Cirque du Soleil, starting as an artist in 1987, and "he is an example of how far you can go with Cirque du Soleil," Heward points out. "In 1990 he became the combined director of casting and the studio. In 1993 he became an artistic director. He took a leave of absence to go home [to London] to do the Millennium Dome show for a year and a half. So he came back to us with all new baggage and his experience with Cirque to guide this new team."[20]

This new creative team's process of conceptualization, Heward points out, was different from that of their predecessors, mainly because of the director's stage experience. "Because of Dominic's written work, and because he's directed actors specifically in the field of theatre, his approach tends to be a little bit different. So it will really be a marriage of two approaches for the creation of the show."

This was to be the first Cirque production to be directed by someone who was not a part of the original creative team, and although the idea of using a totally new director would seem to be somewhat terrifying, the terror was ameliorated by wedding the director's newness with the experience of Watson. "The director and the director of creation go into this hand in hand," Heward explains.

In attempting to differentiate between the functions of these two artists, she explains, "you have to look at the director's ability, not only to create for himself from a staging point of view, but his ability to draw out the best from each of the people on his creative team."

But the qualifications for the job go far beyond mere creativity. "I honestly did not ask for an idea," Heward says of her initial interview with the new director. "The question was do we think that philosophically this director can fit with a Cirque du Soleil model and be able to work within this framework. When you do this for the first time you have to be extremely present. It's not something that you can do by long distance or something you can do by fax or whatever. So being here was a big factor. Dominic was prepared to come in full-time during the last year of production.

"So the development of complicity, the feeling that when you talk to this person, there is a spark and a flame, which is similar to the passion that you have," Heward continues, "is essential. For me and Guy Laliberté, Cirque du Soleil's founder, our first conversation with Dominic was just a general one about his relationship with his family and colleagues, his general creative process, his objectives in life, because doing a Cirque du Soleil show is not investing two or three months in a theatre project. Doing a Cirque du Soleil show is a commitment for two years of intensive work and ten or twelve years of follow-up, being constantly interested in the evolution of the show, maybe not always on a daily or even a monthly basis, but available at the end of the telephone to answer questions. We may have a query about the original concept of the show. We may need a new costume because we have a new key player or we need to write a new piece of music."[21]

Cirque du Soleil's production of *Dralion*, for instance, required that the entire troupe of performers be changed, according to the company's agreement with the Chinese Cultural Ministry, after the second year of its run. "This was easier because we could do so internally to a large extent," Heward says. "In other words we knew the profile of the show when we went to cast the kids in China. Murielle Cantin and Bernard Petiot, then the casting director and studio director respectively, went with me to China and auditioned the kids. They all came from the same troupe, but we auditioned them individually. We negotiated with the troupe director. 'We want this one and not this one.' But the bottom line on this process is the director. When a director becomes involved, he or she must be committed and open to follow up on his or her show for a long period of time. Some people let it run and die. Cirque du Soleil does require a bigger commitment, so you want to be sure that the person is prepared to commit for a long term and that the show somehow fits into his long-term career development. We want to invest in players with whom we think we can work, not on one project, but on future projects."[22]

In contrast, the director of creation, a role unique to Cirque du Soleil, coordinates the activities of that creative team and provides the link with casting, because "casting is something that is done 24 hours a day, 7 days a week, year round here. The casting director, the training director, and a whole bunch of production managers all need to be kept up to speed. They need to feel a link to this group of creators who come in *temporarily* to create a show. They need to know what the director is looking for in characters. What the acts in the show will be. The casting department and the studio also participate in that process. They will generate ideas for the consideration of the creative group. They will say, 'We saw this, this, and this.' They will offer a panoply of ideas, hundreds of ideas, but at some point in time they need feedback so they know where they are going.

"Andrew plays a tremendous role in ensuring that all the conceptors have the information that they need to do their work. So very often it's going to be

Andrew who is going to sit down and look at twenty hours of videotape propositions from the casting department, or it will be Andrew who will spend the time down in the studio looking at the acrobatic research and development or artistic research and development and say, 'This is the direction we want to head in,' or 'no, we are totally off the mark here.'

"So Andrew's role is also creative and his creativity lies in the knowledge that he has accumulated in the thirteen years he has been with Cirque du Soleil, his acrobatic expertise, and the knowledge and creativity that he has proved time and time again within the context of other Cirque shows. He is a guide for everybody who is outside of the creative group, and he is also a guide for the creative group itself if it gets stuck and bogged down."[23]

He must make sure that all members of the creative team possess a sure sense of the Cirque du Soleil style, or as Heward puts it, "the Cirque value and what we are looking for in a show, because we don't necessarily expect someone like Dominic to know that when he walks in the door." And that's what's terrifying about placing a production in the hands of someone who is not intimately familiar with what Cirque is all about. "Andrew's job, therefore, is really to ensure that this creative group is conscious of all this. This is not pure theatre that we are doing. It's not pure acrobatics. It's not pure circus. It's a marriage of all the above.

"Through the training process, different people, whether it be a coach, an artist, a creator, or an assistant, will all contribute in their own way to this process. It's Andrew's stimulation that is going to bring that out of people, but Dominic is going to have to make the ultimate choices. The director is always king with his creative team, and where he really becomes king is when we hit the rehearsal period. Until then he receives the same nurturing from the director of creation [as any of the other artists]."[24]

The individual acts for *Varekai*, Heward pointed out, were fusions. "Some of them were born not necessarily from individual acts but from group acts that we have seen—small group acts (two and three or four people) that we want to amplify and take to a new direction. At this point we are not looking at specific acts that exist outside of Cirque du Soleil."[25] Nor does it seem likely that they will be doing so in future productions, for most of the individual acts have already been seen and considered, used, or rejected.

★ ★ ★

In the overall evolution of Cirque de Soleil's productions, the creative thrust has been toward creating a seamless amalgam of story and acts, fusing circus into the structure of a narrative.[26] This process began with *Quidam* in which Dragone subtly attempted to break away from the revue format in which each act had a definite beginning and ending. This was accomplished with a thematic thread or threads that ran through the production. O took the process one step forward. All of the acts overlap and cross over into each other through the use of characters and images that may seem tangential or peripheral to the featured acts themselves, but are in fact central to what Dragone is trying to achieve. This approach, Heward says, is a challenge. "We thought we would get there maybe in five years. I think now, in ten."[27]

Although Franco Dragone has left Cirque du Soleil to establish his own creative studio in his native Belgium, where he has begun producing shows for a variety of producers, the creative process he established during his tenure with the Canadian circus has set the pattern for all of its productions that have followed his departure. The problem for Cirque du Soleil since Dragone left has been finding creative talent equal to the level of artistry he brought to the company's productions.

★ ★ ★

Before discussing the process by which the productions of Ringling Bros. and Barnum & Bailey are created, it is necessary to look first at the man who produces these shows. Kenneth Feld's role as producer is unique in the world of the circus. In the theatre, the producer options the rights to produce a play and then raises the money to finance that production. He hires all the artists, from director to actors, and provides the means for them to do their work under the best possible circumstances. Once the creative personnel are hired, a theatrical producer may never again take part in the creative process until such time as he sees what it is that his money has bought. If he is dissatisfied, he can take certain steps to rectify the situation. He can fire the director, replace actors, bring in play doctors, but he cannot, by reason of the contracts he signs with the various artists' unions, actually change the play without the playwright's consent.

As producer of The Greatest Show on Earth, Kenneth Feld, along with his daughter, Nicole, who joined him as coproducer in 2004 for the 134th edition, exercises many of the same prerogatives as a theatrical producer. In almost all other circuses, except for the Big Apple in recent years, the producer and director is usually one and the same person. At the Big Apple Circus Paul Binder has stepped back from that dual role to function solely as producer, although the financing of each year's production is raised by the not-for-profit corporation, rather than the privately held enterprise over which Feld presides.

Thus by virtue of the fact that he is putting up what amounts to his own money to mount each new production, Kenneth Feld justifiably wields an extraordinary amount of power. He is not merely engaged in the creative process of a new circus each year; he is protecting his investment in it. To do that he must be a keen observer of trends. He says that he reads, goes to the theatre, carefully watches how shows on television are rated, and basically tries to see everything.

The Feld organization does a great deal of market research, using focus groups in various parts of the country. These focus groups help the organization not only in the mounting of its marketing and advertising campaigns, but also in deciding what elements each new production should include or emphasize. One of the things contemporary audiences seem to want, according to Ringling research, is a seamless production, and the best way to achieve that, they have determined, is through a unifying score that moves through the entire production.

Feld makes no bones about having the final word here. "Ultimately what the public sees is an extension of my taste executed through the work of many other people," he says.[28] And it takes a lot of time and hard work. The level of Feld's involvement has increased over the years, gaining momentum as the creative staff that prevailed under his father's leadership died or were dismissed, and, for a time, a string of directors came and went.

★ ★ ★

Steve Smith is one of the few directors of The Greatest Show on Earth who came up through the ranks. A 1971 graduate of Ringling's Clown College, the same class as Tim Holst, vice president for talent and production, Smith eventually came to serve ten years as the program's dean during the early '90s. When he learned of the proposed theme for the 123rd edition, which was to feature children, he was so excited by the idea that he wrote a memo to Kenneth Feld throwing his hat, as it were, into the ring for the job of directing the show. He was then interviewed by Feld, who asked him to articulate how he envisioned the theme being realized. After considering how that vision would mesh with what he and Holst had already come up with, Feld awarded his dean of clowning the job of director of The Greatest Show on Earth.[29]

Beforehand, however, Holst had already engaged a number of acts that featured children. The problem for the director was to find ways of tying all these seemingly disparate elements together. In effect, he had to "create the scenario that made some kind of sense.

"Now, because we're spectacle, we can't be very intimate with our storytelling, but we can still tell a story with a beginning, a middle, and an end that the audience can get. It must be very simple when you're working on a canvas as large as a circus arena, or it will get lost. But we can direct focus anywhere we want, because our lighting equipment allows us to do that. We can focus down to a single clown, David Larible, and a little girl in the audience, a plant, who was going to run away and join the circus." Thus, in Smith's vision, David Larible had become the Pied Piper.

Smith's circus, Ringling's 123rd edition, was called *Children of the Rainbow,* and in addition to focusing on children, the production was also intended as a celebration of 200 years of circus in America, thus complicating the matter of theme somewhat. To introduce the historical note, the opening production number became a celebration of the circus's history. Smith and his creative team came up with the idea of using the symbol of the sunburst wagon wheel as the unifying element. Everything in that production number, from the showgirls who wore wagon wheel skirts that rotated, to the Chicago Kidz who came down the track in giant wheels, to the umbrellas that were painted like wagon wheels, carried out that design element. The floor coverings in rings one and three were supposed to elevate and look like big tops, but, as Smith discovered, "they ended up looking like tacos" because, as they were raised, they folded themselves in half. "Unfortunately that was an idea that didn't pay off so well, but in the conceptual stage, it sounded like a great idea," Smith says. The opening also featured a number of children from the show, which introduced the theme that would be developed throughout the major and later spectacle.

The "spec" began with an original song, "Flying in Your Dreams," which was sung while Vivian Larible performed her aerial act high above the heads of her brother, David, and the little girl he had supposedly taken into the ring from out of the audience. They watched the act together, sitting in a pool of light on the ring curb. This then segued into a huge production number featuring more original music and forty kids.

To make something like this happen takes an army of creative people because, as Smith says, echoing sentiments we will hear from the Big Apple Circus's Michael Christensen, "It's one thing to conceptualize and dream up these ideas, and it's something very different for the people in operations to say how this is going to work."

"My hat goes off to Kenneth," Smith insists, "because he included [Larible], an artist from the show, in these production meetings. It made a lot of sense, because we got to hear from the source. We could say, 'Here's what we want you to do, David,' and since he was sitting right there, he could say, 'Yes, I can do that,' or 'I have a problem with that.' It just helped us to move forward a lot faster."

The early meetings were usually held at the corporate headquarters. "We would go to Vienna [Virginia] to have a big meeting with Kenneth to make our presentation of our initial ideas, show him some rough sketches or renderings of costumes, play him samples of the music, and get his input [into these matters]." This would be followed by smaller meetings, which would attempt to deal with Feld's reaction to what he had just seen and heard.

"Some stuff he loved; some he actually hated, and said 'I never want to see that again.' It was pretty clear if we were on the wrong path or the right path. So we would take our notes, leave, and break up into small groups focusing on whatever aspect it was that we were trying to change or alter or throw out.

"We also kept in touch with each other so each of the areas was keyed into what was going on. That way it didn't come as a surprise to the scenic people if, say, we were changing the costumes in the opening number. And so," he says, sounding very much like Franco Dragone, "it was really my job to be like a cheerleader to keep everything going and everybody connected to the process so that we were all on the same page every time we came back to Kenneth. What made that difficult was that we were all, all over the country, all of the time, and this was at a time when cell phones were just coming in so we didn't quite have that advantage yet."

Sometimes, Smith was forced to defend an element or detail he thought he wanted and needed. The only thing really worth defending, Smith insists, is the integrity of the artistic vision. It must be something that is needed to help the show move forward. "So you choose your battles," he says. "There are some things worth fighting for and some that absolutely aren't.

"Kenneth doesn't want five train cars in the spec; he wants three. Okay. We can live with three. Other, not so tangible, items, the ephemeral things, like a quiet little moment with David and the little girl really weren't so difficult to defend. I just had to show Kenneth why it was important to bring everything down to this one sweet, gentle moment so that everything else that took off from there had a base to start from. You need to be that small to get that big, so that you got something to compare it to. Kenneth is very open to that if you can explain why it's important. But if you can't tell him, you're a lost cause, and I think that's only fair. You have to be able to articulate what it is you are after."

After that introductory moment, Smith's "spec," the circus's major production number, was carefully laid out so that it kept building dramatically. By the time it got to the "Children of the Rainbow" number, all of the kids who had been performing were circling the hippodrome track and signing the words of the song in American Sign Language. "These little touches are not cut and dried; this is intuitive. I had to say, 'Trust me here, boss, because I know this road is right.' That's a huge, huge risk to ask a producer to take. This was a multimillion dollar production, and I was asking him to trust me on my *intuition*! What you really have to do in those production meetings is act out what's going to happen. You have to create the scene; you have to create that environment; you have to create that emotional hot button, in order to sell the idea to everybody—the designers, too."

Around August, prior to the January debut, Ringling's creative team convenes in full for the white model meetings usually held in Palmetto, Florida, at the offices of the Hagenbeck-Wallace Co., that branch of Feld Entertainment that builds the sets and props and floats for all of the organization's shows, ice shows as well as circuses. The white model is a two-dimensional, paper facsimile in miniature of all the elements of the various production numbers. The model is built by the Hagenbeck-Wallace Co., and it derives its name from the fact that the figures are not colored. At these meetings every element is put together for all to see for the very first time. There is usually more than one such meeting, as elements are refined, eliminated, or added. Once the model, and the designs it represents, are green-lighted, the designs then go into the shops, and the Hagenbeck-Wallace team begins immediately building all the pieces.

The white model meetings are held at this time because all the elements that make up the physical production have to be on the floor ready for rehearsals in late November. "Once you hit the ground running at rehearsals," Smith explains, "you don't look back. You can't, even though enormous changes are about to happen, because Kenneth *will*, without hesitation, cut something that he had agreed to in that final white model meeting, something he had committed the funds, time, and energy to build. When he sees it on the floor, and it doesn't work for him, it's out. And there's no question about it. You can fight it. But why? It's sitting right there in front of you, and he doesn't like it. If it's not an integral part of your production, let it go and move on is my feeling.

"Kenneth once said to me, 'Don't be afraid to fight me.' He wants his directors to articulate what they want, but you better be able to deliver. To me the challenge is to stay positive, because when you're in this storm of criticism and mayhem and chaos, with things changing every day, it's difficult not to start thinking, 'This is not the way we said it was going to be six weeks ago,' and that is a very difficult job."

Anyone who has worked in the theatre will recognize the kind of tensions and conflicts that Smith describes. They are not at all unusual. The difference is that when dealing with a production like Ringling Bros. and Barnum & Bailey, everything seems magnified by the size of the show itself. And then, of course, "We had the added attraction of five interpreters," Smith adds.

"And I have to mention Roy Luthringer, choreographer on my show. The strength of having Danny Hermann and Phil McKinley (the directors who followed Smith) is that they are stagers. They understand choreography. They can not only envision what they want the picture to be, but they can also make it happen. So they are better suited in many ways to be the solo voice. Let's look at the floor. There are only so many ways you can go. You can come in the back door, go around and back out the back door. To make it interesting for two and a half hours, you need somebody who is very inventive."[30]

With people like Hermann and McKinley providing the staging, it should be pointed out, the Ringling circus has come to look more and more like a piece of musical theatre. If Kenneth Feld decides this is the kind of circus his audiences want to see, choreographers turned directors will continue to be the most successful at staging this circus just as people like Bob Fosse, Gower Champion, and Michael Bennett have been the most successful directors of musical theatre.

During the four weeks of rehearsals in Tampa, Florida, the individual acts begin their day's rehearsals as early as 8 a.m. The remainder of the morning is usually given over to rehearsing the animals or perhaps the flying acts. Rehearsals for the production numbers begin at 11 a.m., when the floor has been cleared. These run until about six in the evening. Following a break, the creative team begins its daily production meeting with Kenneth. Here they go through the voluminous notes from the day and the changes that will have to be made the next day. With a cast of upward of one hundred humans, a crew of seventy-five, numerous animals of varying species, the logistics involved in dealing with it all are staggering. "It's a major team effort," Feld agrees.[31]

At Smith's very first rehearsal, all of the pieces—props, floats, scenic pieces—were placed on the floor so the entire company could see what the major spec was all about. "For European acts and other foreign acts," Smith points out, "this is all very odd, this three-ring concept, so they need to be shown: 'This is how you fit into the picture; this is what I need you to do, because you are part of the whole picture.' As artists you must treat them with a great deal of respect, because if you treat them as a body in a production number, that's what you will get.

"You must tell them, 'I need you, as a professional, to participate in this production as fully as you would in your own act.' I showed them the white model, and I had their names on cards next to the little cutouts and said, 'This is you; this is where you fit in,' so it's not some abstraction. It's a tangible thing. Now, do they still fight it? Of course they do. This idea of production numbers does not sell very well. So I beg, plead, cajole, be funny, stand on my head, whatever it takes, because you don't have time to hand hold that much. I will lend myself to being available for comment, and I'm sensitive enough to understand how long it takes to perfect an act. But this is a big show, and everyone coming into it understood and knew when they signed their contracts that they would be expected to participate in these production numbers.

What I'm trying to get them to do as an act person is to be an actor, to participate fully."

All of this, of course, has to be communicated through five different interpreters. "That became a challenge," Smith vividly recalls, "because I was never sure what information was getting through and what wasn't. For all I knew they were telling them, 'Don't listen to the little, bald man.'" (Smith is a little, bald man.) "It was also a challenge because you had to keep repeating yourself. I think it was harder for Roy as choreographer to try to teach some of those production steps through so many different interpreters. All future choreographers would be advised to learn to count 'and . . . five, six, seven, eight' in five different languages."[32] During the rehearsal period the initial focus is on staging the spec, which takes about a week. But the most difficult aspects of any production to get right are the transitions from act to act, moment to moment, moving from one thing to the next, making it seem seamless and effortless. These moments are first set during rehearsals, but continue to be tinkered with throughout the early portion of the tour.

"Part of the difficulty in getting these moments right is the fact that there are so many purely mechanical problems that get in the way," Steve Smith explains. "It would be much more beautiful if we went from David in ring one to this beautiful girl down in ring three, but we can't do that because there's a giant piece of steel in the way because of the act before and that ruins my concept, but we can't help that because we can't get the truck in there fast enough to get it out. That's why you need a meeting every day to resolve this kind of problem."

As rehearsals progress, costume fittings and alterations continue so that the clothes can be tried out in rehearsals. Wardrobe sets up trailers in one of the arena's anterooms. Four huge trailers serve as dressing rooms. Props, too, need to be finished and worked with and tested. The crews for these departments are working in the building and, if needed, in the arena, and can be counted on to come running.

Once the show opens in Florida and people are paying money to see it, the new show is a living, dynamic entity about to take on a life of its own, but the director and the creative staff are not done with it yet. Not until performances begin is it finally possible to see what the production is going to be. Those transitions and other pesky moments that seem to resist being made to work correctly continue to be tweaked. "You continue to have spot rehearsals, and in some cases eliminate things," Smith recalls. "In the 123rd it was the Karoly horse act. It took too long; it didn't fit in. The producer, Kenneth Feld, had to make a hard choice. He had signed these people to a contract. I don't know what he ultimately did, but it must have been hard to say, 'You know what? The two years you thought you were going to be working here, you're not working here.' Now that's a tough pill to take. But it was the right decision for the show. But some of those things you don't know, even after all those production meetings, even after you've thought it all out and you've made the white model sets. You put it on its feet and you say, my god, this doesn't work."[33]

All the extra rehearsals and the fine-tuning are accomplished in anticipation of the opening in New York. The new show's real opening night is held in Madison Square Garden. The reviews it garners there will be a part of the show's press kit for the next year and a half on the road. Normally the director will conduct one or more full rehearsals to buff and polish in New Jersey or Long Island, the dates the show plays just prior to coming into Manhattan.

Officially, the director's duties conclude once the show finishes its Florida dates. After New York, the show's performance director (the circus's equivalent of the stage manager) can fiddle with it while it's on the road. He will make any temporary changes necessitated by the idiosyncrasies of the various buildings in which it will play. Something may be too big and not be able to get through the portal. The weather may influence other changes if the animals are not housed in the arena proper. Those practical decisions have to be made by the performance director on the floor at the moment.

"It seems to me that as a director, when you're dealing with a logistical monster like Ringling Bros. and Barnum & Bailey, you need to understand that this show is going to move, and it's going to keep moving for two years. It's going to play venues vastly different from one another, which can change the content of your show. And that means you have to conceive of something that's going to work in many different formats and still be able to get the story across."

In addition someone has to keep after the cast almost every day to remind them of the message the director had tried to impart during rehearsals. By the three hundredth performance, it's old hat, except for the audience that is seeing it for the first time. Some of the performers begin to "call it in," as the saying goes.

"So you have to keep after them constantly. I don't know any other way. Currently Ringling has someone sit at each and every show with a headset that is connected to all the lighting and sound technicians and takes notes and gives those notes after each performance.

"What needs to happen next," Smith believes, "is that acting needs to be brought into the venue in the training process worldwide, because Cirque du Soleil has elevated everything to a level where the audience expectation is such that they want a story. Just as with any skill you learn in the circus, there is a technique and skill to acting that really needs to be a part of circus training."[34]

Philip Wm. McKinley is the most recent director of Ringling Bros. and Barnum & Bailey to have any staying power. He has enjoyed the longest tenure of any director since Richard Barstow, who began staging the show in 1952 and remained until after Irvin Feld's death in 1984.

McKinley's longevity may be attributed to the successful working relationship he has enjoyed with producer Kenneth Feld and Tim Holst, as well as his own creativity. "What's great about Kenneth," he says, "is I've never found him unreasonable. He's brilliant. Nobody knows the three rings better then he does, having grown up with that format. The new team for the 132nd was just mesmerized by him. He's just so perceptive about what he wants for the show. What's been stimulating for me is the fact that he's an active collaborator who tells you what he wants. He does know what he wants. Only occasionally he will say, 'I just don't like it. I don't know why. This just isn't what I want.' And I'll say, 'Okay, we'll accept that.' Because I do that, too.[35]

"I've always been that kind of person, and that's the kind of producer I prefer to work with—very direct, in your face—because then you know where you stand. The mistake that many people make in working with a creative individual like Kenneth is trying to guess what he'll like. That's a mistake every time. I put the show together the way I think it is going to work, and then we all sit down and debate it for whatever reasons. Kenneth said a couple of times the reason he keeps me on is because I argue with him." The same is true even when working with actors, McKinley says: "You better be able to stand up for your idea. And that's all that Kenneth asks."

One of the problems that Ringling Bros. and Barnum & Bailey has been facing for nearly fifteen years is how to react to the technological and artistic changes that are coming to the circus. "It's become more and more like the theatre," McKinley argues. "We are in essence borrowing certain traits from the American theatre. We've obviously added lights. The idea is that you take contemporary improvements to support the show, but you don't let them overpower the performance. It's a circus that has become theatrical rather than a circus that has been theatricalized, in the sense that the theatre has overpowered it and taken over, which I think is the difference between The Greatest Show on Earth and Cirque du Soleil. Cirque is a theatricalization. It uses circus arts in its theatricalization, but it's close to being its own form, and because it lacks a ring and animals it's not really a circus in its purest form."

To keep the circus vital, McKinley has often said, "Let's go back to our roots, back to the more traditional aspect of it. I would love to put sawdust all over the arena. That way the people would walk down on the floor and get the real feeling of circus. I would like to start commentating, like at sport events,[36] because I don't think people realize how hard it is to do what circus performers do. I don't think they are aware of the athletic ability, the difficulty of mixing animals. I don't think they understand the natural behavior of the elephants in the manège. These are things that they do in the wild. So my thing is [trying to figure out] how we can educate, because the smarter the audiences, the more they will come to us."[37]

How McKinley came to be the director of The Greatest Show on Earth reveals something of the thinking that goes into producing a circus on the scale of Ringling Bros. and Barnum & Bailey. According to McKinley, Tim Holst called the director's agent, Bret Adams, regarding another of the agent's clients. Adams suggested that Holst give some consideration to McKinley as well. The only problem was that at that moment McKinley was in Tokyo directing a production of the musical *Hair*. Since the circus was in need of a director as soon as possible, Holst decided to pass on McKinley. Nonetheless, when McKinley returned to the States, he was informed of Ringling's interest, and Adams assured him that he would try to set up an interview for the future.

About two weeks later the agent received another call from Holst, this time saying that the show had lost its first choice for director. The quick-witted agent replied, "No, you haven't seen your first choice yet." A meeting was hurriedly set up between McKinley and Holst. It took place at a Manhattan diner located at Tenth Ave. and 42nd St., the following Wednesday morning.[38]

There were enough positives in McKinley's background to convince Holst that he had found a likely prospect. The future director had been raised on a farm in Illinois and had been around animals all his life. His grandfather was one of the first to raise buffalo and then beefalo. As a boy, McKinley had owned and cared for horses, dogs, a monkey, and even a pet pig. Besides that, he had worked in Germany, France, and Japan and was used to working with people in different languages. Finally there was the fact that he had directed a number of large-scale theatrical productions in such places as the St. Louis Municipal Opera and Kansas City's Starlight Theatre. Recently he had staged one of the Broadway Cares shows, an AIDS benefit with 300 people, which he had put together in a day and a half. So obviously he could work fast as well.

After the two men had talked for a while, Holst told McKinley that he wanted him to meet Kenneth Feld. He then proceeded to take his cell phone out of his pocket, punched in the number, and handed the phone to the surprised director. While on the phone with Feld, McKinley was asked to come down to Vienna, Virginia, the following Monday so that they could meet and talk further. In his frantic preparation for that meeting, McKinley talked to everybody he could think of who might be able to give him some insight into what working for the circus and Kenneth Feld might entail.

Once introduced, "One of the first things Mr. Feld asked," McKinley recalls, "was if I had any questions. I said, 'Yes, one. Why are you trying to be everything but a circus?' and he said, 'What do you mean?'"

In the course of his research, McKinley had watched several videotapes of past performances. "They had a lot of rock and roll, modern, contemporary music in them," McKinley observed. "I just thought the thing people love about the circus is the fact that although it changes, there's a constancy about it. What families love is that they know they can take their kids today and have the same experience, the same emotional experience that they had had as kids with their parents.

"I'd seen other companies that thought they needed to step into the modern world and by doing so they lost their identity." McKinley felt sure the circus needed to preserve the purity of its art. "If I do nothing else," he proclaims, "it will be to make sure that America becomes more aware that circus is an art form and not a theme park attraction."

And so, when Kenneth Feld asked McKinley to explain what he meant, he told him: "The circus to me is its own thing, an art form of its own. It doesn't need to duplicate or replicate anything else. "

Kenneth Feld was just about sold. McKinley was told what talent had been engaged for the coming show and was asked to come back in two weeks with some ideas as to how he would use these various acts. "I spent three days in Sarasota going through the warehouses, the library, and the museum, looking at old programs, trying by osmosis to pick up whatever I could," McKinley says. "Then after about the second day I went to Tim and I said, 'I have this idea. What about a sideshow?'" Holst was immediately enthused and proposed taking the idea to Feld at once. McKinley protested that he wasn't quite ready to make a presentation, but Holst insisted, and they caught Feld as he emerged from a meeting concerning his next ice show. "I just sat down and said, 'What about this?' and threw it out and that's pretty much how our relationship has been ever since, very collaborative, very hands on."[39]

★ ★ ★

Michael Christensen is the cofounder and creative director of the Big Apple Circus. During the show's early years, he often performed some uncredited directorial work behind the scenes, alongside Paul Binder, who in the first two decades of the show's existence directed every one of the circus's annual productions. As the institution has grown in recent years, the roles of both Binder and Christensen have evolved and expanded. "More and more what we find ourselves evolving into is the traditional roles that artistic and creative directors have in most arts institutions," Christensen explains.[40]

"We are responsible for putting together the creative teams that we feel will embody and engender the creative spirit of the Big Apple Circus. Paul has final approval of the composition of that creative team. Together we hire the directors and the acts. We create the themes, and then we take a more distant role in putting that show together, rather than sitting there at every rehearsal and getting involved with every detail in front of us, which we would do if we were directing a show."

The creation of a new Big Apple Circus production begins with one or another of two activities. The first of these is thinking about themes. "They can be informed by our imagination, our experiences, or by a particular act," Christensen offers by way of explanation. "Sometimes we will book an act before we have any themes. We may feel it's a fantastic act and no matter what the theme we've got to have that act. The killer acts come first and then we tie them together with the theme.

"Or maybe there's a theme we've wanted to do for a long time and all of a sudden it hooks up with an act we've found, and we say, 'Hey, that would be good for that theme,' and we do it. If you don't have the artists, you don't have the show.

"So in the first stage of creation, getting the backbone of the show in place is getting the show booked in terms of acts. That process happens simultaneously with the creation of how these acts are all going to be linked together in some form by the theme."

As the process moves on down the creative road, the creative team is assembled and the show is written. This involves putting the acts in order and creating the links between them. Oftentimes these links are dictated by the needs of each act when it appears in the ring. Rigging needs to be set up. "What we have to do is decide whether we want to focus on that, or distract from it or mask it," Christensen says. "These decisions are made at this point in the process. Paul, the director, and I are usually the writers. When Paul is not involved in the writing, we do our presentation for him."

Along the way the process is continuously documented. Dominique Jando, who was for a time the show's associate artistic director, disseminated a continuously updated synopsis of where the show was, at any given moment. Any time there is a meeting of the creative staff or further input, he will revise that synopsis so that it is always current.

"We have a very large picture of Grock [the legendary Swiss clown] on the wall of the room where we meet," Christensen says, "and what we do is we take sticky papers and write down the components of the show, each one on a different piece of sticky paper. We have one section labeled 'R' representing reprises. When everything is on the board, we start playing on Grock, moving papers around, rearranging the order they will appear in the show. When we need a reprise [a relatively short piece of clowning], we grab one from under the "Rs" and see how we like it, looking for variety and making sure the needs of the acts are met. Each reprise has a time written on it, how long it will take. We play around until we come up with an order we can live with at that time, and then Jando cranks out the latest synopsis. This process continues on until the first day of rehearsals, and we have a final synopsis."

While all this is going on, the designers are doing their preproduction work, drawing their inspiration from various artifacts—photographs, clippings, art works, mementos, films—that Binder, Christensen, and the director have collected.

After the show is written, a script is presented to Paul Binder, general manager Guillaume Dufresnoy, and Tom Larson, the technical director. "If everyone loves it," Christensen says, charting the progress of the creation, "we present it to the designers. They make notes. Then we have subsequent meetings with the designers to address such issues as budget and time lines. The designers cross-pollinate and take each other's work into account."

After final approval of the designs and budgets, the new production is presented to the current company who may have a role in it, so they can start rehearsing any new acts before the start of rehearsals in Walden, New York.[41]

★ ★ ★

Christensen worked closely with the director, Guy Caron, on the 20th anniversary production. Caron at the time was working as a freelance director of circus and spectacle, after having served as Cirque du Soleil's first artistic director. He had previously worked with the Big Apple Circus as a consultant three years before Christensen thought of their directing together.

During those years, the two men found that they got along really well. "We have a similar means of communicating," Christensen says. "There was a wonderful rapport, evident from the very beginning. Eventually Guy expressed interest in directing one of the shows with me and put this forward to Paul [Binder], who also thought it was a good idea, and so Guy signed on to direct two productions of the Big Apple Circus, one of which I would co-direct with him. It was a wonderful opportunity to step forward."

Caron, who sees the clowns as the links that hold a circus performance together, says that he particularly wanted Christensen as codirector because the clowning had been Christensen's special concern on the Big Apple Circus for many years. As a codirector, Christensen would be able to provide a comfortable transition in the show's ongoing artistic evolution. "Michael is my guideline," Caron said, during the show's rehearsals in Walden, N.Y. "He gives me the spirit and flavor of the Big Apple. Whenever I go too far, he pulls me back and says, 'That's not the Big Apple Circus.'"

Caron was pragmatic in what he hoped to accomplish with the Big Apple Circus. It wasn't so much where the show was going that concerned him as much as how it went about getting there. "I didn't come to change the show," he explained. He was more interested in changing the process rather than the product.[42]

The reason for the concern over the process at the time that Caron and Christensen first collaborated was because the 20th anniversary show was the first to be rehearsed and put together in the company's new creative center in Walden. Previously, each season's new acts were rehearsed at Floyd Bennett Field in Brooklyn. Prior to the show's traditional opening in Reston, Virginia, all the elements of the new production—the setting, music, lights, sound, staging, guest artists, and company acts—were put together in just ten days.

Having the facilities of Walden at their disposal changed all that for the creative staff. It afforded them a luxury virtually unknown in most performing arts institutions. During the show's seven-week stay in the bucolic village of Walden, the lighting designer and crew, the composer and the musicians, the stage manager and ring crew are all in residence, along with the core company and some of the guest artists.

Before taking up residence in Walden, however, every company member will have received a letter of welcome and a synopsis of the new show, with his or her own contributions highlighted. Prior to moving to Walden, usually in the early spring, the directors will meet with the new company to explain the concept and their individual parts in making it come alive. All of the artifacts that had stimulated the directors' thinking are shared with the company, as are preliminary costume sketches. Depending on the theme, this meeting may also include a movement rehearsal.

The first company meeting in Walden is held on or about August 15. The rehearsals in the big top there are held under much the same circumstances as those that will prevail during a performance. The ring crew moves mock-ups of the actual props around as needed, on cue, so that their timing will be as precise as that of any of the performers.

The lighting plot that will be used in the ultimate performance is already in place at this time. Follow spot operators, as well as the other electricians, participate in every run-through, and the lighting is constantly being adjusted (sometimes merely through trial and error) in consultation between the designer and directors as the performance evolves.

This method, which Caron brought from his experience with Cirque du Soleil, is used because Caron feels so strongly about the importance of the show's lighting design. Whenever the designer sees something that stimulates a new idea, Caron will temporarily halt the proceedings so that he can be shown what the designer has in mind for that moment. The change will be discussed, discarded, modified, or incorporated before the rehearsal moves forward again.

In the meantime, the musicians who will play the score on tour are rehearsing in the music studio under the tutelage of the musical director, who is also at the directors' elbow ready to discuss and make any changes or adjustments that may be deemed necessary by alterations in the performance's changing scenario.

Each of the rehearsals is videotaped. These documents of the performance's ever-changing status are studied each night by the performers and the creative team, just as the daily rushes might be studied by a film director.

In Walden, "we make the transition from what we've been doing in a room all by ourselves to the reality of live performers in the ring," Christensen points out. "The translation of comedy into the reality of clowns in a ring surrounded by an audience is very difficult. Some things translate readily and others don't translate at all. You see those differences very clearly in the rehearsal process. You have to decide what to keep and what to throw out. It is a process that never ends. The process becomes even more refined when you add an audience. There are constant discoveries."

After the dress rehearsal in Walden, "we literally give Paul the keys, which means he is now the guardian. He is now the steward, the director." At this point the director's contractual obligations have ended.

The need for any further changes that become apparent during the run will usually be taken care of during the big breaks in the touring schedule, between the so-called tryout dates in Reston, Virginia, and the opening in Lincoln Center, and then again before the Atlanta run.[43]

Of his experience as a full-fledged director, Christensen says, "One of the things I discovered while directing was that directing clowns is not as easy as being a clown. It was a lot easier to have the vision than to realize the vision, what with all the personalities one has to deal with. The first show was a much easier go than *Happy On!* [the second show he directed with Caron]. There was a ready-made theme there for us in the 20th anniversary show and Grandma's birthday party. So it was more straightforward.

"In *Happy On!* Guy and I had a very clear vision of what we wanted the show to be like, inspired by the Spike Jones craziness. As it turned out, however, the process was a series of setbacks, one after the other, and they never stopped right up to opening night. It was the single most difficult experience I've had with the Big Apple Circus.

"Part of it was because of the various contractual negotiations. Then it was the musical director; we didn't know if we had a band, or which acts. The Chinese [acrobatic troupe] was very inexperienced when they showed up. They had never worked in a circus before. After a few months they really grew up and gained a professionalism that was not there in the beginning."

He has also learned to be adaptable. "A lot of times in the midst of the process you can get attached to an idea that you should have long since discarded and gone on, using it as a stepping stone to the next idea," Christensen admits. "I learned from this experience, happily, that I do have a facile ability to do that. A lot of ideas are like pushing a car up a hill, when what you need to do is cut it loose or get a new car, and the sooner the better."[44]

★ ★ ★

Like the other companies under discussion here, Circus Flora has incorporated all of the theatrical arts in its productions, but to this mix it also adds various concepts of the dramatic arts, as well. Cecil MacKinnon, the director and star of Circus Flora, divides her time between the theatre and the circus. When working in the theatre, she notes, "I have a script to pore over long before rehearsals begin; the next step in the process is to cast and confer with the designers. Then I begin the collaboration with the actors in rehearsal. In the circus I have found that the collaboration is more fundamental and constant than it is in the theatre. That is because in the circus, the collaboration includes creating the framework of the show itself."

The creation of each new production of Circus Flora begins with discussions involving MacKinnon and the show's cofounders, David Balding and Sacha Pavlata. More recently general manager Holly Harris is also involved in this process. These individuals make all the decisions about the performance together and through constant consultation. "Our show, as a result, has a sort of antihierarchical style that can take a while for performers, new to us, to grasp," MacKinnon explains. "My particular province, the plot, the movement from one act to another, and the clown acts, overlaps constantly with those of both David and Sacha. Decisions about acts and their order are made by all three of us. No one person can decide a show's structure. That involves a mix of concerns." The danger and intricacy of the acts involved add complexities that must be taken into consideration, as well as any required rigging changes.[45] Other considerations to be taken into account include any performers who appear in more than one act, the presence of animals, and the transitions from air to ground or vice versa. A final consideration is the circus audience, which is very different from a theatre audience and, therefore, dictates a different approach than would be used in the theatre.

As might be guessed from the preceding, Circus Flora considers itself to be a theatre-circus, and through the more than dozen years of its existence its creative staff has been working to make this a fusion of two truly equal halves, neither dominated by the other.

From the very beginning, the performances of Circus Flora have been narrative driven. For the first several years of its existence that narrative took the form of an annual installment of a serial that told the story of a circus coming to America. Loosely based on historical fact, the fictional circus family was known as the Baldinis (which began as a play on Balding's name, but like many such jokes, it stuck, and the name lasted for several years). In successive shows the plot followed this fictional circus family as it arrived in the United States, met Uncle Sam, traveled west, ran into buffaloes and native Americans, made its way down the Mississippi to New Orleans where brigands nearly annihilated the troupe, and finally set sail through the Caribbean, where the family was attacked by pirates. Ultimately the Baldinis landed in California, where their adventures were left.

"When we put together Circus Flora's first show in 1986, we had a writer who worked from the improvisations that I did with Hall Hunsinger," MacKinnon says, recounting the history of the show's early years, beginning with its appearance at the Spoleto Festival in Charleston, South Carolina. "Patty Swanson was the director at that time. David had already hired the acts, and the design work was completed separately. The music was found and arranged for a brass band. As we toured that first show, acts would leave and join, and the script would have to change to accommodate the comings and goings. We would improvise any changes and then fix and set them until something else forced another change."

As Circus Flora grew, the same creative model was retained, but MacKinnon took over the direction from Swanson and the process evolved into a "way of working." In 1988 Miriam Cutler was hired to compose an original score.

"Through those years, working with a variety of partners—primarily Michael Preston [who later joined the Flying Karamazov Brothers] and Merry Conway [a Le Coq trained clown]—I would work in a studio in New York for a couple of weeks before rehearsals, and together we would evolve a loose story line," MacKinnon says, continuing Flora's own saga. "I have also been joined at times by Giovanni Zoppe, Tomas Kupincek, Felix Blaska, and Alex Pavlata.

"During this time, we would have chosen the acts or been rehearsing new acts with performers who, by now, formed a loose company and tended to return to Flora from season to season, particularly Tino Wallenda."

After completing the Baldini saga, MacKinnon took up a detective story. For that show it was she and Cutler who talked through the plot during a weekend retreat together. "Our inspiration was our rooster, Pappagallo, who played dead with remarkable élan. He would lie on the ring curb with his little feet straight up and allow the follow spot to linger on him as he lay there motionless. This inspired me, and the 'crime' of the detective story became not a murder, but the case of The Frozen Rooster. (Various other characters also became frozen into statues, but no other animal actor had Pappagallo's unique talent.)

"Flora, the elephant, was our leading character, and I think it was Miriam who came up with the idea of calling her Inspector Floreau. After that weekend, Miriam sent me tapes of themes and music, which our band rehearsed separately. When we all came together in St. Louis for rehearsals, we had a plot, music, and acts to integrate.

"Performers new to Circus Flora are warned that they will have to use the show's music and costuming. This was very much an issue in the beginning, but has become much less of a problem as this idea is increasingly the norm in circus," MacKinnon relates.[46]

As the creative process continues, Janine Del' Arté, the band leader, and MacKinnon work closely weaving the spoken and visual elements of the production together and setting the music cues to create a unified piece in which the acts, the music, and the text all tell a story.

A few years ago Hovey Burgess, who had been working with Flora as a juggling instructor, became the show's "dramaturg," a term borrowed from the theatre. What that meant in this context was that he was expected to come up with raw material, which MacKinnon could then twist and shape into a plot for a circus performance.

For example, when the plot wandered west, Sky de Sela, a very talented young woman, was a member of the company. Burgess discovered, through his research, that Adah Isaac Mencken and two other women were performing in that area of the country as independent female performers in the 1880s. That information helped establish Sky's character. On another occasion, he researched the World's Fair in St. Louis and the hootchy-kootchy in particular, details of which were used in the plot development

For a few years the staff rehearsed the next show as it performed the current one. (But for Miriam Cutler, no one in the company is exclusively a creator. Everyone also performs.) "This has advantages and disadvantages," MacKinnon points out. "It does allow us to try out new acts and expand or discard ideas quickly as they can be tried out almost immediately. In this way all fifty or so people connected with the show are involved from the beginning in its evolution and have a stake in it.

"I do not strive for tight control. I try to create an atmosphere in which people feel free and empowered to contribute their ideas," MacKinnon explains. "It is difficult in the circus ring to try out ideas that don't immediately pay off, and a large part of my task is to encourage performers to try new things anyway.

"I have," MacKinnon says, "over the years, thought a great deal about this style of directing, its pains and strengths. The dynamic of not controlling too much and yet making the choices needed is constantly tugging at me. I try to allow for a variety of performing styles and to present them with tolerance and humor. I aim for a production with a freewheeling, warm, inclusive feeling, hoping to keep the joy, as well as the awe and admiration that all circuses can inspire."

To further illustrate her creative process, MacKinnon spoke in detail about the making of the show that served as a bon voyage party to the show's namesake, Flora, the elephant. "The idea of its being Flora's last show made me want to do it about her. I usually base the shows on fact, historical fact, or some other kind of fact. I was inspired by Jean de Brunhoff's *Babar*, not any one of the stories, but the tone of them all. That was what interested me. Besides, I also liked the fact that the stories have a very simple narrative, without being sentimental. And I loved the image of the rear of an elephant scaring away a rhinoceros. I loved that image, and so I drew it and sent it to David [Balding] and Flora's trainer, Raul, about three months before we started rehearsals so that they could get Flora used to backing into the ring.

"I usually start working on a new show in February if we're going up in April, and I write the scenario for myself before I get to St. Louis, before all of the acts are there. Sometimes, depending on the year, I actually get together with the composer. We send material back and forth, and since we've been working together for so long that seems to work pretty well.

"When I get here and see the acts, I start figuring out how to weave them all together. And to do that, I have to change my scenario. You have to be very flexible, so I give myself something to start from and then I throw it out and basically start all over again.

"When I write my first scenario, I have some idea of what the acts in the show will be. So I establish a running order and then talk to David and change it around, and then we finally change once again when we're here.

"We do seek certain acts because of a specific skill that seems to work into the scenario. We always have something specific in mind when we hire them.

"I don't generally show what I have written to anyone else except the composer or someone who knows we aren't necessarily going to stick to what I have written. People tend to think that if something is written down, that's it. And that's not the way it is in my head at all.

"As the show's narrator, that leaves me free to say absolutely anything I want. That's a great freedom to have. The words are written quite late. I'm still moving things around in my head for the first three or four performances. And of course there are always things [like unexpected mishaps] which I have to cover, and I'm pretty used to doing that. As long as I know the world I'm in really clearly and the kind of story it is and the kind of thing I'm talking about or dealing with, I feel I can cover for most anything. It's an actor's problem.

"We rehearse for five days, with all the acts and the band. That's a crucial thing, the band, because it's almost a musical dialogue.

"What's always difficult is that for every cue you have to coordinate the movements of about forty people. And usually if something goes wrong with a cue, it's because someone had to solve some other problem that came up at that moment. Circus people tend to solve a problem on their own, but if you get them to talk to each other, they can figure out how to solve it a little more quickly with several people. You have to walk them through it, too. You can't just talk about it."[47]

★ ★ ★

Jeff Jenkins and Julie Greenberg are both natives of Chicago. Julie graduated from the University of Illinois with a BFA in theatre and then went on to study Shakespeare at the National Theatre of Great Britain. She was also a member of the first American company to study and tour with the Kabuki theatre in Japan. Jeff, on the other hand, went to Ringling's Clown College right after high school and toured with The Greatest Show on Earth for two years.

Upon ending his association with the circus, Jeff moved back to his hometown, Chicago, intending to start a Loop theatre, hustling acting roles wherever he found them. Eventually their paths crossed, and Jeff invited Julie to join his company of actors to practice tumbling and clowning. After working as a team for nearly five years, they married in 1999, and finding their own union mutually satisfying, they next decided to serve as matchmaker for the circus and theatre.

In 1994, however, before that could happen, Jeff was offered the job of running Vermont's youth circus, Circus Smirkus, while its founder Rob Mermin was on a sabbatical, serving as co-dean of Clown College with Dick Monday.

The couple took it on together. "We brought a theatrical background to Circus Smirkus, which it didn't have before," Julie says. "We started choreographing acts and directing them to tell a story." By the time they ended their two-year stint with Smirkus, they had a trunkful of new skills they had picked up from the Smirkus coaches, and then upon returning to Chicago, they quickly discovered they had nowhere to use them. To refresh their creative spirit they started going around looking at what was being done in other theatres around Chicago. Disappointed in what little physical theatre they saw, they decided they would do something to make up for that shortcoming and set out to write a show of their own. "We were very full of ourselves, pretentious," Julie admits. That was in January of 1997.[48]

They began by exploring what it was that bothered them about what they were seeing elsewhere. Finally they started writing about things they knew something about. For Julie it was the theatre, and for Jeff it was circus. What they arrived at was a parody of serious theatre, filtered through a clown mentality.

"We came up with the idea of a classic acting company doing a classic scene, a kitchen-sink drama, which happened to be straight out of *A Streetcar Named Desire*. We wanted the circus to literally bust down the door and walk in and have the circus performers try their hand at drama and vice versa, each making something better than they could have done working independently.

"Out of the eighteen people we thought about asking to join us, we got none." Instead, they turned to a group of people they had been working with in Chicago at the time. Some of them came from circus, some from theatre, some even came from opera; one was a carpenter. "We couldn't offer them any money," Julie points out, but they were interested, at least tentatively. "All we asked was that they bring some kind of skill. We didn't care if they could act, so long as they had some kind of skill, which was our first mistake," Julie says now. "Because although we found out we could take great performers and give them a skill," there was no way to turn an acrobat into an actor if he was not imbued with the needed spirit and energy.

In an effort to keep the company together, "We put some of them up in our spare bedroom." The script evolved as an attempt to accommodate the people involved. Ironically, for all its catch-as-catch-can improvisations, the show clicked on stage. Offstage, however, Jeff quickly adds, "the company couldn't have been more dysfunctional. Some of the people in the show brought acts they weren't too excited about changing to fit our show." It was a classic case of life imitating art. This was the kind of marriage no one would have given a chance of succeeding, but it worked, at least onstage. Offstage the tensions were never resolved. "When it took off, we didn't have the foundation to keep a company together, but suddenly there was a company, whether we liked it or not."[49]

The performance that ultimately came to impress Chicago theatre critics grew out of a three-page outline. Most of the comedy, although not written out, was planned in advance, and the only changes concerned whatever acts the two could get to plug into the script. As with other circus directors, the couple not only wrote their show, but also directed it. The distinction here was that they also starred in it, and to make matters more complicated, there were very few production people backing them up in the technical departments.

After the first six weeks of turning away as many people as they could squeeze into a sixty-seat theater, the couple knew the show had to go on. A move was made to the Ivanhoe, a larger, more expensive theatre. Following nearly a year's run, the couple was exhausted and depressed. "We felt we were the only ones not growing," Julie says. "We were finished."[50]

During that remarkable run at the Ivanhoe it happened that Paul Binder dropped by to see what all the fuss was about. He was so taken with the show that he invited Jeff and Julie to join the Big Apple Circus as clowns. They were flattered, but decided to decline. Four months later an offer came from the Big Apple Circus looking to buy out the Midnight Circus lock, stock, and barrel. Instead of accepting that offer, Jeff and Julie wound up licensing the rights to their show for what eventually was to become *Oops, The Big Apple Circus Stage Show*. That contract, the two concur, gave them renewed confidence in their work, for it validated what they had been trying to do, and it gave them the financial wherewithal to keep doing it.

Once their show closed, the couple opened a studio of their own in an old firehouse, which was where Nyangar Batbaatar found them. A gifted acrobatics coach, Batbaatar began to attract others. Without having to go out looking for them, a new company of people who shared the couple's vision was beginning to take shape around them and their studio.

"We ran the studio like Hovey Burgess did with his on the Bowery," Jeff points out. "Anybody who came could participate, but they had to do something. Nothing was organized. They came out of the woodwork. Some of them were legit actors who wanted to do something more physical. We had a dozen or so regulars. They were working out just for the sake of working out." Even when no money was involved, they kept telling Jeff and Julie, "Whatever you need, we want to be here."

A short time after closing their first production the couple was approached to do a new show, which was to open the season at Chicago's Theater on the Lake. "The city had committed a lot of money, which was more than we ever had," Jeff remembers. "We felt burnt out," Julie adds, "but we had to sit down and write a new show. We held auditions and found some great people. We discovered they're out there."[51]

This time Jeff and Julie worked on the script with a writer, and miraculously, everyone got along.

★ ★ ★

In the development of the Midnight Circus, the studio has played an important role. "It is our big sandbox," Jeff says jokingly. "We have all our toys there."

"Having a studio is important, a necessity," Julie says, embroidering the thought. "It's ours. There's lots of tradition and history there." It is also home base, a place the company members can identify with and know that they are welcome there. In the company classes, it is especially gratifying to the couple to find themselves perfecting their own skills alongside people who share their commitment to a particular style of performance.[52]

It is something of an understatement to say, therefore, that a studio is an essential element for any circus company that hopes to develop an ensemble style and production technique. Even on a scale much reduced from Cirque du Soleil, what happens in the Chicago studio of Jeff Jenkins and Julie Greenberg is the equivalent of the research and development that takes place in the Montreal facility.

★　★　★

This matter of developing a narrative for a circus performance has proven tricky for all who have tried it. Tandy Beal, a choreographer turned director, has also employed a story line in a number of the shows she created for the Pickle Circus because she saw it as a way of providing cohesion to a group of seemingly disparate acts. Instead of submerging the circus artists in imagined characters, however, she believes that the story line must be loose enough to allow the audience to identify with each act or performer as his or her own self, rather than as a particular character. "The audience must recognize and empathize with the real person in front of them doing the act," she says, "because if the performer in a precarious act is seen as a character rather than as a person who is actually doing something electrifying, then it is a bit like the unreality of the movie when you know the hero will make it through any difficult situation."[53]

For her, the plot provides a jumping-off point. In her production of *Tossing and Turning*, the acts and the comedy were based on the central character's insomnia. The clown, Jeff Raz, was Everyman trying to get some sleep, and Diane Wasnak was the twin image of the Sandman who tried to put him to sleep and the Mischief Maker who kept him awake. The acts were the dreams.

In *Jump Cuts*, the clowns Raz and Wasnak were lost in a movie studio and kept stumbling into the sets of various movies: a western, detective, romance, adventure. The set, costumes, and score would transform themselves to provide the appropriate atmosphere, and the acts would emerge from each new environment.

Tandy Beal is also one of the two most successful circus choreographers. The other is Debra Brown, who has choreographed nine of Cirque du Soleil's most important productions. Their work is significant in that, for them, bringing choreography to the circus meant more than simply devising dance combinations for a group of dancers who tended to be more decorative than integral to the overall production. It meant imposing on circus performers a dancer's obsession with making every move beautiful.

Despite the similarity of the aesthetic they each bring to choreographing a circus, they approach their work from opposite poles. Beal comes to the circus from the world of dance, Brown from competitive gymnastics.

Tandy Beal's dance background has had, she admits, a significant impact on the way she works with circus performers. "Coming from many years of dance," she explains, "my eye is trained to see movement, dynamics, form, timing, and showmanship, and my craft is to shape those elements to the best advantage of the performer and the show. As a choreographer, I was trained to work carefully with music, and in my particular background with the Nikolai Dance Theatre, with lighting as well. This has been a rich resource to mine in making circus shows. I use these tools all the time.

"In the circus I find that people are often trick oriented, so I have to take a different point of view than I do when working with dancers. I try to get the performers to see the narrative of what they are doing and how it can be enhanced to make their tricks look better. I tell the circus performers that phrasing is what makes their work look beautiful. If you can phrase something with an inner song, then it sings to the audience.

"I have found that there is a density to most circus performers' bodies. They are very mesomorphic and very strong, but not very fluid—contortionists excepted. I work with them to keep fluidity in their musculature and to allow their minds to move fluidly through their bodies. I also teach them the basics like pointing feet, projecting into space, projecting outward no matter how fearful they are, and how to work with rhythm, which is not always a part of their training."[54]

There are other differences between dancers and circus performers and athletes. "With ballet dancers," Beal points out, "you must be very specific. They want to know which foot to start on, where each finger should be placed, how their head is to be held. When you are working with a wirewalker you have to get into the kinetics of how that works. When you switch to the trapeze it's a very different use of gravity, so you have to figure out what that feels like." As a result, Beal is cognizant of the fact that consideration of the body dynamics is essential, both in realizing a particular trick and in making it look beautiful.

"I have to think about how my shifting an acrobat's placement will affect a trick," Beal admits. "I have to ask myself who am I to go in and mess with an acrobat's placement. Often, however, where the weight is placed can be a matter of style rather than function. I'm still feeling my way through that," Beal confesses.[55]

★ ★ ★

Debra Brown, on the other hand, having studied and competed as a gymnast, says she knows in her body what each move feels like. "I am very comfortable in the world of acrobatics. Even though my body hasn't done all the flips that they have, my body has flipped, so I have a kinesthetic awareness of where they travel."

Born in Toronto, Debra Brown grew up wanting to be a gymnast. Once she saw someone perform a cartwheel, she was determined to be a gymnast. The skills essential to realizing that ambition were essentially self-taught. She and a friend would watch gymnasts and acrobats on television and then try to figure out how to do what they had just seen. Her friend would always try the move first, "and I would analyze why she fell flat on her face. That's how we trained."[56]

In university Brown finally got to work with a very strong coach and learned to do gymnastics properly. She competed in all four women's events between the ages of thirteen and twenty-one.

After receiving a degree in physical education from Western University in London, she went on to earn a fine arts degree in dance from York University in Toronto. She then moved to Vancouver where she continued studying dance and performed with modern dance companies and trained gymnasts. Several of those she worked with were on the Canadian national team; two went to the 1984 Olympics.

"I worked with the same gymnasts for eight years," she says, "and we started to develop a style because they knew my work so well." That style soon began attracting attention. Eventually she became the choreographer of the Canadian national gymnastics team. One of the people she worked with, Laurie Fong, won the gold medal at the Los Angeles Olympics.

At that point, she began looking about for other challenges, and someone suggested she go see Cirque du Soleil. In 1986 Cirque came to Vancouver for the children's festival, "and I snuck under the big top at intermission and saw the second half. And I said, 'This is really cool; they're trying to do the same thing I am doing, only in circus,' trying to make gymnastics artistic."

The next day the individual artists appeared at the Canada pavilion, and she gave several of them her business card. It was 1987, and the troupe had just been invited to the States, and had, therefore, decided they needed to add a choreographer to their roster. It also happened that Andre Simard, who at that time was the national gymnastics coach, was sharing an office with Guy Caron, then the Cirque du Soleil artistic director. The men's national gymnastics team trained out of the same center in Montreal where the circus school trained. So, as it turned out, Simard was in the office when Caron was handed Brown's business card by one of the clowns to whom she had given it the day before. "I know her," he told Caron. "She would be a good person to hire."[57]

So in 1987, Brown came to Montreal. "It changed my life, and my coming in added a taste they didn't have before," Brown confirms. Over the course of the next sixteen years, she believes, "each creation was a theatrical evolution of ourselves, in movement and visuals and everything, so collectively I think we have evolved together in the field of circus. Collectively we went further with each new show."

Part of that evolution has been a growing acceptance of dance as part of the circus performance. "I think *Mystère* was first," she says. "We hired six dancers for that. It took an adaptation that would allow me to create a schedule that would suit dancers and cater to their rhythm because it's very different from that of acrobats. They need a class in the morning, and then they like to rehearse after class. Even their rhythm of warming up is different. Acrobats don't need a dance class in the morning. They need their own type of warm-up to prepare them for their physical feats, so normally everyone does their own different warm-up. But dancers are used to doing the same vocabulary."[58]

Quidam, O, and *La Nouba,* the last shows created by Dragone and his team, of which Brown was a prominent member, contain the most actual dance of all the Cirque du Soleil productions. One of the reasons for *Quidam* having so much dance movement is that the choreographer spent far more time with the performers than she had in the past. "I was seriously invested in the show the moment the artists arrived. Usually they train for six months, and then we go into full production." The reason for her early involvement here was that a group of Russian artists had been brought in to create the banquine number. No one in the group spoke anything but Russian, and none of them had worked together before. Brown speaks English and French. "And so," she confesses, "I was really nervous because this was the first group number using Russians that we would create in the studio. So I started with them right at the beginning. Maybe that's why it's so choreographically heavy."

One way of getting people to move, Brown believes, is by motivating them with music. "I had to create a rope skipping number for all those Russian men. So what we did was to play great music and everybody started skipping and had a lot of fun because they enjoyed the music. I didn't know what I was doing. I had never choreographed skipping, but I knew how to work the stage and spacing.

"Music is a great way to get people loosened up. Find something that they can respond to. When I was working with René [Dupéré] it was very different from working with Benoit Jutras. René would create lots of little themes, and I would take them to the rehearsal and put them on, and whatever felt good I would take back to his studio the next day and say, 'We need something more like this.'"

Although she makes no claims to being a dancer, Brown has, in fact, studied dance, both modern and ballet, and even maintains her own modern dance company, Apogee. "But," she insists, "I use everybody else's talents. That's one thing that is great about the circus. We don't give them choreography, but we use their talents and their physical features. So I can work with almost anyone. One of my strong points is getting non-movers, people who are not dancers, to move, because I think of it more as movement than dance. I love getting them to move in a nonthreatening way."

When she worked at the Metropolitan Opera providing choreography for a production of *Ghosts of Versailles*, music director James Levine complimented her on her nonthreatening way of getting opera singers, who would prefer standing stock still when belting out their arias, to move. She has also worked with Madonna and one hundred ballroom dancers in Prague on the film *Van Helsing*, with Hugh Jackman.

"My own philosophy, my own point of view about movement is that I'm not a dancer; I don't consider myself a 'dancer'; I consider myself a 'mover,' and so I don't carry an air of training with me to intimidate them. In addition, you have to be adaptable; you have to try different things."[59]

When working with gymnasts Brown makes it a point not to use dance vocabulary with them. It makes them feel awkward and out of place, because their training is completely different from that of a dancer.

Brown's use of music to stimulate movement is an idea Beal would also endorse. "Developing musicality," she points out, "is the crossover between dance and circus skills."[60] And that, of course, is where the choreographer comes into the picture.

It is difficult for Debra Brown to be specific about how she goes about creating "beautiful movement" because she insists every single show is different. "It all depends on the dynamics of the cast, the nature of the equipment that you're dealing with. There are so many variables that no circus [production] is ever the same, and it depends on my involvement. If I start in the beginning, I have more time to integrate, which is very healthy. Sometimes it's so difficult that I can't really move on an act because it needs both me and Franco to put it together. There are moments like that when I need his help to adapt it to the stage."

"Often in the rehearsal process, I start with the artists before Franco. When we created *Quidam* he gave me one word, 'simplicity,' which I kept in the back of my mind. With *Mystère* it was birds mating. I don't think he gave me a word for *O*. It was more water, obviously. He gives me these loose outlines, and he trusts me to start to research because choreographically, it's my milieu, acrobatic dance. I have a lot of freedom.

"I know Franco, when he starts working with the performers, will get hooked on maybe two or three pieces of music, and he'll try many different elements to that music. And then he'll find a color that he likes." On other occasions she and the director will work with a particular act. "Sometimes we work from scratch and create the act. Sometimes the artists have the basis of an act, and we change it and sometimes, as for example when the Chinese came over, and they had an act, we'll just stage it to fit into our show. I'll just change little things. So there are different degrees to what I do, and there's no one method to how it begins."

Perhaps the most vital part of what Brown does is getting to know the artists she is working with and determining what they are capable of doing, both as dancers and as circus performers. "But the process goes beyond just exploring personalities and individual ability." The array of novel apparatus that Cirque has created and used in its productions has forced further exploration and experimentation. "Some of it [the apparatus] has been new, and I would never have had the opportunity to explore it elsewhere, so you have no choice but to experiment in the here and now. I'm one of the few choreographers in the world who got to do research on so many different elements, working with people on so many different apparatuses."

As far as the individual artists are concerned, Brown says, "I get to know them during the process when I start the rehearsals. I usually visit the training sessions, depending on what act needs more time acrobatically. Sometimes an act needs more time to get the tricks together before we're ready to deal [with movement]. Now the studio is changing its methods. They start artistic and acrobatic right off the top from day one. And all the artists get both types of training right away, so it's not separate, these are the tricks and this is the artistic part.

"I think that the most important thing about the creative process, and this is what Franco used to say, is your intuition, what you bring. And I couldn't agree more, and perhaps that is why we were able to work together for so long. We used our intuition on stage." And, apparently, they also trusted each other's intuition.

After thirteen years of working with Franco Dragone, Debra Brown took a break from Cirque du Soleil before returning to work on the company's Las Vegas venture, *Zumanity*. During her time away from the company she worked on a variety of projects. Of her position now, she says, "I'm really on the outside as well as on the inside. That's probably why I've been able to continue working here because I'm on the outside and inside."[61]

★ ★ ★

In addition to the directors and choreographers who are responsible for the style and substance of an entire production, there are also artists who create individual acts for one or more performers. These acts are, in effect, mini-performances that may tell a story but always have a beginning, a middle, and a conclusion. The two principal exponents of this art are Valentin Gneushev, whose work has been seen in circuses around the globe; and Alla Youdina, whose work has been featured in several productions of Ringling Bros. and Barnum & Bailey Circus and Circus Smirkus, the Vermont-based youth circus.

Although not a performer himself, Valentin Gneushev for a time stood virtually alone in the world as the preeminent creator of circus acts. No one else can match the number, variety, and quality of the acts he has had a hand in sending out into the world. Like many of the people involved in today's circus, his background is in the theatre as well as the circus. After completing his studies at the state-run circus school in his native Russia, however, he abandoned the circus to take up study at the Moscow Theatre Institute, where he apprenticed himself to several of the theatre's leading directors for six years. He then returned to his first love, the circus.

It is not surprising, therefore, to find that his circus work has been influenced by his theatre work. The acts he has developed are often inspired by the artists whose work he admires: Charlie Chaplin, Federico Fellini, Marcel Marceau, Picasso, and Wagner.

Many young people have come to him, seeking his services, many more in fact than he could possibly accommodate. As a result, he has had to be selective, and the first thing he looks for in a young artist, he has said, is an interesting personality. He must, he says, be able to see something in the prospect. Sometimes that "something" may be a quality that will turn others away. There is an old saying, "crazy like an artist." He seeks out that craziness.[62] Of course, one cannot discount an artist's skill level, which is a crucial consideration, but for Gneushev there is also a matter of "feeling" and the artist's sensuality, to which he is extremely sensitive.[63]

Gneushev is himself a highly cultured man. Completely lacking modesty, he compares himself to Michelangelo. He, too, sculpts, he says. He has to chip away at what does not belong, to get at the essential artist that is embedded in the stone. Most directors, he points out, are very aggressive. They change things. But, he says, as fond of metaphors as he is of classical references, it is necessary to stain your hands to spill blood when being creative.

In describing his creative process, Gneushev says he must first observe the artists who come to him, and evaluate absolutely everything about them, to the extent that, in the end, he will know them completely: their past, their present, and even to the point of being about to predict what kind of future they will have. At that stage, it is essential to let the artist be natural and open so that he can "feel" him. The next step is to take those qualities he has intuited from the potential artist and exploit them. With the juggler Tsarkov, for instance, he observed his mechanical gestures, and made use of them. He then created a commedia dell'arte-type of character, like Picasso's *Red Harlequin*, and asked the artist to perform within a tight circle where he seemed to be in his own world, separated from the audience.

With Vladimir Kehkaial, who presented a sensational strap act with Cirque du Soleil, it was different. He was obviously a strong, attractive body-builder-type, with something inside him that suggested the demonic. Inspired by that, Gneushev took a painting called *The Demon* by the Russian artist Vrubel as a source of inspiration. He stripped the artist's costume down to little more than a jockstrap and allowed his flowing mane to hang wildly about his shoulders. So successful was the act that Kehkaial quickly left Cirque du Soleil and headed for Las Vegas, and eventually to London where he starred in his own show and has spawned many imitators.

Vasilyi Demenchukov originally wanted to do an act in which he would be a cosmonaut. In observing him Gneushev took note of the fact that, for some strange reason, he always had cakes in the trunk of his car that he was taking to his friends. As a result, Gneushev created an act for Demenchukov in which he climbs a stack of chairs, which gets higher and higher, and all the while he is balancing a tray with a cake on it. Thus Demenchukov became the man who delivers cakes.

Once accepted by Gneushev, the artist is expected to submit himself completely to his vision. Is there something of the Svengali to the man?

His artists, he insists, are not passive objects that he molds to his taste. The fact that the artist has to open himself up and show him everything about himself, Gneushev claims, is a form of participation. If the director's instincts are correct, the artist will follow naturally, even to the extent that, Gneushev says, the artist will believe that what he got from the director came from himself. This certainly was true of Tsarkov. He came to Gneushev and told him, "You see, I was right to choose red!"[64] And this is the point: if the creation is to ring true, the proposition will seem to have come from the artists because it is an obvious proposition based on who they are.

In the creative process, Gneushev will also help the artist develop new tricks or expand his or her skills through the use of qualified trainers in order to accommodate the director's vision.[65] The length of time Gneushev spends with an act varies according to its needs. The Peresvoni, a flying act known as The Chimes, needed only ten days to put their act together, insofar as the concept (or the metaphor) and the choreography were concerned. All the movements and the choreography, along with the music, were prepared on the ground, before the troupe went aloft. The most important part of the process was adapting the rhythm of the music to the rhythm of the tricks or vice versa. When he works with an individual, however, the approach is different. Then it becomes a question of probing for feelings and that sensuality, a process that can be quite time consuming.[66]

Fiercely independent, Gneushev has insisted that he does whatever he wants in regard to larger projects. Sometimes projects, like his full-length but ill-fated production Cirk Valentin, which quickly died in the confines of a New York theatre, do not work out. "Life is difficult," he glumly concludes with a shrug.[67]

Life has at times proven so difficult for him that in order to support his appetite for the finer things it has to offer, he has left the circus for other employment not connected to the performing arts.

★ ★ ★

Alla Youdina is known in the circus world for the imaginative acts she created for Ringling Bros. and Barnum & Bailey. Those acts include the "Chicago Kidz," the "Spider Web," and "Women of the Rainbow." Her work with Circus Smirkus has been documented by the Disney Channel's *Totally Circus*, a series that ran on national television during the summer of 2000. She worked for both Ringling and Circus Smirkus, often simultaneously, for ten years.

Another product of the theatre and like Gneushev something of a poet who deals in images and symbols, she was Ringling's most significant bridge to the "New" circus and its main link to what was left of the Russian state circus and its pool of finely trained performers.

After her performing days ended, Youdina completed graduate study with a thesis on theatre imagery and worked as a dramaturg selecting plays for Russian theatres. By 1990, she was a top executive in the All Union Administration of Circus Programs in the Russian Federation.

As a director capable of providing not only the artistic vision, but also the physical and mental training required to make something imagined into something real, she consistently proved herself to be, during her years with the Feld organization, its creative ace in the hole.

Youdina's contributions to the Ringling performance, for a time, earned her a position in the Ringling think tank. She would come into her own at that point when, after the overall direction of the show was decided, the individual acts were considered. "At this point," she says, "it is like shuffling a deck of cards and throwing them on the table to see how you can play with what you have." Then, she says, her mind is working like a computer, "but my ideas do not come from the moon. They grow out of my background and experience as well as the needs of the production." Eventually she must turn the imagined creations into reality.

She trained several of the acts she created for Ringling at the home she built in Vermont before integrating them into their shows at the Tampa, Florida, rehearsals. Although she was always given complete artistic freedom when creating a new act, she did have to keep in mind the demands of a strict budget, the safety of her performers, and meeting deadlines.

When Youdina brought the training standards she learned in a subsidized system to free-market conditions, she learned that the free market affects not only the training of acts, but also the ways in which they are presented. Youdina has often been frustrated when her work has been compromised by the requirements of the productions in which they have appeared. "The time is always too short. We always start too late," she says with some regret.[68]

"The Spider Web," for instance, which she created for Ringling's center ring, was a problem from the beginning and ended up at the end of the arena where its effect was considerably diminished. She built the rigging herself with the help of her two sons, and had only four months before the act's scheduled debut to get it ready. When it came time to decide on the placement of the acts within the overall physical confines of the arena, "There are so many bosses," she sighs. "It is a contest to see who is the stronger. I am always in the weaker position because nobody knows what it is that I have done. Nobody has seen it before. By the time the web was hung, at the end arena, and everyone saw the act and could appreciate its worth, the lights were already in place and their positions could not be changed to accommodate a change in the position of the web's rigging."

The "Women of the Rainbow," designed to demonstrate Russian composer Alexander Scriabin's theories of color and music, was reduced to an act in which seven women did simultaneous solo trapeze, a remarkable feat in itself when one considers that the timing of each trick varies with the size of the performer.

Like her husband, Eugen Youdin, a professor of mathematics at Moscow University, Youdina is academic in her approach to her work. All her acts are built around clearly articulated ideas that are developed in a series of drawings Youdina creates before rehearsals begin. During rehearsals she adapts this vision to the particular performers with whom she is working.

In 2000, Ringling eliminated her staff position, and she took a leave from Circus Smirkus, sending her career into a new phase. She is still creating acts, but not as a staff member of a circus organization. Instead, she has become an independent contractor. "I love it," she says. "For the first time, I have no bosses."[69]

★ ★ ★

Tandy Beal has observed that "the circus is a very complicated art." So many complex elements—the individual acts, heavy rigging and equipment, the lights, music, costumes, sets and props, the characters and often some form of narrative—must be woven together as a seamless totality. The image of that final entity resides in the imagination of the director, and it is his or her job to turn that image into a real, living, three-dimensional creation through a process that varies, as we have seen, with the artistic idiosyncrasies of each director who has taken up the creative challenge of the contemporary circus.

NOTES

1. Franco Dragone, telephone interview with the author, April 1, 1999.
2. Dragone interview.
3. Lyn Heward, personal interview with the author, Montreal, Canada, August 20, 1998.
4. Heward interview, May 15, 2001.
5. Both Heward and Patrice Aubertin confirm this in separate interviews with the author in Montreal, August 20, 1998.
6. Heward interview, August 20, 1998.
7. Heward interview, August 20, 1998.
8. Dragone interview.
9. Aubertin interview.
10. Witek Biegaj personal interview with the author, Montreal, Canada, August 20, 1998.
11. Steve Ragatz, telephone interview with the author, January 4, 2003.
12. Ragatz interview.
13. Ragatz interview.
14. Ragatz interview.
15. Biegaj interview.
16. Ragatz interview.
17. Biegaj interview.
18. Dragone interview.

19. Aurelie Heiden, personal interview with the author, Orlando, Fla., July 20, 2000.

20. Heward interview, May 15, 2001.

21. Heward interview, May 15, 2001.

22. Heward interview, May 15, 2001.

23. Heward interview, May 15, 2001.

24. Heward interview, May 15, 2001.

25. Heward interview, May 15, 2001.

26. Stewart McGill. "Introducing the Alchemist," *Spectacle* (Fall 2002): 49.

27. Heward interview, May 15, 2001.

28. Kenneth Feld, telephone interview with the author, May 10, 1999.

29. Steve Smith, personal interview with the author, New York, March 29, 2001.

30. See Philip Wm. McKinley's discussion of this matter in chapter 4.

31. Kenneth Feld, personal interview with the author, New York, March 31, 2001.

32. Smith interview.

33. Smith interview.

34. Smith interview.

35. Philip Wm. McKinley, personal interview with the author, Edison, N.J., April 9, 2001.

36. This was accomplished in the Hometown Edition beginning in 2004 and later added to the Red Unit in 2005.

37. McKinley interview.

38. McKinley interview.

39. McKinley interview.

40. Michael Christensen, personal interview with the author, New York, March 9, 1999.

41. Christensen interview.

42. Guy Caron, personal interview with the author, Walden, N.Y., August 28, 1999.

43. Christensen interview.

44. Christensen interview.

45. Cecil MacKinnon, personal interview with the author, St. Louis, Mo., May 21, 2000.

46. MacKinnon interview.

47. MacKinnon interview.

48. Jeff Jenkins and Julie Greenberg, joint personal interview with the author, Chicago, January 26, 1999.

49. Jenkins/Greenberg interview.

50. Jenkins/Greenberg interview.

51. Jenkins/Greenberg interview.

52. Jenkins/Greenberg interview.

53. Tandy Beal. "Weaving It All Together," *Spectacle* (Spring 1999): 17.

54. Jean Schiffman. "Spotlight on Tandy Beal," *Dance Teacher Now* (October 1994): 36–45.

55. Beal, 17.

56. Debra Brown, personal interview with the author, Montreal, Canada, May 14, 2003.

57. Brown interview.

58. Brown interview.

59. Brown interview.

60. Beal, 17.

61. Brown interview.

62. Valentin Gneushev, personal interview with the author, Elena Panova translator, New York, March 15, 2001.

63. Dominique Jando. "The Master Builder of Circus Acts," *Spectacle* (Spring 1998): 16.

64. Jando, 17.

65. Jando, 17.

66. Jando, 17.

67. Gneushev interview.

68. Robert Sugarman. "Alla Youdina, Weaving New Webs," *Spectacle* (Fall 2000): 26.

69. Sugarman, 26.

· 2 ·

Designing the Circus

Since a circus is essentially nonverbal, the most direct route to realizing the director's vision is through the images he produces, and in this the designers of costumes, lighting, and décor are critically important. For Cirque du Soleil's Franco Dragone, his costume designer Dominique Lemieux was an indispensable collaborator, almost, in fact, an extension of the director himself, in that she provided Dragone with hundreds of sketches, suggesting not just costumes, but groupings and images, in much the same way that a painter does preliminary drawings from many perspectives before actually putting paint to canvas.

Nonetheless, but for a brief period in the forties and fifties, when the Ringling Bros. and Barnum & Bailey Circus was designed by Miles White, who created not only the costumes for the production numbers but the individual acts and the décor as well, the work of costume designers was not always given much consideration by circus producers. Soon after White's tenure with The Greatest Show on Earth ended, the show abandoned the policy of providing costumes for all the individual acts. Only the wardrobe for the specs was built especially for the circus. It was not until the late '90s that management reinstated the policy of having costumes for individual acts specially designed. Once again a single designer would bring a unified visual scheme to the big show.

Director Philip McKinley provides some insight into how this transition was managed: "What I kept hearing from people was that it was hard to watch the show because they didn't know where to focus their attention." He soon came to realize the value and power that a single color can have when it appears in three rings. The best example was the teeterboard acts on the 129th edition of the show that used red and black in all three rings. "When you saw it on the floor, all that red made your eye relax. You weren't so distracted with a lot of color, and you thought, 'Oh, I'm watching the same thing; I'm not missing anything.' We needed to make everyone look like we put them together."[1]

This return to a unified design scheme was first accomplished by Pascal Jacob, who designed two productions for Ringling Bros. and Barnum & Bailey, the 126th and 129th editions, as well as *Barnum's Kaleidoscape*.[2]

The first French designer to create the costumes for Ringling Bros. and Barnum & Bailey since Vertès in 1956, Jacob started his career as an assistant director in France, working in both opera and theatre. Around 1990, he decided he wanted to do something different. "I started to design costumes, because for me it was very exciting" to be able to touch the fabric and then to imagine that somebody would be wearing it as a costume. "That's something incredible, especially for me, because I am not able to sew. Not at all. I'm just a designer. It is fascinating to me that somebody can cut and build a costume from a piece of fabric that's lying on the table. That's a big part of my fascination about costumes."

In 1984, ten years before he started to work for Ringling, Jacob wrote his master's thesis on the American circus. "I never, even in my dreams, expected actually to be working one day for Ringling. In my thesis I wrote about Don Foote and Miles White and Max Weldy, and the costume designs for the show in the past, so I was very involved in the spirit and feeling of the American circus, the huge shows and big tents. When I met Tim [Holst], it was like meeting a part of history for me." And being hired to design such a show was "an adventure, because before everything, I am a circus fan."

To make the experience even more unbelievable, not only was this Jacob's first assignment for Ringling, it was his first in America, and his first design assignment of any size anywhere.

Tim Holst first met Jacob in Paris at the Festival Mondial du Cirque de Demain, where the future designer was working with Swiss circus historian Frédéric Bollman in a bookstall. Bollman had asked Jacob to create some kind of decoration for the booth, which ended up reflecting some of the designer's ideas of what the circus should be like. Holst saw the sketches and asked who had done them. Jacob declared himself their creator and was handed Holst's business card and an invitation to come to New York the following March for the Ringling opening.

Jacob hesitated and promised to tell Holst the following day whether he would accept the invitation. "Of course, the next day I said, 'Yes, I will be there.' Two days before he was to leave for New York, Jacob received a terse fax, "Don't forget to bring some sketches." The day after the opening, Jacob was shown into a small makeshift office set up between the tiger cages and the elephant picket line. Kenneth Feld was there along with fifteen or so other people. "I put my sketches on the table, and he flipped through them," Jacob recalls. After just a few minutes he was dismissed with a simple, "Very nice, thank you for coming."

For the next five years this scene, with minor variations, was replayed again and again. "Each year I met Tim somewhere, in China or Paris. Paris was like a rendezvous, and each year he asked me more questions. He would tell me what the theme of the next year's show was going to be and then he would ask me if I could do some sketches for the opening? And I would always say, 'Yes, of course.' One year he was in Sweden with Mr. Feld, and he called me in Paris and said, 'We would like to change the elephant act, and do it to some Michael Jackson music. Can you do something in ten days? I will be in Paris with Mr. Feld, and we can have a meeting at the Hotel de Crillon at 2 o'clock.' So I did the sketches, and I met Mr. Feld in Paris for ten minutes again. I showed him my sketches, and he asked some questions about the use of leather and some stones, and then he said, 'Okay, thank you very much, see you.'

"And then one day in Paris again, I think in 1995, we were at Cirque d'Hiver, and Tim asked me if I had some time the next day. He needed to speak to me about something. The next day we sat down at his hotel and he said, 'I think it is time.'"

After discussing the terms of the contract, it was decided that they should meet next in Baraboo, Wisconsin, at the Circus World Museum and Research Center. "Since it was my first show with Ringling," Jacob points out, "Tim asked me to go see one of the units and after that to join him in Chicago and then to go up to Baraboo."

On that trip Tim Holst also brought along Danny Herman, the director, and the scenic designer Robert Little. Since the 126th edition was to feature Arianna, the human arrow, the medieval theme would dominate the second part of the show. "So we were looking at how the circus had previously been able to transform medieval things into a circus theme."

★ ★ ★

Jacob's involvement in the creative process employed by Ringling at this time included many discussions with the director, who usually brought his own ideas of color, line, shape, and period to the table. These discussions were quite different from those that might take place between a theatrical director and his designer. "When it's for the theatre or the opera," Jacob points out, "it's more intellectual; it's more a projection of the vision of the director about the play, what the play is saying. In a way the circus is more open; with a circus you can do anything. It's a part of a dream. When I started working for Ringling, the first thing Tim Holst told me was, 'You have to dream now. Afterwards we can find ways to make it possible. But before that you have to dream.' It was a good introduction into the circus world," Jacob acknowledges.

"The first year we had a lot of meetings," Jacob remembers, "starting in Baraboo and then in New York just after the current show had opened." The first production meeting was held in Vienna, Virginia, about a month later. Following that there was a meeting about every three weeks until August and the white model meeting. After that the bidding process for the construction of the costumes was begun, and the contracts let to various shops. In order for the costume companies to bid intelligently they must meet with the designer. "My first such experience was at Eaves Costume Co. in New York," Jacob recalls. "It was very impressive for me to be at a table with all the people from Eaves, looking at the sketches and their saying, 'So tell us; what do you want?'"

The theme of the major production number for Jacob's first circus was the rain forest, "so it was easy to dream." The theme came from the show's director, Danny Herman. The evolution of the show from concept to actualization was a slow process, Jacob recalls. It began in Baraboo in the dead of winter, hardly an atmosphere conducive to conjuring up tropical vegetation.

After about three or four meetings it was decided that there would be four sections to the rain forest production: flowers, insects, birds, and trees. Jacob recalls being overwhelmed with ideas. "That is why I did so many sketches, because sometimes you have a good idea, like for a clown with flowers everywhere, but then you think we can do the flowers in another way, which means another sketch. So I did maybe two hundred sketches for the thirty or forty different costumes that were actually made."

The color choices were always a bone of considerable contention, and their selection amply illustrates the extent to which the producer micromanages every detail of his productions. "I tried, as much as possible, to put as little of the color fuchsia in the show as possible, but I think Kenneth loves fuchsia. Maybe two weeks before we started construction, I received some sketches with some notes which said things like 'for number 25, change the color from yellow to fuchsia, and add some pieces of fuchsia on number 26. And can you do the shoes in fuchsia for 45?' This kind of thing. At this time we changed the color but not the concept of the costume."

The directors, on the other hand, influenced the choice of colors even more profoundly, because, as Jacob insists, "they have the vision. They are the first ones involved in the process. I remember for the rain forest, at one time, Danny wanted it to be a trip to the Himalaya mountains, and we started with very pale blue and silver and white costumes, and Tim was ready to ask the Chinese to build some kind of traditional lion, but in white." That early vision, however, was discarded along the way.

"Phil [McKinley, director of the 129th] works the same way," Jacob says. "I spent two visits at Phil's house in Connecticut talking about costumes and colors and shapes. It's a very long process, but it's also a very comfortable one for me because I am not alone, ever." Creating a new circus each year is a very collaborative effort. In that way it is very much like the theatre.

"When I say we had a lot of meetings," Jacob explains, "I am talking about the official meetings, but each time when I was in New York, when I was in the shop, I would spend an evening with Danny talking about the show. I remember one evening, on the Fourth of July, just before the fireworks, when we spent a lot of time talking about small details, every color, very small changes."

Although the costumes are a collection of small details, ultimately they are what make it possible for the designer to fill a very large space. The arenas in which the Ringling circus performs are, as Miles White before him understood, "big empty spaces." It takes a lot of color and activity to fill them. In addition to the costumes, the rain forest spec, like all of the circus's production numbers, also featured several floats, and as a consequence, Jacob worked very closely that first year with scenic designer Robert Little in his studio in Sarasota, Florida. "I spent a lot of time in Sarasota because if he had an idea for a float, it was very easy to say, 'Yes, and maybe I can do a costume in the same way.' It was a very comfortable way to fit the costumes and the set pieces together."

Finally it was time for the new production to be previewed by a sizable portion of the staff of Feld Entertainment. "The white model meeting is something very special," Jacob says with emphasis. "They put up a huge table with everything on it to scale, each ring and the aerial frame. And you have different rows of people sitting around the table. You have the director, costume designer, the producer, Tim, all the very important people in the first row. After that you have the assistants. After that, more and more people: the marketing department, the press department, about fifty people in all, and everybody is looking at the table. And you have another table on the side, with all the silhouettes of everything that is in the show, the costumes, the wagons, everything. So Kenneth is in his place, looking at everything, and I remember Phil started to sing the entire score which was already done, and the assistants were moving all the silhouettes. In that way we were seeing the show, but without any colors, and everybody was able to understand what Phil wanted. I think it was very important to do this, at this time.

"I remember for the rain forest the big deal was the aerial act, the spider web.[3] We spent a lot of time with the model to see what was possible. In the beginning the idea was to put three of them up, but it was going to be too expensive. We talked a lot about everything in this white model meeting. In the

Living Carousel [the 129th edition], we spent something like twelve hours. At the end of the day Tim came to me and said, 'You know what? Mr. Feld has some time now. Can you show him your sketches for *Kaleidoscape* again?' I said, 'Yes, sure.' So we spent maybe two more hours talking about *Kaleidoscape*. It was a long, long day. But it was very important because at this time everybody is on the same track: media, marketing, merchandising."

As we will see from other accounts of the white model meeting, it can be a traumatic moment for costume designers. Jacob managed to escape relatively unscathed. "For my first circus we cut the skirts for the girls in the medieval tableau. I designed some very long skirts, after something I had seen at the Metropolitan Museum. They decided they were too long and a handicap for the dancers. It was a big change, but I think the only one. For the Living Carousel I think we kept everything. For the rain forest production we lost a float. Kenneth didn't like it. It was a big, blue snake. It's still in the warehouse."

The aforementioned bidding process begins after the white model meeting, when the sketches are approved. It is here that the designer faces a whole new set of seemingly endless and critical choices.

As a neophyte designer Jacob confesses to being very nervous and uncertain about some of his choices. "The first time I was in New York I was thinking about color and fabric all day and all night, too, so I spent a lot of time in the museum and in the zoo. I was looking at the medieval things in the Metropolitan Museum in New York searching for something close to what I wanted to do. And I kept thinking, 'Maybe this is not medieval.' Now, of course, it is 'Who cares?' But that first year I was very concerned about the correct period. I kept asking myself, 'Is this a good way to do this? Is it correct? Is it medieval or not?' I was going crazy. I took some pieces of fabric from the costume shop and brought them to my hotel room and put them under the lamp on the table. I was trying to decide between some gold pieces or maybe some combination of golds, and I put my hands over my eyes, and I said, 'One, two, three. Yes, that's fine.' I did that hundreds of time, just to be sure I had chosen a good combination because the next day I was supposed to say which fabric I wanted to use. One particular choice involved the costumes for fourteen dancers so it was a bunch of money, and I had to be sure, so I did my small repetition every day, every night.

"I also found a good idea in the Central Park Zoo. I was designing the blankets for the elephants with big, green leaves, and the first sketch was nice, but I felt that there was something missing, so I spent some time in the zoo, and I saw in the rain forest building a very nice combination of leaves, so I said, 'That's it.' I went back to the hotel, and I did a new sketch and I sent it to Eaves, and I said, 'I think this is better.' Danny said, 'Yes, it's better but it will be more expensive,' so he decided to send the sketch to Tim, and get his reaction. Tim called me and said, 'I have something from Eaves, a new sketch. Why?' I said, 'because I think it is more beautiful,' and he said, 'Okay, that's a good answer.'"

Jacob faced the same sort of decisions with the Living Carousel spectacle of the 129th edition. This time, in addition to selecting from the hundreds of fabric samples, he also had to choose the stones with which the costumes were to be embroidered. First the people at Eaves asked how many stones he wanted. Then it was a question of their size. Small, medium, or large? The first time Jacob was asked about size, he came back with a question of his own. "What is the meaning of *medium*?" Pressed to make a selection he looked over at Holst, who said, "Give a good answer."

Then there was the matter of the dyeing. The designer had to decide whether each costume could be made from fabric that already existed or if it would have to be dyed to his specifications. This process of making selections is carried on in each of the houses that builds the costumes for the circus: Michael John, Eaves, Parsons Meares, Penn and Fletcher (who worked on an elephant blanket as if it were an haute couture creation) and later Barbara Matera. Once the costume companies know what the designer wants, the bidding process begins.

The bids are eventually sent to Holst who inevitably, it seems, must tell the designer, "We have to cut." In making those cuts one had to take into consideration the fact that the more work any one of the shops was given, the better the price they were able to offer. Once the cuts are made and the contracts let, the designer will receive a list of which costumes are being constructed by which shop.

"And then I go back to New York with my assistant," Jacob concludes, and we do it again in each shop, but now we know exactly what design is supposed to be executed by which shop. So this is the time to pick out the fabric. This is another part of the dream, because when you're in a big shop, like Parsons Meares or Eaves, you say, 'Okay it has to be red and gold, but I'm not sure if it will be in silk or velvet.' 'No problem,' you are told. 'Come back in three days' and when you do, they have an entire table of reds and golds laid out for you.

"Costume designing for the circus is the story of tables," he says, recalling the white model meeting and those conferences at the costume shops. "They have a big table, and everything that they can find in red and gold is there. Everything in every kind of fabric, and you can say at this time, because it's your job, 'You know what? Maybe it would be better in blue.' And they will do it all over again in blue.

"Or you need velvet. There are fifty different samples of velvet, with every kind of trim. Silk? Okay, sixty more. It may be cotton, or some very strange fabric. That's very comfortable, too, because you can say, 'Let's do a combination.' Most of the shops the circus uses are able to do that."

For both of the shows that he designed, Jacob also created some of the costumes used in the individual acts, more for his second production than the first. When working on such designs, one major consideration is always what the performer must do while wearing it.

"For the spec we don't care so much. It could be big and bigger. It's not a problem, because the artists don't have anything to do in them but walk and be happy. But for the acts it's more difficult. For the Living Carousel show, I did the costumes for the teeterboard acts and for the horseback acts. We tried to match the three rings to each other. The three Hungarian horse juggling acts were part of the opening, so we had to create a transition from the opening to the beginning of the show and slowly go into the spec. In those costumes we used white, with some touch of pale blue and yellow that would take us to the pure white and gold of the spec.

"When designing a whole show, you have to consider other things like the progression of color. That's a big question because it's a big empty space; it's huge. For the three-ring circus you have to create something, a complete feeling for the show in an empty space. So we work with the lights and the costumes. The floor is gray, pale gray, so it's perfect for colors.[4] We can really play with the combinations. That's a big part of the conception: the colors. Because if you try to do it in black, it's dead, but you can add some touches of black like an accent. For the Living Carousel, it was white and gold. It was not white and gold and something; it was white and gold. Think about that. It was *white* and gold, and so you have to think in terms of different kinds of white and some different kinds of gold, too, but it has to match in the end, so it's not a noncolor show. The rain forest was yellow, red, green, and blue—and fuchsia.

"For the medieval section we did a blanket with a dragon on top with gold lines running through the blanket. Eaves decided to make a sample, so we came and saw the sample under light, and I said, 'The gold seems very flat to me. Can we try to do something more textural?' The people at Eaves agreed and said, 'Let's look at the other samples.' Once again we looked at the table with the samples, and I picked out at a very nice fabric with some small gold roses running through it, and it was very nice. I said, 'I think it would be better in this,' and they of course said, 'Okay, we'll do a sample. Can you come back tomorrow?' When I saw the new sample, I said, 'That's it. Don't change anything.'

"Six months later, I saw the blanket from the seats. Could I see those small roses? Of course not. The original gold would have been fine, but it was a good experience.

"Perhaps no one cares that the roses are there, but when you pay attention to the details, even if you can't see them directly, they are part of the construction of the costume, so when you look at the costume it seems livelier. I was looking at some costumes in the exhibit hall in Baraboo, and I was able to examine them up close. I was looking at the Chinese costumes and another one for the 'Living Unicorn,' from two different designers. The Chinese one was very nice. It had a wig made of velvet, but the way it was done, it looked like hair. They could have used only black spandex on the head, but the velvet gave it a wonderful texture. The Living Unicorn was a very good spec, but if you look at some of the pants, they were just spandex. You look at it and say, 'It's spandex.' But when you look at the Chinese costume from a distance, you can see the difference. Of course you can't tell it's velvet, but you see there is something, whereas when you look at the costume from the Living Unicorn, you say, 'Okay this is spandex.' And that's it. You see the surface of flat fabric, and that is why I think you need to be very careful about details.

"When we did *Kaleidoscape* with Barbara Matera and Parsons Meares, I remember some small details from Barbara Matera. They did an epaulet for one of the costumes, and they did something incredible with just a small piece of fringe, because each line was different so that in the end it was something moving and different. It was just an epaulet on the costume, but you can feel it. That's very important. I think that's why *Kaleidoscape* was so impressive for the audience, because we paid attention to many, many details, and Kenneth was very attentive to that as well. He was always telling us to be careful about small things. *Kaleidoscape* was a very good, exciting experience for me because we built a circus. When you work for the big show it already exists before you got there. And it will exist after you. For *Kaleidoscape* we had the sensation of building something from nothing. We saw everything coming in that we had dreamed, and each day was different, seeing more and more of what we had made with the costumes and the set coming in from the shops.

"Coming from the European circus, working with Ringling was very exciting. There is no circus in the world that spends as much money and that allows you to be so free. The budget for each show was about one million dollars."

But it was not just the generous budget that made it possible for Pascal Jacob to realize what he had set out to create. Had it not been for Tim Holst, he might not have completed even one show. "Tim is like my father in America," Jacob says without hesitation.

"I remember one meeting that involved about forty people, and my sketches were up on the wall and most were in white, because I had wanted to bring as many sketches as possible, and I didn't want to color them at that point. So we started the meeting and Kenneth [who understood intuitively that color is the first and most important ingredient in circus design] pointed to one of the sketches and asked, 'What color is this?' I said, 'Maybe yellow.' He said, '*Maybe* yellow?' and I said, 'Yes.' It was a disaster. He said, 'What can we do? Why do we need a meeting now, when nothing is finished?'" Jacob was sure that it was the end of his career with Ringling. "It's a good thing I have my ticket home," he thought to himself.

Feld continued the production meeting, but he never said anything more about the costumes. Then Robert Little showed him a float in white. "It was horrible," Jacob recalls. "It was a very long day, and after the meeting was over, Tim said, 'Can you come into my office, please, for a moment?' I thought I was finished because I didn't have a contract." There was nothing more than a verbal agreement. "And here I was in Tim's office in Washington, very tired. He said, 'It's been a long day, huh?' Then he handed me some papers. It was my contract, ten pages long. 'Could you sign it? And when you do, you will find you have a check waiting for you next door.'"

At one point, looking back on his first assignment with Ringling, Jacob recalled Holst saying to him, "That was a big job." Jacob unhesitatingly agreed. "I mean," Holst added, making sure the designer understood the point of what he was saying, "it was a big job for me to keep him from firing you." He was, of course, referring to Kenneth Feld. "He kept saying," Holst added, "'he's too French; I don't get it.'"

It took some doing on both their parts, but eventually the French designer and the very American Ringling circus came to understand each other very well.

★ ★ ★

Increasingly, as circus performances become more sophisticated and complex with each technological advance, the artist whose work has had the greatest impact is the lighting designer.

Luc Lafortune is a French Canadian who has been the lighting designer of each of Cirque du Soleil's many productions with one exception. In order to expand the company's team of "conceptors," he stepped aside to allow his assistant Nol van Genuchten to design *Varekai*.

Lafortune's approach to his work, unique in the world of lighting design, is, however, typical of the way in which every member of the Cirque du Soleil team conceives his or her contribution to the overall effort.[5]

"Essentially I don't do a plot," he says by way of beginning the discussion of his creative style. "The way that I work with lighting is very unconventional. I don't know what the reason is exactly, but the method that is accepted in the industry, in entertainment, whether it is theatre or musicals or dance or anything like that, is a method that I'm not particularly comfortable with." Because of the false deadlines the traditional method tends to impose on everyone, and because of its dogmatic insistence that there can be no other way of creating a lighting design, he says he finds such an approach "quite restrictive."

"The way that a lighting designer typically works," he reminds us, "is that there are a few conceptual discussions with the director and quite often they are rather late in the process when scenic choices have already been made, which, of course, have an impact on the lighting and more often than not the role of the lighting designer is put into a secondary role."

Most lighting designers, therefore, are more concerned with illumination than with other aspects of the creation, which, he concludes, "is kind of sad, really. The difficulty with such an approach is that it doesn't give a lot of room for creativity because it relies on a structure which is quite rigid. What I mean is that typically in theatre or dance you may have two or three days of what we call lighting sessions where you are doing levels with the director. And essentially that's pretty much where you compose your cues. I think that is the most ludicrous way of working because it puts everyone under the gun while you're sitting next to the director for two or three days. It's always hell. You've got a bunch of people waiting around doing nothing, which just adds to the frustration. Frustration is something that doesn't have to be voiced, but it is always keenly felt when it's around, and it really undermines creativity."

In most theatrical situations, however, this is the only method tolerated. Lafortune, however, refuses to work in that manner. (See the following discussion provided by LeRoy Bennett.) What has made it possible for Lafortune to reject this system at Cirque du Soleil, Lafortune points out, is that he has had "the luck of working with my mentors Franco Dragone, the director, and Michel Crête, the set designer. They didn't work in that manner, so I was lucky to learn from people who didn't adhere to this rigid methodology.

"So the manner in which I work is not so much as a lighting designer, but really as a designer and creator, particularly early on in the process with no specificity attached to my art form, meaning I don't concern myself with the lighting early on in the process. To be quite honest, I really don't give a damn about the lighting early on in the process, and very few of the discussions I have with the director and the other designers have anything to do with the lighting. It has everything to do with the intent, the intention behind the show, what we have to say, and hopefully we have something to say. If we are doing shows and have nothing to say, then we ought to stop doing shows. So the discussions have to do with a whole lot more than lighting. It's about life, about a premise, how we feel about certain things. And based on those discussions, we move into the specificity of our individual art forms, meaning the set designer then concerns himself more with the scenery. I concern myself more with the lighting, and so on and so forth.

"I think you can only design lighting, or scenery, or anything else for that matter, once you have a consciousness of what the whole intent of the show is, once you are convinced of the premise or intention. Otherwise, the choices that you make as a lighting designer in regard to colors, textures, levels of saturation, or obscurity become just a matter of mechanics, and then quite often the lighting design is one of illumination rather than one of conveying emotion and reaction."

That means, of course, that the lighting designer, like all the other creators, must be intimately involved in even the earliest discussions of a show's intent. The form these discussions take is aptly described by Lafortune. They are, he says, "a debate."

It is "like a group of friends or a bunch of acquaintances sitting around a table, whether it is in a bar late at night or a café, and discussing world affairs. And the discussion goes back and forth with people cutting into someone else's conversation or cross talking. So it's a very lively process. It has nothing to do with the type of fixtures that I'm going to be working with; it has nothing to do with the kind of colors I'm going to be choosing, but it has *everything* to do with finding a premise that will motivate the colors that I'm going to be working with, the textures that I'm going to be applying onto the environment, the quality of light that I'm going to be specifying for that particular show. Is it a warm light? Is it a harsh light? Is it a cold light?

"These choices become almost instinctual, if not intuitive, only after you've had a discussion that has more to do with the premise and emotion than with anything else. If those discussions are not had early on in the process, if there's no debate, no exchange of ideas, then you can't make the right choices in regard to colors, textures, or quality of light because your choice becomes an irrational one. You think, 'I have this type of fixture available or that type of fixture available,' but who cares? It's not the kind of fixture that is available to you that ought to motivate your decision, but rather the premise behind the show, what you're trying to say. Once you're convinced of that, then the choices become automatic. You know which colors are right."

But even when he gets into the matter of choosing and placing the instruments, Lafortune's methods are unorthodox. "Even then [I do not work] quite like any other lighting designer. More often than not I deliver a light plot on opening night. I don't concern myself with making a light plot. The only reason I make a light plot is so I can keep up with all the work that I've done, so that I know where all my stuff is, so I can find my way when I'm looking for one particular fixture or another. But I don't really work off a light plot.

"Quite often what I try to do is maintain a very close [working relationship] with the set designer. Because most of my work is really inspired by the environment, I don't concern myself too much early on with the acrobatics per se, because, and I don't mean to demean the importance of the acrobatics, but quite often the acrobatics are not the driving factor behind the premise of the show. It's content, but it's not necessarily intention.

"Eventually at some point in the game I have to concern myself with acrobatics, of course; you have to. If you're designing lighting for someone who is walking a tightrope which could be ninety feet across but only a half inch wide, and they have to do a salto on it, you have to address the lighting at some point as it relates to the performance. But more often than not what I do is design the lighting around an environment, a scenic environment. And I design it in a very intuitive manner."

To illustrate what he means, Lafortune offers an analogy often used in the lighting industry, which suggests that lighting is like painting. "The manner in which I work is very intuitive because another concept that I reject is that there's a light board programmer and a designer who calls the shots to the board operator, which to me is completely ludicrous, because if lighting is like painting then the designer is the one who should be operating the console because he knows it intuitively. He knows what the channel numbers are for his various projectors, and he just lets his hand move around the console based on his intuition and his inspiration for that moment, and he creates images. How can you say lighting is like painting if you're the one sitting behind the console operator with your channel sheet calling numbers, waiting for the reaction time? It's like having a painter who is blindfolded, and someone else is guiding his paintbrush. It doesn't make sense. If in fact it is like painting, then it needs to rely a lot on intuition.

"Intuition is such a great part of design, whether it's lighting, scenery, or costumes. The downside of intuition is that because it doesn't have a chronology and because there are no logistics to an intuitive process, it's also an intimidating process.

"If you're cooking something at home, it's pretty darned simple. You follow the recipe, and a chronology of events shows you the way. When you're designing lighting, if you do it in a much more intuitive manner, that chronology doesn't apply because the events themselves become an imposition, and the downside to that is that because you don't have a map to see you through the process, sometimes it can be rather intimidating. But you have to accept that."

Lafortune often lectures to student designers, and he tells them, "When you're all freaking out because it's not coming together, you can feel your temperature rise. It happens to everyone. It's part of the process, and when I tell them that, they get a sense of reassurance knowing that professional designers go through that same damned process.

"I am absolutely convinced that people who design, whether it's lighting or anything else, and don't freak out at some point, it's because they are doing things that they have done over and over again and are not being creative. So if you're true to your nature and are going to be a creator, then you have to accept that at some point the process will get a little intimidating, but you'll find your way."

He does not, however, entirely dismiss the importance of the technical side of lighting design. He also tells his students, "All the knowledge you can learn in school about the mechanics of lighting, dimmers, types of fixtures, beam angles, foot candles, colors, levels of saturation you need to know in order to be a lighting designer, and that knowledge is a tool that will help you design lighting. But it's only the media. You can have the largest pallet available to you, but unless you have something to say, it's going to be absolutely useless. Later at some point, when things start falling into place, and you start doing the programming, then you can start applying the logistics so that other people can take your show out and run it for whatever amount of time it needs to run.

"But the person running the consoles also needs to have an understanding of what motivated your choices; otherwise, all you're asking for is someone to push a button. Over time all your cues will be executed in a very mechanical manner. So the first thing the board operator needs to learn is what motivated you, what your intention was. What are we trying to convey? They need to have an understanding of why they're doing what they're doing."

Before getting to that point, however, and after the initial discussions have run their course, "Once we have had that debate, as I like to call it, I spend a lot of time with the set designer talking about the scenery. I collect images, which I propose. The images may sometimes just reflect an intention or a feeling or a mood for one scene or another. So there's all this exchange. Of course, all these things I also propose to the director, and that starts channeling the direction that the design is going to take, so based on that I can start making choices about the types of fixtures and type of colors. But I also work with the set designer, who provides me with samples of the environment, and we go through a process of verifying all sorts of colors and textures and various lights on that. So it's a very long process of verification, but the verification is very important. Because nine times out of ten you're going to be wrong, but we accept that. That's what we do."

Cirque du Soleil is, of course, open to the kind of experimentation this method implies. Most theatrical ventures are not. "There's something about our industry, meaning the arts, that sometimes makes us think of ourselves as some sort of elite, and we're not, you know," Lafortune insists. "So the things that we do, sometimes we get it right, and sometimes we get it wrong, but if we have that openness, then we are able to verify things and say, 'I thought this would work, but it doesn't; let's explore another option.' With the people that we have here at Cirque we have that luxury to explore and verify various options, so that by the time we get into rehearsals we have a pretty good idea as to where we're going and where we're going to be hanging fixtures and which angles serve us best and which are advantageous to us.

"When we go into rehearsals we have some semblance of a light plot. Maybe fifty percent of our rig is up there and then we start turning things on. We're talking about the beginning of rehearsals in the scenic environment. Not technical rehearsals. We don't really have technical rehearsals. This part of the process can go on for as little as a month and up to four months. When we did *O* in Las Vegas we were in there for four months with the scenery and lighting. The last tent show I did I was in there for just one month."

Although much of Lafortune's work is done in close collaboration with the other creators, there comes a time when he prefers to work alone. "The best time of day to do [the painting] is late at night when there's no one out there. But I'm always there when the director is staging the actors, as well. I paint then, too. If I see something, and I think I have something that can support it or make it stronger, then I will approach the director and say, 'Do you want to see this? I got something that may work in this scene,' and sometimes he'll say, 'No, no. I don't have the time right now,' and other times he'll say, 'Sure, let me see what you got.' So it's a very fluid process."[6]

When the traditional technical rehearsals do arrive, it is quite late in a very lengthy process, approximately ten days before opening night. Even at Cirque du Soleil these rehearsals tend to look and feel like those in more tradition-oriented venues. "Usually it's quite the mess. Everyone walks out of the first one with his head bowed. But that's what you've got to do. You've got to try things, to see what works and what doesn't work. We're not that great at what we do that what we do is perfect the first time we do it. I think we're very good at what we do because we allow ourselves to make mistakes."

★　★　★

Lafortune earned a degree in fine arts from Concordia University in Montreal. Originally he had hoped to be a scenic designer, but during his first semester in school he was assigned to work on a production of *The Threepenny Opera*, in the lighting department. During the day, however, because he knew how to weld, he would also help build the scenery, which was constructed of steel. "So I would weld the scenery during the day and in the evening do levels, and it was quite peculiar because as I was welding and looking at the scenery I would think, 'This is not going to be pretty at all, and somebody's going to get his head served on a platter.' And then in the evening we would go and do levels and all of a sudden this thing became just magnificent. And not only was it beautiful, but it had a number of personalities, a number of interpretations, so I discovered that you could do a whole lot with one static piece of scenery with the lighting, and that totally impressed me."

That started him studying lighting rather than scenery, which he believes is "also related to the notion that as a teenager I drew a lot, and all of my drawings were made with charcoal, black and white. I played with levels of light and the absence of light, so I think when we started working with light at the university, I kind of picked up on that, and it became very interesting to me.

"One thing that I detested was the logistics of lighting," he confesses, making his current working methods more understandable. "We had a lighting design class in which we would learn about dimmers and hookup sheets and whatnot, and I couldn't be bothered. But in a way it worked to my advantage, because I didn't learn to adhere to a method early on that was very academic, so when I started designing lighting, I relied more on my intuition and on what I didn't know rather than on what I knew. There's an expression: 'She didn't know it couldn't be done, so she went ahead and did it.' And that probably accounts a lot for the manner in which I work in lighting."

Lafortune offers one other important suggestion: "Surround yourself with people who are experts in things that are important to you."

After graduating from the university in 1984, which happened to be the year of Cirque du Soleil's first tour, he headed down the usual career route and began sending out résumés to theatres and producing companies. "I didn't want to have anything to do with the circus. To be quite honest, I wanted to do theatre or rock and roll. I wanted to do big gigs with a lot of gear, but my résumé didn't say very much other than Bachelor of Art, so there weren't a whole lot of people out there interested in hiring a student. However, one of the founders of Cirque du Soleil, Gilles Ste-Croix, was also studying with me at the university to sharpen his skills in scenery. He kept on bothering me and saying, 'Come on out with us; it'll be fun.' But I didn't want to work for a circus. I wanted to do something serious. But, since I got no replies, I went out with him as a backstage technician the first year, and the second year I became the lighting console operator. And then, when the third year came around, they were still looking for a lighting designer, and since there is not a lot of cirque history in our [Canadian] culture, it was pretty much impossible for them to find someone who had circus experience in lighting design. But with my two tours, I was pretty much the most experienced person in Montreal. So I gathered all my courage and asked them to give me a try. That was 1986."

In 1987, he designed the lighting for *Cirque Réinventé*, the show that came to Los Angeles and set Cirque du Soleil and its creators (and the circus) on a new course.

★ ★ ★

LeRoy Bennett, who has designed the lighting for several of the recent productions of Ringling Bros. and Barnum & Bailey Circus, is the complete opposite of Luc Lafortune in temperament and work schedule. Consequently his involvement in the creative process is quite different as well.[7]

Whereas Lafortune is involved from day one, it is not unusual for Bennett to be absent from Ringling's all-important white model meeting, partly because of his busy design schedule and partly because of his nature. "Since I started off in rock and roll and circus is a side thing, I'm just constantly jumping from show to show," Bennett explains.

"I can't sit in one place and do the same thing all the time. I used to go out on tour when I first started, and I would do the entire tour with an act. It was fun, in the beginning, but after a while, after you've tweaked the show, and you've fiddled and fiddled and fiddled, at some point you've got to stop. You can only fiddle so much before you start fiddling too much. So once I got to that level, I would have nothing to do but get bored and into trouble."

To compensate for his not being present, the white model meeting is videotaped and he "participates" by watching the videotape. In even starker contrast to the working habits of Lafortune, Bennett will have had no participation in the creative process before he sees the tape. With *Barnum's Kaleidoscape*, however, his first circus for Feld Entertainment, he was more involved because it was a group effort. "It was the first time it had been done," he says, offering his take on what the creators were trying to do. "We were trying to do the Monte Carlo, European style circus."

Bennett came to the circus from Feld's ice shows. He had designed eight of those spectacles, and over the years the producer had talked to him on and off about working on the circus. "So when the *Kaleidoscape* show came up, I thought it would be an interesting way to be introduced into the circus world," Bennett says.

With that shared background of experience, Feld has gotten used to not having Bennett around for the critical white model meetings. "When I first started doing things for Kenneth Feld, yes, he was upset with my not being there, but then he realized I could sit and watch a tape and understand what is going on. And there is communication. There is always communication. Being a production designer and a set designer myself, I understand what I need to be looking for, and if I have questions about what they are trying to do or suggestions, they are always communicated to the set designer."

Ironically, both Lafortune and Bennett started out wanting to go into rock and roll, or, as Bennett puts it, "the music industry." Whereas Lafortune studied theatre and lighting design in school, Bennett had no formal training at all. "I went right from high school into working with a local band," he says.

Although he knew for sure that he wanted to be involved with music, at nineteen years of age he wasn't quite sure how he would fit in. "I definitely knew I didn't want to be on stage, but I wanted to be able to perform without being up there, and I eventually figured it out. I enjoyed being musical and tried to be dynamic, even though I had a limited gig."

After leaving that first band, Bennett worked with a touring lighting company and "learned a lot more technical stuff." Next he worked for an English company out of Los Angeles, and from them he got his first design job with rock star Prince in 1979–80. "I actually ended up working for Prince full-time, doing his movies, videos, and college tours, and as his popularity grew, my reputation grew, so I started getting calls from other bands." Some of the entertainers Bennett has worked for include Tina Turner, Janet Jackson, Nine Inch Nails, and Marilyn Manson. Twenty-five years later, 50 percent of his work is still rock and roll, the rest being divided among the circus, ice shows, and television.

There are, he acknowledges, various challenges involved in meeting the needs of circus performers and still trying to be theatrical. "The difficulty is building a scene or a performance because there is an element of safety involved. So you have to make sure you provide whatever is needed by way of illumination for performers so that they can comfortably do their act. There are some acts that have done their act for so long in full-on, fluorescent-lit rooms that when they suddenly get into theatrical light, it throws them off at first. It just takes time for them to get comfortable in the different environment. Some performers will be professional and come up to the plate and perform under any circumstances. Some of them dig their heels in, but eventually they get there."

The theatricality he speaks of involves creating an atmospheric environment, and in describing this aspect of his work, he resorts to familiar metaphors. "You're trying to create an environment, to paint a picture. The three rings is a huge area, and so you try to isolate these areas and make them different for every act, whatever it is, whoever is performing. You're trying to create something that fits the mood of each individual performance, but also there's an overall theme that goes through the whole circus, and you're trying to weave all that into one cohesive look." In addition, of course, the lighting is also used to draw attention to one particular area of the arena or another.

To do all that effectively, a huge number of instruments or lighting fixtures is used. Some are used strictly for effect. The instruments on the ground are used basically as fill, for the floor area, "because you've got all the chorus girls. They are all over the place, and sometimes the only way you can light them, because we don't have lights way out in the audience and there are only so many spotlights, you have to use the instruments on the floor. They're footlights basically. Sometimes they're necessary." The logistics, because of the circus's physical setup and sight lines, make it almost impossible to hang lights in the positions favored by those who work on stages in theatres. "You have to worry about obstructing, not only the audience, but the spotlights, as well. Unfortunately you've got all these parameters that you have to work around restricting where you can put lights. And even with the footlights, you've got issues because you have animals kicking them," he says with a laugh.

The floor instruments are also used to highlight the aerial acts. Those instruments that can move are used to provide special effects. "Having moving lights, of course, gives you the flexibility of pointing them anywhere at any moment, and using them almost as a spotlight. Even outside of *Kaleidoscape*, in the three-ring circus, we have tried, any time we can, to avoid using spotlights to highlight. Sometimes the follow spots work. It can be fun to watch the spots following the flying trapeze acts; you've got the one movement accentuating the other. But sometimes the follow spots can be very distracting, too. So if you can light in a way that you don't see them, it's good to try."

There are between eight and ten follow spots used in each venue. One or two of the people who operate these spots travel with the show. The local people are rehearsed during the day, so they know whom they're supposed to follow. "In a flying act there's so much going on you need to know which person you're highlighting, and you've got to catch these people before they even take off. They need to be able to see. It's a safety thing as well as being able to illuminate them."

The actual design process, after Bennett has studied the video of the white model meeting, begins with a CAD (computer-aided design) program. This allows the designer to create a lighting plot in a three-dimensional form. "I can do it based on the way the actual set has been drawn out," Bennett explains. "The thing is, the truss layout has to be a certain way most of the time, because the trusses are what they attach the flying rigs to, so there are restrictions, and it is what it is, basically, and so what I do is take that structure and attach the lights and put them into the plot for what I think it's going to take to light certain places in certain acts in certain ways." The hanging plot (a diagram of where all the lighting instruments will be hung) is pretty much fixed, or as Bennett says, "written in stone. I can change a couple of things, but it's dictated by the show itself, as far as what is needed physically to attach the scenic pieces or whatever is needed for the performance." This is another of the differences between the work of Bennett and Lafortune. The latter has a new scenic structure for each show, and is, therefore, presented with different challenges in each show as his lighting positions change.

For Bennett the variations from show to show and act to act come in the cues. "I can maybe alter or augment that structure a little bit. But it's all in the way of placement and most of it is how I program the lights, the colorization, the gobbo patterns, and the timing."

The instruments used consist of the conventional PAR lamps that are used to create washes, or general lighting around the rings and track. The lekos and ellipsoidals are permanently focused, but the rest of the system consists of mostly automated lights, whose focus and color can be changed throughout the performance. "You have a whole list of focus positions for each of these lamps and you end up just touching them up if they are off a bit at any point."

After one of the units shuts down at the completion of its two-year tour, Bennett has about a month to hang the lighting equipment for the new production. He will sometimes come to winter quarters himself when the electric crew is placing the lamps just to make sure everything is sitting where it's supposed to be. And then he leaves. He doesn't get back to program the cues (i.e., decide which instruments will be used at any given moment), until the second week of December. At that time he begins by first programming the entire show in a basic way, meaning that there is something in the way of lights for every act, including all the productions numbers, which he says he can accomplish in seven to ten days.

"I do that separately at night when nobody's around," he explains, sharing another of Lafortune's methods. "They tape the show for us in all the rehearsals. We come in and watch the rehearsals on the tape and start programming them that way, and once we've got that down, we come in and do it real time with the acts and begin refining." That last step involves some amount of stop and go during the rehearsal. Stopping, he says, is "like pulling a big break. You have to be really quick about things, so if there are things that are going to take me maybe twenty minutes, I'll make notes and say, 'Look, I've got that covered.' If there's something that I can do quickly, like spike somebody's position, we'll do that as quickly as possible and come back to it later. With animals in particular you can't have them wait around." Having to take animals into consideration is another of the big differences between the working procedure of Cirque du Soleil's lighting designer and Ringling's.

Bennett says that the 133rd was his favorite among the Ringling shows he has designed, because "for the first time there was a connection between the ground and the air, by using festoon lights, and the tie downs. It was a proscenium stage without actually having one there, and it took away from all the steel tie downs. It became more three-dimensional. Wherever you sat, it just seemed richer." Apparently the producer had been looking for some way to soften the effect of the cold arenas in which the circus played, and garlands of lights (not used for illumination, but strictly as a scenic element) were suggested by set designer Steve Bass.

These lights did prove to be something of a problem for the flying act. "We tried not to be too distracting," Bennett says. "Instead of having this string of black dots when they are off, you might as well keep them lighted." The flying act always presents some difficulty for the lighting designer even without the added strings of lights. There's so much equipment, cables and things, that are hung more or less vertically, and the act covers such a large area. As with the animal acts, "the timing has to be right. You try to be dramatic and take things down in order to highlight something and then bring it back up. That has to be done in a very subtle way, especially with the cat act; otherwise, you'll throw the cats off. Anything distracts them. You know they have ADD. Animals are the most finicky."

Once the show is on tour, the director will continue to fiddle and tweak the performance. If any of his fiddling requires lighting changes, the crew that is left there and given to the designer by the management will take care of it. "We train them, and they understand the show. They know all the cues and understand why the lamps are focused the way they are and what they are doing, so if there is a change, they know how to update the cueing without getting off base and losing track of what is going on. Usually what will happen if something drastic is required, my assistants and programmers who are there with me during the rehearsal sessions will come out and deal with it."

In comparing his experiences lighting rock shows and the circus, Bennett says, "The only area in which I would bring in my rock show experience is with the musical numbers. The entr'acte or anything like that, because it's not performance; it's more a musical at that point, and I treat it as such." Relating his early interest in being part of the musical industry to his work with the circus, he adds, "The desire to be musical comes into play in the circus to a certain extent. Like I said, during the finale or the big production numbers, that's when you can get musical. With some particular acts you can do it a little bit, but it's more like providing accents. It depends on whether the act is musical. It's all act driven, whether you can get away with it or not."

★ ★ ★

Whether engaged from the director's earliest musings like Luc Lafortune; contracted after the theme has been set in place as is the case with costume designers like Pascal Jacob; or brought in, like LeRoy Bennett, to provide the final visual magic, it is clear that a circus designer's contributions are critical to the success of a new production and are painstakingly considered. If a circus's initial impact is visual, however, its next appeal is aural, demonstrating, as one critic has said of another kind of performance, "what one set of sensory organs can do to another."[8]

NOTES

1. Philip Wm. McKinley interview, April 9, 2001.

2. Pascal Jacob, personal interview with the author, Milwaukee, July 13, 2002.

3. See Alla Youdina's discussion of this act in chapter 1.

4. Miles White believed the floor was actually the background, as most spectators looked down at the arena, so he tinted the sawdust to vary the color of his background according to the color palette he chose for his costumes.

5. Luc Lafortune, personal interview with the author, Montreal, Canada, May 14, 2003.

6. This is the method Guy Caron brought to the Big Apple Circus. See chapter 1.

7. LeRoy Bennett, personal interview with the author, Atlantic City, N.J., while lighting the Miss America Pageant, September 15, 2003.

8. Bernard Holland. "Taking a Cue from Pictures to Modern Dance and the Circus," *New York Times* (December 30, 2004): E5.

• 3 •

Setting the Circus to Music

*M*usic has always played an important role in circus performances throughout the world. The first Golden Age of circus music in America began around 1880, when circuses began hiring musicians to travel with the show and provide music for the acts.[1] It was also at about this time that composers began writing music—marches, waltzes, galops, and novelty pieces—specifically intended to accompany circus performers. Circus bands and their concerts were featured prominently in the publicity materials prepared by the shows to lure customers to the big top.

During the 1930s, popular music began to replace what had come to be thought of as traditional circus music, so that by the 1970s, circus music was a hodgepodge of styles usually inserted into the performance only during the final days of rehearsals. That began to change once again with the success of Cirque du Soleil in the mid-1980s. Rather than being an afterthought, music was the starting point. For Guy Caron, Cirque du Soleil's first artistic director, "music is 90 percent of the package. It creates the mood and atmosphere."[2] Or as Eric Michael Gillett, once Ringling's singing ringmaster puts it, music "controls your heart strings."[3]

Thanks to the phenomenal success of the Cirque du Soleil productions, we are now hearing entire scores composed not just for the circus in general, but for a specific circus performance.

Music intended to accompany a circus performance is unique in many ways, but it is closest in form to ballet music. Like dance music, circus music must capture the mood of a particular act and follow its movement, providing crescendos, climaxes, diminuendos, and stops at the appropriate time. But unlike ballet dancers, circus artists may miss a trick and wish to repeat it, or for some physical or mechanical reason take longer than expected for its preparation

71

or execution. So circus music, in addition to the above requirements, must also have provisions for repeats, vamps, and other stalling devices that allow the artist and the music to reach the peak of their performance simultaneously. As a result, melody is often lost in the bargain.

That said, however, it should be understood that there is not complete unanimity within the circus community as to whether the performers follow the music or the music follows the performers. The French composer Bernard Hilda, speaking at the Third World Convention of Circus Directors in Paris, in 1995, said, "Things are changing, but live music is absolutely indispensable to the circus. Take the high school act.[4] Music follows the horse, not the contrary." Of course, the desired illusion is that the horse is following the music; that he is, in effect, "dancing."[5]

Speaking further of the peculiar requirements of circus music, Hilda added, "You have to emphasize the moment when the hat is going to land on the juggler's head or the fall of the chair in the clown act." For generations, meeting that requirement fell to the percussionist who emphasized such moments with the classic rim-shot.

★ ★ ★

Another participant in the same directors' symposium, Tereza Durova, the director of the Moscow Clown Theatre, in speaking of the ways in which music adds to the drama of any act, said, "There is that moment when the orchestra reduces the sound level to emphasize the artist's anxiety [when having to repeat a missed trick, for instance]. It plays sotto voce, and all of a sudden, when the trick is completed, it naturally resumes its original level. The orchestra follows, lives the moment, there is a dialogue and, if only for that, the moment becomes a celebration." And then by way of emphasizing the importance of music in the overall program, she added, in what is something of an oxymoron, "In a collective, the music director should be the second most important person after the director."

Valentin Gneushev, whose work was discussed in the previous chapter, added an observation of his own about the Russian conductor Sokolov, who was six feet tall and had enormous hands. "A very famous juggler got into the habit, at the end of his act, of sending a club toward the orchestra and the conductor caught it and proceeded to lead the band with the club in his hand, then sent it back to the juggler. The audience understood that the conductor followed the juggler's work so intensely that he could join in his act."

But another comment from the director reveals his ambivalence on this topic of who follows whom: "To me it is of the utmost importance that the artist feels the music within his body. And not only feels it, but also releases the music through his act. But he must never become enslaved to his music, and this is why I often change music during rehearsals, so that the artist doesn't become a prisoner of his music."

Perhaps the obvious compromise, and the most precise description of the collaboration of music and artist, can be found in the statement of Evgenia Godzikovskaya, the music director of Rosgostsirk, the official circus agency of Russia: "Circus music is often seen as an accompaniment although the music contains in fact the dynamics of the act." The two, the music and the artist, are collaborators, each bringing something to the creation of a single effect.

The conference's discussion soon moved from the Russians to the French. Bernard Kudlak of *Cirque Plume* explained how this circus's performances are created. "We are lucky to have, within our performing company, the composer of our music, Robert Muny. We are also fortunate to have ten musicians among the fifteen artists in our troupe; five are better acrobats than musicians. The other five are better musicians than acrobats. Therefore, we have many different musical combinations.

"Robert Muny attends every rehearsal, and we invent the music while we put the acts together. Music doesn't underscore the show; it is the show. There is symbiosis. . . . The whole of Robert's compositions must follow a thematic idea. Each melody is the countermelody of the previous one. . . . He always uses the same themes, but transposes them according to the dramatic moment. . . . If circus is an art form, then music mustn't be a mere accompaniment. It must go to the heart."

Kudlak also spoke of the significance of the setting in establishing the tone of a performance, a subject for which the symposium's moderator, Dominique Mauclair, could provide a vivid example. He told of the Russian tiger trainer Nikolai Pavlenko, who normally used the music of American jazz great Dave Brubeck. During the course of filming a video program *Les Enfants du Volyage*, one of the barns of the German circus impresario Franz Althoff, where the film was shot, was transformed into an open space without bars or boundaries. When the film was finally edited, everyone working on it agreed that the Brubeck score no longer seemed appropriate in the new setting, and the music was changed.

In support of Kudlak's insistence on the collaborative nature of circus work, Luo Baoshan, deputy director of China's Red Army Acrobatic Troupe, spoke of the situation in his country that might be deemed the ideal collaboration. After the People's Revolution and the organization of the acrobats into government troupes, each troupe was assigned its own orchestra, allowing students to practice to music. "In the creative process," Baoshan said, "we create the music while we practice. When the director has an idea, the composer makes a dummy for us to work to and afterward he writes the completed score." In addition to having their own orchestra, the acrobatic troupes have the opportunity of working with any Chinese composers who will then work expressly for them and thus develop a repertoire.[6]

★ ★ ★

Each of the composers who work in western circuses has found his or her own individual approach to solving the problems that grow out of this unique collaboration of musicians and circus artists.

The first American circus to use music especially composed for its performances was the Pickle Family Circus beginning in 1974. Harvey Robb, who worked as a musician in every one of the company's shows, provides a useful comparison to the music of the traditional and contemporary circuses: "In a lot of other circuses, musicians will play through a book of tunes. There's no sense of the contours of the show—sometimes a tune will stop in the middle of a phrase and then there'll be a fanfare. The end. With our circus [the Pickles] everything is carefully considered, selected, and composed; sometimes—not often—the action is edited to fit the music. It's all integrated."[7]

Jeffrey Gaeto, one of several Pickle composers, adds, "I find myself more and more working with images of the type of movement that will be going on. I see acrobats, and I get a meter, and after a while I realize it's six-eight. Traditionally, trapeze is three-four, waltz time, but we've been trying to break that up a bit, to use four-four some of the time and save the three-four for when the trapeze starts to swing. Lorenzo Pickle [the show's cocreator and star clown] was always four-four; he's got that four-four walk. There's a lot of improvisation. Quite often it's like everyone is soloing at once. I remember a clown act. I was handed a piece of paper with eight bars on it with the chord names, and that was it. After a while, a lot of the music in the show becomes a group composition."[8]

The Pickles fancied themselves a collection, and so music composed by a committee of the whole is entirely in keeping with its politics. The first composer to write for an American circus as a solo artist was Linda Hudes, who might rightfully be called the First Lady of American Circus Music.[9] She began writing original music for the Big Apple Circus several years before Cirque du Soleil had even come upon the scene. Having to produce a new score every year has also made her the most prolific composer of circus music. After nearly twenty years with the Big Apple, she undertook the assignment of writing the score for *Barnum's Kaleidoscape*, a show whose creative process is described in detail in a later chapter.

★ ★ ★

Linda Hudes and her husband, Rik Albani, began working in New York with their own band called Linda Hudes's Power Trio, playing many of the city's most famous rocks clubs like CBGB, Max's Kansas City, and the Mudd Club. Occasionally, Albani substituted in the early bands of the Big Apple Circus. After a year he was made the show's musical director, and Paul Binder, being an adventurous soul, came to hear the Power Trio in one of their club gigs. He was so impressed he asked them to work for his circus. It was just the opening Hudes needed.

Hired by her husband to be part of the circus band, she quickly became excited by what the circus was trying to do. "I told Paul," she recalls, "the Big Apple Circus is so original and creative, it should be just as original and creative musically." Thus began a nearly twenty-year collaboration in which Linda Hudes was the first person to compose an entire original score for an American circus. "And to be a woman at that!" she says with enormous pleasure. "There were so few of us." Now, she thinks, the idea that a circus should have a score composed specifically for its performance has pretty much caught on.

But the fact that she was working in a circus did not alter her style. "We saw it as just another venue. We were creating music for the circus, not circus music," she explains. "I saw no problem in going from the Kitchen [an off-off-Broadway theatre] to the Big Apple Circus to the Boston Pops with the same music." That music is what she calls "classical rock."

She was trained as a classical musician at Hartt College of Music in Hartford, Connecticut, and the New England Conservatory before moving to New York. Her husband's background is jazz and classical music. Besides playing the rock clubs with their trio, Hudes also wrote music for several modern dance companies at such venerated venues as La Mama and the Brooklyn Academy of Music. "We never expected to be in the circus. It was beyond my wildest dreams, and I am a pretty wild dreamer."

Those early years at the Big Apple Circus were special. "It was very thrilling to be there in the very beginning, working with young, high-energy people, very fresh, very New York. We all put everything we had into it. Going from thirty shows a season to three hundred was thrilling."

Hudes's relationship with the Big Apple Circus ended when Guy Caron was hired to direct the circus's twentieth anniversary production. "I have a strong style and voice," Hudes explains. "He has his own voice. He handed me a disc and said write something like this."[10] Hudes demurred, and Brigitte Larochelle was hired to take her place.

★ ★ ★

Like all the other composers who found themselves with an assignment to write music for a circus, Brigitte Larochelle does not have a circus background. Before coming to the Big Apple Circus, she had worked as a theatrical music director and had extensive experience as arranger and choral and music director for several productions of Cirque du Soleil, hence the connection to Guy Caron. For the Big Apple's 1999–2000 season, her third with the show, she provided the music for the production *Bello and Friends*.

Before the show began its five-week rehearsal period in Walden, N.Y., Larochelle says, "The music for the show was always in my head, for five months in Montreal, even while I worked on other projects. Michel Barette [the show's director] and I met just a few times during that period; for some parts he suggested examples of what he wanted, and for others, he just said to me, 'Go where you want.' Sometimes he asked me to listen to a CD, but that stopped my creativity," a sentiment expressed by almost all of the composers considered here. "Our best discussions were more about the words which suggested a style, a color, a spirit, and established a tempo. Once we had an understanding about a piece, he trusted me and gave me freedom to do my own work."[11]

For the individual acts, she worked from the videotapes provided by the guest artists. This was so that she could synchronize her work with what she saw on the videos, building musical sequences to the big trick in each act. "By the time we got to Walden," she recalls, "there was still a lot of work to do." She composed the music for a hand-balancing act set in a restaurant even as the two performers were in the process of putting the act together. The music for Katja Schumann, the Big Apple Circus's star equestrian and wife of its founder Paul Binder, was written in Walden as well. Schumann's equestrian acts cannot be put together until the previous season has concluded; otherwise, the animals would be confused by having to rehearse one act and perform another. Another of the musical changes that occurred in Walden was a result of a personnel change. "We had to change all the music for the Jungle Frolics elephant act, which had been planned for two dancers, because one of the dancers quit. The very last piece of music she wrote was composed the night before dress rehearsal."

The show's star, Bello Nock, recalls Larochelle's having asked him what he wanted to come across in his act and the kind of music he preferred to work with. By way of answering, he described his act to her. "I'm a character who falls, but then gets up and keeps going, and is still optimistic. I take the hit without getting hurt, and I want the music to help the audience know that. And I want each hit to be augmented by a natural drumbeat, not by some artificial special effect. The drummer, the percussionist, and the bandleader all have monitors of the live performance, and I'm very consistent, so they can easily follow my falls."[12]

Many circus performers resist having to work with new music, especially if they have been using material that they have found to work successfully for them in the past. But as is often the case with the new circuses, the Big Apple wanted all new music. Nonetheless, Bello confesses, "I love the classics."

Bello wanted to use his own theme for climbing the swaypole, but he agreed to listen to anything new she could come up. She tried four different pieces, but Bello felt they just weren't right for him. But she insisted there was something missing from the music he was using. "She felt that I needed 'tension music' when I stood up at the top of the pole. So she gave me that," Bello adds. "But I kept the 'Blue Danube' swaying music because it has always worked so well."[13]

In spite of such comments, according to Larochelle, most performers, however, don't depend on their music very much, except perhaps as cues for the opening and closing of an act. "The job of the band is to follow the performers," she said. "I gave the musicians a video of each act during rehearsal and the written parts of the music. In performance, they have video monitors to watch the acts in progress. I've lettered sections of the music A, B, C. If an act goes long, or the performers have to repeat a trick, Rob [Slowik, the conductor] can take the band back to a letter to repeat the music as necessary. This is sometimes the case with the animal acts, for instance," or with the aerial act formerly known as the Flying Jesters, for whom Larochelle wrote nothing less than a rock version of a medieval court dance, bright and fast, with trembling interior builds and holds and releases.

"I use the waltz, but I also like rock, swing, and Latin. I try not to go the way we're 'supposed' to go. I make a lot of different propositions from what is expected. Sometimes they are taken, sometimes not."[14]

A good deal of the music Larochelle was asked to write for the Big Apple Circus was intended to produce some excitement when not very much, other than set or prop changes, was going on. Larochelle wrote the music for all those transitions while in Walden, obviously a very busy period for her.

During the opening of *Bello and Friends*, the show's music was provided by an old calliope that stood in the ring. It played a lilting, nostalgic waltz, and as the music was being cranked out, ringmaster Paul Binder invited the audience to imagine an ordinary, vacant lot, about to be transformed into something extraordinary. The show proceeded to move through fourteen different musical selections that were often funky, almost always up-tempo, with the farandole (a French word for dance in which the dancers are in a line, holding hands) that came to be titled "Medrano Fantasy" as a finale.

★ ★ ★

In its production titled *Dralion*, Cirque du Soleil fused ancient Chinese acrobatic tradition with the brand of high theatricality that the company has established as its hallmark. It was something of a risky project for Cirque du Soleil, as it introduced a new creative team to replace the familiar lineup headed by Franco Dragone. In Dragone's place, Guy Caron installed his old colleagues along with his extensive knowledge of Chinese acrobatic arts. For his composer, Caron choose newcomer Violaine Corradi, who won the job after sending the company a demo tape. As a final audition she was asked to write twenty minutes of music for a video she was given, and she had two weeks to produce it.

In the show's early period of gestation, Corradi says, "I worked very closely with both Guy and Julie Lachance, the choreographer. We knew we were getting Chinese numbers, many of them quite developed, so I had to write for acts already existing. I watched technical videos of work and made demos of my early ideas. We put these on our working table. If they were no good, then it was back to work! With the ribbon [or tissue] sequence, for instance, I wrote the music first, and from that source came the number. We really worked in both ways. With the overture, I recall, we went through many stages of fine-tuning, adding a few bars here and there—timing to the last second and then blending with the lighting and so on."

Her background, she says, includes tracing "world-beat" music and exploring the music of a wide variety of cultures. Her goal, she explains, "is to create a fusion of past music with contemporary means." As it turned out, *Dralion* was the perfect forum for her to pursue this goal, linking, as it does, the cultures of East and West, the traditional with the contemporary. As a result, her score borrows from traditional sources and moves into the electro-symphonic realm of a world yet to come. "I was inspired by Central European music and able to explore an acoustic and electric synthesis, enabling technology to encounter traditional sounds," is how she puts it.[15]

After its premiere in Montreal in 1999, *Dralion* continued, as is the practice at Cirque du Soleil, to be considered a work in progress. Corradi confirms that a lot of editing continued to take place. "For two or three months we tuned it continually. From February to September we were moving all the time, which is the beauty of a Cirque show; it is a live being, and even though I continually revisit, the musicians have to take responsibility for the daily onstage changes, so the music can adapt to the action. Unlike a Broadway show, the whole scene varies nightly," she explains.

The most unusual aspect of Corradi's score is its use of a countertenor, a rarity in opera, let alone circus. "What happened," Corradi explains, "was that Guy Laliberté [Cirque du Soleil's founder] wanted to use a countertenor, and he asked Guy Caron and me to move in that direction. I had to compose for that range [in effect, a male soprano]. Finding the singer was very hard and certainly out of my own arena. Erik Karol was working in Paris and came from an alternative vocal background. By the time we reached Santa Monica, I had been asked to add a female vocalist to share the score with Erik and, I believe, the blend is beautiful; he has a wonderful range, and she has a low frequency which marries very well."

Corradi continues to visit the show every two to three months, but talks weekly with the bandleader and receives regular e-mail reports of the show with detailed notes, sometimes requesting fifty seconds of new music here, twenty there. In San Francisco, several months into the show's run, Corradi was working on changing the music for the clown entrée, a continuing and pesky problem in this production.

"Nothing is like Cirque," Corradi concludes. "It is like being part of a harmonious tribe."[16]

★ ★ ★

From the slickest and most extravagantly financed circus company in the world, we move to the company whose work most resembles folk art, the impecunious but creative Circus Flora. For most of the sixteen years it has struggled to survive, its composer has been Miriam Cutler. Her story amply illustrates the reluctance with which traditional circus people sometimes deal with the issue of original, contemporary music and the kind of adaptability it takes to make it work.[17]

"I come from theatrical street theatre," Miriam Cutler announces, establishing not only her credentials, but also her personality. "That was my real background as a performer. The '70s in L.A. was an incredible time. There was so much talent out on the street doing what we called 'hits,' showing up somewhere and just starting something, creating a show anywhere."

At the time she was introduced to the show's producer, David Balding, in 1988, she had a swing band, with a steady club gig in town. "David and a few other people [from the show] came to see my band, which was fun, very high energy, hot playing, with a lot of audience banter. After the show, David invited me to come out to see him. It was my first time to see this beautiful red and white striped tent, and I just said, 'Oh, this has to happen.'"

During her visit to the show she and Balding chatted as he took her around to meet Sacha Pavlata, Flora's cofounder, and James Zoppé and Flora, the elephant. "I thought I was in heaven. At the end of the day I had no idea if David liked me. I thought he was going to want to hear some music and tell me to send him a reel, like they do in L.A."

Instead, she was offered the job on the spot. "I was aghast," Cutler remembers. "But that's the way David is. He just totally does things from his heart. He had good vibes, and he liked my friend, and he just hired me. I went home dancing. But then I thought, 'Now what?' I think I had been to one circus in my life. I wasn't really a big fan of three-ring circuses. But I was aware of the Pickle Family. I'd seen them and every kind of street theatre like the San Francisco Mime Troupe and others. That was my sense of circus."

She began by meeting Patrick Swanson, the show's director. During that initial two-week visit, Balding, Swanson, and a few other people talked about the show and possible themes. The new composer also talked to some of the key performers, taking notes and sketching out their acts and the energy each needed and the effect the music was to provide. Cutler went home with videotapes of the Zoppé act and the Wallendas. "I sat down and tried to imagine what they'd need. I had to learn. I had to learn about 'ta-daa.' There's a whole thing to 'ta-daa' and knowing when and how to do it and when not to do it."

And then there was the matter of "etiquette." That eventually had to be worked out with the conductor and the band, so the choice of musicians was critical. Janine Del'Arté, the show's first conductor, has stayed on over the years and, in the estimation of Cutler, "has become a really incredible circus conductor. She's very tuned in." But she had a lot to learn, too, "picking up on the performer's signals, being sensitive to the inherent danger in some of the acts."

The band that first year consisted of just four sidemen. "I would say, 'Please, David, just one more,'" Cutler recalls. "The first year we got a musician from St. Louis. He played guitar and fiddle. He added so much that David realized we had to have a violin. Sacha keeps asking when we are going to get trumpets. I love brass. I think the European style is much more brass, and I would love to incorporate that, and hopefully if we mount a bigger show with better financing, we can."

Prior to Cutler's arrival, the music heard during a performance of Circus Flora consisted of various kinds of standards. "It was," Cutler sums up, "limited stylistically." Her idea was to give the show a big orchestra sound by using synthesizers. "At the time it was cutting edge. We bought a midi setup, two keyboards and drums, and Janine on woodwinds. I think it was pretty exciting. It was big, but of course it brought new issues and challenges, like the sound system."

Such equipment did not exist around Circus Flora before Miriam Cutler came upon the scene. Nor, for that matter, did the concept of original music. Cutler met with Balding prior to the start of the season hoping to guide him through the process of selecting an adequate sound system. "But, of course, someone came along with some deal. It was not the sound system that we needed, but it was the sound system he bought, so we tried to make it work."

The band was organized and rehearsed in Los Angeles. Aware that once they arrived on the circus lot they were going to have to deal with issues other than their own, Cutler decided they needed some time to work together before departing for St. Louis, the show's home base. Another reason for getting together beforehand was that no one in the band had ever worked on a circus before. "We were a great team," Cutler says with pride. "Everybody that I got involved really resonated with this experience. You can't just have regular musicians; you've got to have people who understand this lifestyle and appreciate it and appreciate this adventure. That was the biggest success I had, finding those people. They were incredibly diligent and respectful when they came to the show.

"In L.A. we became a factory, printing out music madly, not knowing how it was going to be used or whether it would work. I remember the printer going at all hours printing out music and my cutting and pasting, trying to make things work." With all that was involved in getting ready, the band ended up having only one rehearsal during which they all actually played together before it was time to join the show, expecting that the tent and bandstand would be ready when they got there so that they would be able to rehearse for a few days on their own. There was time scheduled to do just that, but, not surprisingly, things did not turn out quite as planned. The bandstand wasn't built. There was no power. "We couldn't even play one note."

The reason may very well have been a conspiracy, fueled by the suspicions of the show's more traditional staff members who harbored some resentment toward the whole idea of an original score by someone from outside the circus family. One of the performers in the show, who had been put in charge of building the bandstand, seemed especially resentful from the minute the musicians arrived. Cutler kept trying to get him to finish the bandstand so the band members could install their equipment. "There was this resistance right from the beginning," which Cutler shrugs off now. "I tried really hard to push, and I realized I couldn't. There was so much going on, different concepts of what different people on the lot thought the band should be and do. But David always had this very strong belief that it had to be an original score, and it had to be a unique circus score sound. It took us a little time, but we did win over the performers, and I think most of them are pretty pleased with how [the show's music] has evolved."

Obviously the situation called for the implementation of Plan B. Balding persuaded Virginia Smith, director of historic sites for St. Louis County Parks, to get permission for the band to rehearse in one of the houses in Faust Park. "The acts would come in, and we would talk them through their music." But there was still no tent. And no bandstand.

The tent wasn't up because the show was going to Poplar Bluff, Missouri, for its first date, to which the band traveled as a unit in an RV. "We figured we'd travel down to Poplar Bluff, get set up, and do a sound check because we had never set up with the sound system. I hadn't even seen it. I didn't know what it was, and it was to be a really big part of making this work."

As one might expect, the tent went up late, and the weather forecast was none too promising on opening day. The band did not get to load in their gear until fifteen minutes before the first show, and there still wasn't a bandstand. They worked on the floor, madly trying to connect cables, never having used the sound system before. "The sound guy wasn't much help. He didn't know about us; he didn't know about midi gear, and I'm thinking, 'I can't believe this is happening.'"

Once set up, the sound system immediately produced the horrible squawk of feedback. By this time people were coming into the tent. Finally the band and sound crew worked their way past that, got the system turned on, and managed to get some sounds to come out. "They weren't very good, but we got sound." The show was on. It was, according to Cutler, "Total chaos. I was madly calling cues. Music was flying off the stands, people were throwing it at each other, and I'm dancing trying to get the drummer into it. It was total chaos."

And then the tornado hit.

Tent poles started leaving the ground, but the band kept on playing or trying to. The crew and anyone available, including Cutler herself, started sitting on the tent poles trying to hold them in place. Meanwhile, the audience, mostly kids, seemed totally oblivious to what was happening. "Somehow we got through the first show. We grabbed our gear and pulled it out of the tent really fast," just before it blew away.

"We came back to St. Louis, licking our wounds, wondering if the bandstand would be ready. And then we saw it. I thought the guy who built it was just trying to get even with us or something because it was so scary and rickety. I know it was designed safely, but for people from L.A. who are not really circus people it was something else. I was the only one who was really a theatre person, used to climbing around rigging and stuff. So we lugged all this heavy equipment up these little rickety stairs with only a rope handle rail. When we get up there, it shook, and every time the drummer played, it shimmied and stuff was moving around and falling off, and when Flora would come through as she got bigger, it was really scary."

Undaunted, Cutler and company attempted to cope. "Sometimes between shows when we were trying to have a rehearsal, the power would be off. I think there was resentment that we were electric, and some people wanted a brass band. So that was our very first week or two of a nine-week run that happened to span the drought in the Midwest. We all wanted it to be great to please them, but it took a while to get it going."

Cutler, Del'Arté, and most of the musicians persevered and managed to hang in there for the next twelve years. During that time the music, as well as its level of acceptance, evolved. It went from being overly dependent on the midi to the use of stronger themes with more musical individuality, created by featured instruments like violin and flute. "I like to write a lot of active interaction for the pieces. Instead of just having a band up there that jams and grooves, I think it's important to have strong themes that the audience can really connect with. The band is very disciplined in the sense that they know it's not about getting into a funky groove. Janine really understands that this is not what it is about. It's about staying within a certain theatrical style, which I think is really important because the performers need to know what to expect. And the audience wants melodies that are really strong and recognizable with a through line."

But even as her tenure continued, Cutler rarely enjoyed the luxury of working like her colleagues on the Big Apple Circus or Cirque du Soleil, watching videos, counting measures. Instead, "David would call me up and say, 'I have this much money; write me some music.' Every few years he'll have a budget that I can write a whole show, like when we did *Back to the Bayou*. It had a running theme, and I was pleased with that. But many years he doesn't have a budget for that, so we piece it together. Janine told me we now have a trunk of music that weighs about seventy-five pounds.

"In the beginning I used to fly out and help put all the pieces together, but Janine is very good. She pulls from what we have. She may call me and say, 'I just can't find anything for this act,' and I'll say, 'Okay I'll write something. What do you need?' And I try to fill it in. Janine gets here and has two days to pull it together. So she pulls what works."

When Cutler does have an opportunity to write something new, she designs her music, she says, "in a modular way. I learned very early on to forget about things developing. What I try to do when I write is give the band enough material, way more than they'll need. And then basically Janine calls it as she's watching the acts. She follows the acts. The band learns the sections, and when she sees that a change is needed, she'll just say, 'C,' and they'll go into C section. It's like street theatre. You work with what you have, and if something comes up, you just make it great."

What Cutler has found over the years is that basically there are certain kinds of acts that have a certain energy or style to them. Some are very specific, and others are more generic. Over the years, too, Cutler and her music have become an accepted, integrated part of Circus Flora. "We worked very hard to win over some of the performers, to get them happy," Cutler concludes. However, performers do show up with a stack of their old music and Balding will categorically refuse to allow them to use it. "That's what makes the show special," she insists.

Cutler would like to do more. "The Wallendas' [high-wire act] really needs new music. That music was written in 1988, and their act is different now." And in that happy world where dreams come true, she would like to write a full score again. "Because I've gotten better at what I do. I would love to focus on strong thematic material that leaves people humming it when they leave the tent. To me there's no finer moment than when the audience is clapping with the music in time with an act. That, to me, means I'm doing my job, and the band is doing their job. The act is happy and the audience is happy; everyone is in one space."

One of the qualities that has helped to make Miriam Cutler and her work become accepted by circus people is her sensitivity to their needs, the "etiquette" of the circus, as she calls it. "A lot of times different acts want different things. The Wallendas have specific needs. Janine and I have learned never to play loud when they're trying to work on a certain dangerous part of the act. For me that would seem like the place to fire up and go like gangbusters, but they taught us what we need to know. We must be very respectful of their needs. This band is really very good at it."

★ ★ ★

But sensitivity to a circus act's needs alone is not enough. Circus bands must also be, as we have seen from Cutler's experience, enormously flexible. "Animals don't perform to time. Neither do flying acts and high-wire acts. That's why circus musicians must be more flexible than those in the pit orchestras of a Broadway musical," says Michael Starobin, who composed the entire score for Ringling Bros. and Barnum & Bailey's 129th and 130th editions, and then the 133rd and 135th. In addition to the music itself, "the musicians," he says, by way of tribute, "make a tremendous contribution."[18]

Although Ringling Bros. and Barnum & Bailey has always used special material in its performances, it has only been in recent years that the show has moved toward using an entire original score. But that did not happen over night, as Kenneth Feld readily concedes. It was not until Phil McKinley became director for the 128th edition that the final step was taken.

In the meantime "different composers have helped the evolution," Feld explains. "You go where you have the talent to take you." One of those talents was Eric Michael Gillett. "His level of talent opened the way for us to do more," Feld acknowledges. "He [Gillette] brought a new dimension with his vocalizing," and because of that Feld eventually agreed to have material arranged especially for him.[19] But, according to Gillett, it took a bit of finagling.

"When I first started singing in the circus it was in arrangements not for my voice, a tenor." That was because, Gillett says, "Kenneth Feld had never really heard me sing when he hired me." So he didn't know what his new ringmaster was capable of with the right arrangements, in the correct key. Gillett set about to change all that.[20]

"I was told that Cy Coleman [the composer of the musical *Barnum*] was supposed to write the song for Gunther Gebel-Williams's farewell tour," Gillett relates. But it never happened; Coleman was busy elsewhere, so the house composer leapt into the breach. What he came up with was something less than a showstopping tune, which had to be rewritten. "I saw an opening and knew I had a chance to influence the direction the music in the show would take," Gillett says. "After the Gunther Gebel-Williams tour, I began developing a cabaret show. During our New York run, Kenneth came to one of the shows, and for the first time he saw that I could really sing, and he came to understand what could happen to a song if it were arranged and charted for a specific voice type and voice style."[21]

Having earned a new level of respect, Gillett took the opportunity to introduce Feld to his songwriting friends, Gerald Sternbach and Lindy Robbins. "Eric surprised me," Feld admits. But he agreed to listen to a song that Sternbach and Robbins wrote on speculation.[22]

"What we did," Gillett says, continuing the story, "was to get David Larible to talk to his sister, Vivian. We asked her how she would like a song written for her act, something specifically for her. 'Someone will sing it to you,' we told her; 'it will be romantic and beautiful,' and Vivian fell in love with the idea. So we explained the act to Gerry and Lindy. They went back home, and Lindy had the lyrics: 'Flying in Your Dreams.' We took it to Kenneth, who bought the song and hired Gerry and Lindy, and for the next several years they wrote all the songs for the show."

What that did, Gillett believes, was "allow us, for the first time in many years, to take the music and let it be thematic throughout the show, repeated as underscoring, etc. So you got a texture that controlled the audience's heartstrings, but they were not necessarily aware of the control. That was the biggest change to come over Ringling music in the last thirty years."[23]

The producer's interest in music has evolved as well. Of Hudes's work in *Barnum's Kaleidoscape*, he says, "I think she did a wonderful job interpreting what each act had to bring and what it represented, and then giving it a contemporary feel, still keeping in touch with traditional roots.

"The reason I hired her was that I used to go to the Big Apple Circus every year and there were always two or three pieces that I thought were great. When you're looking at someone else's work, you can never be absolutely sure where the inspiration is coming from. But I knew she had talent, and I thought it would be interesting to see if she could do a whole show. On *Kaleidoscape* she has proven herself to be a perfectionist; she was so well prepared. There were very few changes once we got into rehearsal."

But it isn't just the composers who account for the enormous advancement in the big show's music. "One of the greatest elements in the progression of the music performance is the new sound system," Feld says. "We have invested a lot of money into it. In order for the audience to appreciate the music more fully, we now have a system that I would put up against anybody, anywhere, in any venue. The sound in *Kaleidoscape* is the best in any tent in the world."

Why such an investment? "Because," as Feld insists, "the music drives the performance. It will always be that way. The energy of the music is vital. I go in there and am concerned if it's not right. Performers are not always aware, but it is a very, very important part of a circus act, probably 50 percent of the act."[24]

★ ★ ★

Seven years after Gillett brought in his friends to provide special material, composer Michael Starobin and lyricist Glenn Slater were placed in charge of writing a completely original score and lyrics for an entire production of Ringling Bros. and Barnum & Bailey. The creative process out of which Ringling's 130th edition came into existence began for Starobin and Slater eleven months before the show's premiere in Tampa, Florida, when they initiated their discussions with director Phil McKinley. "We talked about [the director's ideas] from a theatre writer's point of view," Slater explains, "about character, setting, and plot. I don't actually write anything until the summer, because until then there are still lots of things percolating."

One point of discussion with the musical team is the placement of the various acts in the program. In the 130th, Slater points out, there was no place for any of the less spectacular songs like those in the previous year's Red show with Catherine Hanneford handling some of the vocal chores along with the ringmaster. Originally they had tried such a song for the liberty act in the new Blue show and to introduce Sara (the tiger whisperer). These songs were to have been sung by the ringmaster, but they were dropped in winter quarters because it was felt that they delayed getting into the actual act for too long.

By August, Slater and Starobin were working in collaboration to create whatever songs might be used and Starobin was working independently on the rest of the score. For the 130th, McKinley wanted to find a way to have some audience participation. That ultimately led to the "Can You Say Circus?" number. "I wrote the title," Slater says of his collaboration with Starobin. "Then Michael wrote the music, and I added lyrics later. Some ideas for songs come from the marketing strategy that Kenneth has in mind. The themes come from Kenneth." Those discussions led to lyrics proclaiming the show's third century and its designation as a living national treasure.[25]

Starobin composed about 90 percent of the music used in the 130th edition, which included material for all of the acts and the specs. The only acts he didn't get involved with were the clown gags, which were put together by the band with special effects and recognizable tunes.[26]

In his talks with McKinley, Starobin was asked to write some new music for the Quiros's high-wire act. They had a set act and had been using the same music for the past fifteen or twenty years, so they were very uneasy about the prospect of changing it, but "McKinley wanted to try a different design element," Starobin recalls. "He wanted something from the '30s in Fred Astaire's style, jazz, but it had to fit the same structure of the act. I watched a videotape of the act and listened to the music they had been using. I was listening for tempos, and timing the length of each part of the act.

"I wrote something light and happy that I eventually felt was too light; there was no sense of danger in the music. I had to modify what we were doing to get something stylistically new, but true to the essence of the act."

That, in brief, is the composer's basic problem, according to Starobin. "Finding a new musical style, yet staying true to the fact that it's for a circus act. The first thing in writing the music is to balance it with all the other elements that affect your music: the structure of the act, the timing, performer's personality, etc."[27]

Lyricist Slater echoes that sentiment. "The most important thing for me is to remember that it's a circus, a very old tradition, and a way of thinking about entertainment that doesn't exist anymore. It is low tech, upfront, 'amaze me' kind of show business. I try to capture that feeling, what it must have been like to go to a circus 100 years ago and put it into words. I try to capture that sense of wonder people must have felt and translate it into something contemporary."[28]

Starobin, unlike some of the other composers who work for circuses, does not employ many repeats in his score. "I tend to write in 32- to 64-bar phrases," in other words, in strong melodic structures. The strap act in the

130th edition, he points out, has no repeats at all. In the beginning he works loosely for timing, maybe adding a few measures here or there, or cutting, providing more than enough music instead of repeating. To avoid a repeat in the Quiros's act he added a bolero when they are on the bicycles.

For the tiger act, the idea was to go against the stereotype of a traditional tiger act. "We didn't want a sense of danger; we wanted it to be warmer and friendlier, in order to suggest that this tiger act was different. For the swings and traps we decided to go gospel because it felt right."[29]

Production numbers, like the opening, require a good old-fashioned march or, as in the case of the finale, an old-fashioned cakewalk structure. With the finale, Starobin feels, anything can happen. For one thing it can't be timed. The cannon music, Starobin points out, is played over and over, sometimes louder, sometimes softer. The bandsmen really need to watch the conductor, and as they become more familiar with the music they can adapt to his cues much more readily.[30]

The team of Starobin and Slater came together to work on the circus. Prior to that assignment they had worked together only once before. Kenneth Feld found Starobin first. At the time that the composer and the Feld organization became acquainted, Starobin had been working as an orchestrator for Sondheim and Disney. Starobin and Slater had previously met while working on a Disney movie together, and when he was asked to recommend a lyricist, Starobin immediately thought of his most recent collaborator. They wrote a song on spec for McKinley for the 129th edition. He liked it, and they were hired, but the song was replaced.

Before writing any lyrics for that first show, Slater says, he did a great deal of research at the NYC Public Library for a month or so, "getting the history, trying to capture that tone of voice." That Barnumesque voice, Slater says, is what he has tried to capture in his lyrics. "So you have extraordinary rhyming, verbal tricks, alliteration, the words mimicking what the performers do. The ringmaster is sort of in the role of Barnum. He uses that huckster tone of voice."[31]

"A huge amount of [writing and] rewriting is done in winter quarters rehearsals," Starobin says. Having worked as an orchestrator he knows that the music can't be written in stone. Lots of acts are only put together in winter quarters, and it is, therefore, impossible to write for them in advance. A lot of changes occur after watching the acts perform. "You get one image [of an act] when it is described verbally that is very different when you see it."

Of his own work, Slater says, "In rehearsal I write the entire script. I write everything the ringmaster says. The little sung intros are written in winter quarters very quickly.

"After my first circus score," Starobin admits, "I learned to be more flexible, how to stitch sections together, to construct transitions so they could more easily be performed."[32]

★ ★ ★

Any discussion of circus music, however, must go beyond composition and selection of musical settings. Just as important is the way in which the music is used. In many circuses music is far more than a background element supporting the work of the acrobats and animals. It is, as was suggested by the participants of the French conference quoted at the outset of this chapter, an integral part of the performance, the musicians, often doubling as acrobats and jugglers, taking or sharing the spotlight with the nonmusical performers.

In such "noveau" circuses as Cirque Éloize, Cirque Plume, Circus Oz, Les Arts Sauts, and *Les Colporteurs*, most of the artists "double in brass" performing various circus specialties and providing the musical counterpoint to other acts. Each of these circuses qualifies as an ensemble, and characteristically those members of the company not performing physical solos will act as either witnesses or musicians, sometimes, as in the case of David Dimitri, performing both simultaneously. He walks the tightwire while playing a trumpet solo. In either case none of the ensemble is ever completely removed from the action, but in some way or another integrated into it. Solo musicians will often appear next to a featured circus artist, and the two will perform what amounts to a duet.

This aesthetic is carried to new heights (literally) by Les Arts Sauts. This aerial circus takes its musicians, which include a cellist, double bassist, Jew's harp, and a soprano, aloft. Although the musicians do not actually become part of the troupe's extraordinary flying feats, they are physically a part of the rigging and essential in creating the mood and emotions of the production.

The bassist in Circus Oz not only finds himself airborne, but also flies above the stage while sawing away. As in the other circuses noted here, various solo musicians are incorporated into the acts in ways that bring the music to the foreground, sometimes incorporated into the physical action, sometimes providing musical support.

As Bernard Kudlak readily admits earlier on these pages, some of the members of Cirque Plume are stronger musicians than acrobats. That certainly explains why the music is by far the most interesting and amusing aspect of the ensemble's performance. The music is produced by a variety of performers on a startling variety of instruments, in a range of styles that moves from acid rock to music hall. Although it ostensibly assumes a subservient role, the music often asserts itself so forcefully, dramatically or comically, that it is really the true focus of the show.

The best example of the importance of music in the circus performance is provided by France's Alexis Gruss and his family in their *Cirque National à l'ancienne*. A ten-piece orchestra that includes a piano and guitar along with the usual assortment of brass and reeds is placed directly behind the ring, on the same level, rather than in the loft usually reserved for the musicians in traditional one-ring circuses. Each of the male members of the family—Alexis and his two sons, Firmin and Stephan—join the orchestra at various times in the performance or perform featured musical interludes on an assortment of instruments, in the center of the ring. Each is as accomplished musically as he is on horseback or in the classical circus skills. These performances, then, are not merely to demonstrate versatility. They bring a new energy to the performance. Very often the musical interludes provide the transitions between circus displays in the way clowns usually do in other circuses. But never is the music rendered as if it were merely a time killer or filler.

In effect, Alexis Gruss and his family use music in their performances in much the same way as it was during the American circus's "Golden Age." His company's 29th creation, "*Cheval et Musique*" (Horses and Music), produced in 2003, amply demonstrates that music is not merely an adjunct to the circus arts; it is, more precisely, one of them.

NOTES

1. Charles P. Conrad. "The Sawdust Music Man," *Spectacle* (Spring 2000): 7–9.
2. Guy Caron interview, August 28, 1997.
3. Eric Michael Gillett, speech presented to Circus Fans Association of America, Felix Adler Tent, Rutherford, N.J., October 4, 1998.
4. Known more formally as *dressage*, the highest form of equestrian art, hence the term "high school."
5. Third World Convention of Circus Directors, a symposium on *Music and Circus Directing*, Paris, France, January 16, 1995.
6. Third World Convention.
7. Terry Lorant and Jon Carroll. *The Pickle Family Circus* (San Francisco: The Pickle Press, 1986): 95.
8. Lorant and Carroll, 95–99.
9. Linda Hudes, telephone interview with the author, March 16, 2000.
10. Hudes interview.
11. Timothy Jecko. "Brigitte Larochelle Brings a New Brand of Music to the Big Apple," *Spectacle* (Spring 2000): 12.
12. Jecko, 13.

13. Jecko, 13.

14. Jecko, 13.

15. Stewart McGill. "When East Meets West It Is the Music of Violaine Corradi," *Spectacle* (Spring 2000): 14.

16. McGill, 14–15.

17. Miriam Cutler, personal interview with the author, St. Louis, Mo., May 21, 2000.

18. Michael Starobin, telephone interview with the author, March 20, 2000.

19. Kenneth Feld, telephone interview with the author, May 10, 1999.

20. Gillett.

21. Gillett. It should also be noted that the same situation prevailed when Johnathan Lee Iverson first joined the show as ringmaster. By that time, the music had already been written and scored. As a result, Iverson was nagged with vocal problems throughout his first tour. For his second tour the music was written and scored specifically for him.

22. Feld interview, May 10, 1999.

23. Gillett.

24. Feld interview, May 10, 1999.

25. Glenn Slater, telephone interview with the author, March 20, 2000.

26. Starobin interview.

27. Starobin interview.

28. Slater interview.

29. Starobin interview.

30. Starobin interview.

31. Slater interview.

32. Starobin interview.

II

THE COLLABORATION
(CASE STUDIES)

Ringling's 131st Edition

$\mathcal{A}$s with each of Ringling's new productions, the inspiration for the 131st edition grew out of preliminary talks between producer Kenneth Feld and Tim Holst, the vice president for talent and production. Eventually they were joined by director Phil McKinley. "We overlap each other and support each other," Holst says, summing up that relationship. "We all have to interact. There are no silos here. We really have to force ourselves to make decisions together and recognize some of the problems we have."[1]

Kenneth Feld is constantly getting information coming in from all sides: marketing and promotions, as well as talent and production. "Tim travels all over the world," Phil McKinley points out. "He will see an act and get a video and then bring it to Kenneth and say, 'Here is an idea.'" Feld, however, is the one who decides where he wants the new show to go, where his business is going. Because of feedback he was getting from focus groups, the 131st, which introduced Bello Nock to audiences of The Greatest Show on Earth, was purposely geared to appeal to kids.

According to Holst, who says he is often working at least 18 to 24 to 36 months in advance, the groundwork was actually laid six years prior to the 131st's opening in New York's Madison Square Garden on March 30, 2001.[2]

It was at that time that he made the show's first overture to one of Europe's most respected animal trainers, Sacha Houcke. Houcke, however, was not immediately disposed to embarking on a new career in America. Instead, the show won the hand of his daughter, Sara, whom it effectively promoted into a star over the course of several seasons. Like so many Ringling stars she dropped her last name, let down her hair, and became Sara, the "tiger whisperer."

With his daughter royally ensconced, Sacha was quite receptive to Ringling's invitation to come for a visit. While in the United States, he was, of course, also introduced to the Red Unit's menagerie, its personnel, and the train. Houcke was sufficiently impressed with all he saw to agree to come on board as well.

The next step was finding and acquiring the animals Houcke wanted to use in the act he intended to present. Houcke himself began training the animals before returning to fulfill other commitments in Europe. Lisa Dufresne, Holst's wife, took up with the animals where Houcke had left off and continued the training until he returned for the start of rehearsals in November of 2000.

Dufresne stayed in touch with Houcke via the telephone, providing weekly updates on how the animals were progressing with their training and their welfare. As Houcke's surrogate in this process, she carefully followed through on his training instructions and built the act in the manner he had said he wanted the animals presented.

Along with the training, came all the ancillary work. Locating a place for them to work, finding people to take care of the animals, and negotiating salaries had to be accomplished rather quickly. The site chosen was located on property that the show had leased once before near the Ringling Bros. and Barnum & Bailey Center for Elephant Conservation in Florida. The advantage of this location was that it was off the beaten path and, therefore, quiet and away from interruptions. Under those conditions, Dufresne was able to conduct two or three practices a day with the animals without distractions.

At about the same time that Houcke was being cultivated, Holst also began talking to Vilen Golovko, who, along with his father had produced the sensational Flying Cranes in the old Soviet Union. "I had made a definite decision to try to find something other than the classical trapeze act for the circus," Holst says. "We had gone a couple of steps beyond what I would call (with all due respect) the classical or standard Mexican flying act." That meant creating something entirely new, especially for a Ringling show.[3]

Golovko, in need of work and seeing in the Ringling contract a chance to do something as spectacular as the Flying Cranes, was signed more than a year in advance of the time the 131st edition was scheduled to go into rehearsals. Before coming up with a concept for the new act, he was brought in to see the show under performance conditions so as to judge the limitations of the various arenas in which the show would play.[4]

The Russian brought Ringling several flyers who had worked in the by then disbanded Flying Cranes and a new act that had previously had little public exposure. The latter involved the Russian swing, which was eventually used in a much altered and hyped-up, three-ring format. Casting the new flying act, however, proved to be a problem. Many of the people who had worked with the Flying Cranes were at this point either too old or had gone back to Russia. The process of creating the new act began, therefore, by identifying other flyers who then had to be signed to contracts. Finally, and most importantly, the show had to decide if it was willing to gamble on Golovko, himself, who, although his work was well-known and respected, his methods were, as far as the Ringling people were concerned, totally unknown. To ensure his delivering what was required and on time, Holst had to find ways of structuring and monitoring the work.

The basic training for these new acts was done in Tula, Russia. Ringling had what it terms a perfectly legitimate deal with the director of the circus building there. Owing to the economic state of Russia, its circus and its circus artists, all financial transactions, however, were conducted entirely in cash. Out of these payments the building's director was to provide hotel accommodations for the Ringling people along with lights and water 24-7 at the building. "How he handled his money and what obligations he had were his problem," Holst says with a shrug.

Eventually the act completed its training in Las Vegas. Before leaving Russia, however, Golovko had a mock-up made of the costume he wanted. This was then brought to the Ringling costume designer to use as a model. The Russian also gave the show's composer the music of Philip Glass, whose work he has long admired, to suggest the kind of musical setting he envisioned for the new act.[5]

Within that same time frame, the decision was made "corporately" to hire Bello Nock, who was then working on the Big Apple Circus.[6] Kenneth Feld says he had for years been watching and talking to Bello, who for those same years had often expressed a desire to appear under the Ringling banner. "He was perfect for Ringling because everything he does is larger than life, and it works so well in this venue.

"And I knew what I could do with him because I know the diversity of things he can do. That was one of the reasons why we said, 'Okay we have a long-term plan. This is what you're going to be doing for these two years on this show,' and we have a very good idea what he's going to be doing on the following two years on the new show. It's going to be totally different."[7]

Bringing Bello on board was one of the ways in which Feld undertook to act upon the intelligence, previously noted, that he had received from his marketing people. The souvenir program, the billing, and even the traditional Ringling logo were all redesigned to reflect the same marketing thrust that came about because of the production staff's talking to the marketing people.[8]

For Phil McKinley, the 131st edition was his fifth stint at breathing life into a new version of Ringling Bros. and Barnum & Bailey, and by the time he and his creative cohorts had their first formal meeting, he was already well versed in the direction the new show seemed to be going.

★ ★ ★

In the first formal meeting between Feld, Holst, and McKinley, Holst says, "We normally determine the rest of the creative staff that we would like to use, that is, the lyricist, the composer, scenic designer, costume designer, assistants, and so on. And then we decide on certain elements that are going to carry over from the previous show. For the 131st we knew we wanted Johnathan Lee Iverson and Mark Oliver Gebel."[9]

Prior to that, of course, Feld and Holst had talked with those performers they knew they wanted to retain and explored with them ways in which they could be presented that would be different from their previous work. The idea, Feld explains, is "to build stars within the scope of Ringling Bros. and Barnum & Bailey. If you look at this show [the 131st], for instance, we have Johnathan, we have Bello, and Mark Oliver."[10]

McKinley puts it another way. "To me it's very similar to the way Broadway shows used to be done. You had Ethel Merman, and so you wrote a show for Ethel Merman, or you had Mary Martin. Tim and Kenneth gather all this talent and hand it over to me and say, 'Okay, now this all has to go together in some way.' That's the excitement of it. Because you're truly creating from the inside out, as opposed to taking something that's there [like the book for a Broadway musical] and then casting it. It taxes all of my creativity."[11]

As for the new acts, besides those being created by Golovko and Houcke, there was to be a skiing act, which was developed especially for this production, more or less at the same time as the other innovations. This was not the first time the show had had such an act, but, Holst quickly points out, it had been ten years since the last one. "I have that all logged," Holst says in reference to the copious notes he makes daily as each new production moves along its creative process.

The ramp used in the new version is the second generation of what had been used previously. "This thing goes up and down quickly," Holst adds. "But we still had to go through the process of finding the right people to come ski. These are not circus people. They're sportsmen. So it's a matter of adapting. You go through the entire process of indoctrinating them, introducing them, guiding them through the circus process. They are never going to live their whole life in the circus. They're national ski jumpers. It's a completely different mentality, and we have to work with them to prepare them for the day-to-day routine of what's expected. I call them 'hot dogs.' Ordinarily they would work two days a week and that would be it, and then they'd go on to the next thing." So in addition to developing the act, the athletes have to be turned into something approximating artists.[12]

Once the skiers were found, it became McKinley's job to make the act as spectacular as possible. He suggested skiing through fire. Being the "hot dogs" that Holst suggests they are, they were more than willing to give it a try. McKinley had pyro-packs strapped to their ski boots and sent them down the ramp in a literal blaze of glory. "They really went for it," the director says.

That kind of involvement with the acts is, for McKinley, another of the things that makes directing a circus exciting. "I look at an act and say, 'Now what can we do that makes it [more fun]?' I have this term. 'Let's 'Barnum-ize' it. Or 'circus-ize' it."[13]

★ ★ ★

Depending upon how far ahead of the planned opening the work is initiated, most of what has been described here was occurring concurrently with the planning and creation of other circus productions. For a time, everyone's focus was split between two or even three different productions that were in different stages of development at the same time. During November and December of each year, however, the creative team's attention is directed almost exclusively on the show that is about to open, and then in January, the director takes a brief hiatus from the circus. "I usually need to have two weeks away from it all before we hit it heavy again," McKinley explains.

Then, once the design team is set, what happens, according to McKinley, is that "we go to the corporate office and meet with Kenneth, and he gives them [the designers] 'the umbrella,' and we start the collaboration of what the show is going to look like, and basically we get out on the table what the feeling of each act will be. Where we want to go." In talking with designers, McKinley explains, "I don't go to them and say I want you to design a blue and white cape for Sylvia Zerbini, which will be on the horse. I don't do that. I give them adjectives and describe what I want the feel to be. Once in a while I'll say colors. For this show, there was a lot of talk about color because of Bello. We wanted lots of colors all over the place. Then we went off on the gold."[14]

It was the costume designer, Gregg Barnes, who brought up the use of gold as a possibility, setting off a discussion that took the team through several versions of that one color. "I think," Holst explains, "we were trying to get away from what I call jumbo spandex and primary colors." McKinley was sold on the idea and suggested using the gold as the centerpiece. There was also a conscious decision made about how they wanted the girls in the air to be dressed.[15]

In one of the team's periodic meetings, Holst recalls talking about a particular display that he wanted to include in the program. "I knew we would have three troupes performing on the Russian barre," he says. "I wanted something more classical in terms of feeling and style. The next time we met, they [the designers] came back with a feeling for color and texture."[16]

★ ★ ★

For the 131st, a great deal of the early discussion centered on Bello and how he would be used, where he would fit in the opening number, the spec, and finale. Until he arrived in winter quarters in November of 2000, prior to the opening a month later, however, McKinley saw his new star as something of a wild card. "I knew what he could do, but it wasn't until we got to winter quarters, and he actually put it up that I could start to work on it and say, 'What if you tried this and this?' That was difficult for Bello because he'd relied on himself for so long. It was a delicate relationship, figuring out how to work together. It was difficult not only for someone like him, but also for the Europeans because their acts are fifteen or twenty minutes long, and they come to Ringling and all of a sudden we say we want six minutes of their twenty minute act. [That's because] Americans devour everything so quickly and become bored. It's very difficult for [some artists] to understand how, especially in the arena, you have to work so much faster than you do in a one-ring circus. You have to have more in less time. The pace is fast, and that was difficult at first for Bello. He's got it now. He realizes that fast is your friend in the arena, because you don't have the advantage that you do in the one ring where the audience can see your face, your facial expression. Some people do. But for the people way up there in the rafters you've got to give them some kind of body energy before they get it."

One of the themes of the 131st, therefore, turned out to be "energy," and that, McKinley says, was cued off Bello. "He is crazy and frenetic, and I said, 'Let's turn everybody's energy way up.'"[17] While McKinley says the overriding theme of the show was energy, in Holst's words it was "tempo, tempo, tempo. We wanted this thing to move."[18]

★ ★ ★

Around the first of May 2000, the team began looking at designs and design concepts. It was also at this time that McKinley started to work with the composer and lyricist, throwing out titles. "We had one song we never used called 'Expect the Unexpected,' which was going to be the opening. And then we talked about the song 'This is the Circus.' Everyone began throwing out ideas about certain tricks and how things were presented. Putting everything into perceptive Kenneth said, 'Just write the ultimate circus anthem.'" Originally the song "This is the Circus" was to be used only in the finale. Then it was decided to bookend the show with the song.[19]

Craig Safan, the composer, prior to his circus assignment, had principally been active in scoring movies. While his music for the Angels of Fire flying act is generally considered the best music in the show, he did struggle with the songs, which went through several different versions before they were finally accepted.[20] Most of the act music was composed before the acts were seen, using videos for inspiration.[21]

As the star of the show, Bello was brought in on many of the production meetings. The central issue quickly came to revolve around how best to introduce Bello. Feld recalls going through four or five different versions of the opening before arriving at what was finally used. "We tried to bring Bello into the process to find out how he saw himself. What was his perception of himself?"[22]

In the opening finally settled upon, Bello emerges from a soft cube without an introduction of any sort and then bounds over to the end of the arena, where he begins playing on one of the trampolines that is eventually used in the skiing act, providing an easy segue to that number. After the skiers have concluded their performance Bello appears again, this time in a snowmobile that would have set Batman's wings aflutter. The skiers appropriate the vehicle for themselves, using it to chase Bello down the track where he finds a rope ladder that he conveniently climbs, into the seat of a motorcycle he rides up and down an inclined wire.

"It was important for us to establish him at the beginning," Feld says. "But we didn't want to go and say, 'Ladies and Gentleman, here's Bello.' We had to let him establish himself with that kind of cold opening, which in a way was a chancy thing to do, because it was so out of the norm. Now, it doesn't seem so chancy."[23]

Bello believes it was at his insistence that the present opening, withholding his introduction for the first fifteen or twenty minutes of the show, was devised. "In the past they would have said, 'The Greatest Daredevil,' or 'The Greatest Clown in the World,'" Bello points out. "I didn't want the hype to be bigger than what the performance might be. That's why we decided on using just the name Bello."

A hard sell, Bello felt, would have been too difficult to live up to. "We can't really go there," he recalls thinking, betraying perhaps a tiny bit of uncertainty that lurks behind the bravado. "So I said, 'Let's mix a hard sell and a soft sell together and make it a medium sell.' I think that's what we've come up with."[24]

Holst's rationale for the opening was that it was an attempt to forestall the complaints of people who come late and insist they had not been given a full show. So the placement of the opening was intended to keep the latecomers from feeling cheated and to help them get "the biggest bang for the buck in terms of elephant blankets and spectacle."[25] Whatever the motivation behind the programming, moving the traditional opening production number further back into the program satisfied a number of concerns from various people.

But the opening was not the only bone of contention. "We probably went through six different renditions of what the lineup was going to be," Bello recalls. His major concern throughout the planning stages was making sure that there was a reason for him to be doing the things they were asking him to do. He was, in other works, intent on making sure that there was a context or subtext for each of his appearances. Without that he felt he would not have been able to make each moment funny.[26]

This discussion began even before the contracts were signed. "Kenneth and I sat down, talking about what I could do. I told them all the things I can do, but I kept saying, 'I can do these things, but we have to figure out a real reason why.' Like the swaypole act. When you theme it for a clown, you have to think if that theme goes with the theme of the show. So there were a lot of—I don't want to say battles—but they were saying, 'This is good; we've never had this before,' and I kept saying, 'But how does it fit in?' I needed some motivation to be riding a motorcycle on a high-wire. So we had to pick and choose and decide what we wanted to save for another year. I didn't want to do something this year, and then find out next year it would have been perfect, when it's already old hat.

"There was one time when Phil, Kenneth, Tim, and I all sat down in a room and talked about what we were going to do. My wife and I had flown down to Atlanta to meet with everyone. That was in February [of 1999], more than a year before the show's debut, and they said they had never sat down that early before, and that meant we were really well set. But things evolved from there. Personnel changed. First we were way ahead of the game, and then three months before the show was supposed to open, we were still negotiating what I was going to do. I didn't want to do anything that I had done before, especially since I had been in New York with the Big Apple Circus."[27]

One point of early agreement was that the swaypole would be included. Even in the smallest building it could go up twice the height it was under the big top, so that provided the novelty, and since it did not need a big setup, it was a definite asset. "The trampoline I'd done before. It's all about falling, but I'm constantly revamping the motivation on that, so I was happy with that, and they liked it, too." That was another point of easy agreement. "Sometimes they'd say, 'We've seen you do this, but we don't want that [exactly]. We want something like it,' and I said, 'No problem. I'll come up with something.' They didn't know if I could really deliver, but to their credit," Bello adds, "they had faith in me. And there were other times when I said I was worried about something, and Kenneth or Phil would say, 'Don't worry; we'll doctor that; we'll find a theme. We're good at that.'"[28] Obviously both sides of this delicate negotiation had to work at learning to trust each other.

"He [Feld] really wanted the motorcycle on the high wire," Bello says explaining a major disagreement, "but I was used to being on the bottom, on the trapeze, and there's a lot of comedy I can do there. I didn't know if I could make driving the motorcycle funny. I was used to working with my brothers. But they weren't going to be with me this year."

Finally, Feld was moved to reply, "I was under the impression that you could make anything funny." That put Bello on the spot. "Yeeeessss," he replied somewhat hesitantly, having to squirm a bit. "You're right." It was the challenge he needed. "I didn't actually say I could make anything funny," he insists. "I hoped I could, so I had to see his point. That was one of our compromises."[29]

To ease Bello's discomfort, Feld reminded him that he had been making shows for quite some time. "I have a shop in Palmetto and Sarasota," he told Bello. "Those guys do magic. You want fire coming out of the back of your motorcycle? You want confetti cans? You want it to light up?" At that point Bello finally appreciated the extent to which his producer was willing to go, putting all the company's resources into helping him be successful. And then along came an elephant named Bo.

The outsized pachyderm first came into the picture about fourteen months prior to the start of rehearsals. Originally, the idea was that Bo would do the front part of the manège.[30] After his solo turn, the remainder of the herd and the girls would be brought in, filling the three rings. Then McKinley had an inspiration. "What would every kid want to do but play with an elephant?" And, of course, the show had the biggest kid and one of the biggest elephants in the world under contract. "Bello was the perfect solution," McKinley theorized. "Their names both began with Bs and everything started to fit."[31]

Now, in addition to trying to work out how best to present Bello, the creative team also had an elephant they intended to turn into a star. Glenn Slater, the lyricist, later came up with the idea of an interactive song about "Bo and Bello; Bello and Bo."[32] When it was finally determined that Bello and Bo were going to be a team, Feld, Holst, and McKinley met with their star clown, eagerly anticipating his enthusiastic approval of the idea. What they got instead were outrage and indignation. The reason, which Bello never revealed to his fellow teammates, was a misunderstanding that created a classic example of people talking at cross-purposes.

Bello, it seems, had been friendly with a member of the ring crew on the Big Apple Circus whose nickname was Bo. While working together, Bo had approached Bello about getting into clowning. Bello referred him to Tim Holst and even dialed up the VP on his cell phone so the two could arrange a meeting. That, as far as Bello was concerned, was the end of his involvement with Bo's clowning ambitions—until, of course, he was told by the delighted creative team, each one vying for the opportunity of announcing the good news, that Bello would be opening the show, carrying the American flag, sitting on Bo's shoulders. Having never heard of any elephant by that name, Bello assumed they were talking about the inexperienced youngster from the Big Apple Circus who had, apparently, without his knowing it and much to his chagrin, been raised to instant stardom, equal to his own.

To add insult to injury, Bello was further informed that he and Bo were going to be a team, the new Laurel and Hardy. "I was steaming," Bello remembers. "I was so mad I couldn't speak." Finally he growled, "When did I not make myself clear? I work alone! No one can keep up with me. I honestly think I'm a rare breed." In an attempt to calm him, the others insisted upon regaling him with tales of how wonderful Bo was, succeeding only in adding to Bello's fury. "Smoke was coming out of my ears," Bello says now, laughing at the misunderstanding. Finally finding his voice, he snarled, "I explained it to you. If I was going to work with anyone it would be a straight man, my brother, or the announcer." (Bello, of course, had been hoping all along to have his brother hired, as well.) Finally someone said, "But you said you're not afraid of animals."

"I'm not," Bello shouted, and then suddenly taken aback, added, "but what the hell has that got to do with what we're talking about?"

"We're talking about Bo, the elephant," someone explained at last. "What did you think we meant?"

"I don't know . . ." Bello said, somewhat sheepishly, ready, finally, to listen, but avoiding any comment about his erstwhile friend from the Big Apple Circus.[33]

By the time Bello finally understood what they had in mind for him and Bo, the idea of his opening the show carrying the American flag while Johnathan Lee Iverson sang the national anthem ended up being just another one of those ideas for the opening that was discarded. But an act, featuring the newly christened team of Bello and Bo, everyone was dead certain, was going to be in the show no matter what it took to get it there. Bello, on his part, saw it as something of a gamble, and the odds against its working were increased owing to the awkward complication that the act that could not be put together until the show was in winter quarters.

Larry Cardin, who handled Bo and presented him, had the advantage of having been around the show for two years. He had also worked with Bo before, but since the elephant was working on his father's show prior to joining

Ringling, Cardin had to go home and learn Bo's act before he had even met Bello. Having never had the advantage of a prior introduction, therefore, Bello was understandably nervous about whether the animal would even tolerate having him around. After all he was big, and he was a male. "I wasn't sure he'd like the smell of my hair spray," Bello says.[34] As if to add to the suspense, Cardin and Bo did not arrive at winter quarters until a week after everyone else. Bello was supposed to be the headliner, but everyone was acting as if the star hadn't arrived on the lot yet.[35]

To make matters even more tense for Bello, he had, by that time, heard the words to the song that had been written for this new comedy team that was supposed to rival Laurel and Hardy. "The greatest team the circus has ever known," was how the lyrics put it. Bello wasn't quite as confident. "I wondered if it was going to be the biggest embarrassment the circus had ever known. I barely knew the elephant, and he looked like he already had an act of his own. And I had my act. How were we going to mesh?"[36]

Once the two finally met, McKinley advised Bello to stand back and watch what the elephant could do and then decide what he could do that would fit into the elephant's repertoire of tricks. "Bello was great about that," McKinley says. "He really developed a lot of the act, the somersault and the elephant's shaking his head and all that. That was Bello!"[37]

Needless to say, Bello was considerably less optimistic than the director. In fact, he was nearly frantic the first time he and the elephant rehearsed together. "I was going, 'Hey, can we do this? Can we do this?'" he says, recalling the early stages of his work with Bo and his trainer as they explored ways of becoming the "Bello and Bo" already celebrated in song.

The show had set aside an hour a day for the two to rehearse together in one of the rings, in full view of everyone, and Bello was uncomfortable working in so public a space on so private and delicate a matter as trying to be funny. Cardin suggested working outside in the middle of the field on the fairgrounds, a notion Bello quickly seconded. As they began, the trainer showed Bello Bo's trunkful of tricks. He also coached Bello on what to look out for with the animal, how to approach him, and how to get him to respond. During this crash course in Bo's idiosyncrasies, Bello says, "We started to get to know each other." And although it was Bo and Bello who were supposed to be the team, in an odd way the two men also meshed together well: Larry, the straight man, raised in a family of animal trainers, and Bello, the natural-born clown.

While creating their pachydermic pantomime, Bello was instructing Cardin in the fine art of comic timing and reaction. Whenever Bello had an idea, he would explain to Cardin what he was trying to do and what he wanted from Bo. Finally "I got him [Cardin] to laugh." That was enough to tell Bello he was onto something that could be developed further. Then, "we would go show it to someone else, and if that person laughed, we'd go show it to Kenneth to see if he liked it."[38]

Working together got to be so much fun and so all consuming that Bello remembers driving to Virginia from New York with his wife and spending half the time on the phone or the car's CB talking with Cardin about what more they could do with Bo. "Like with follow-the-leader," Bello points out. "I walked across the plank and so did Bo. And I knew he could say, 'No,' so I figured if I did a cartwheel or a backward somersault, and he said, 'No,' that would be funny. I wanted to have him follow me and do three things and then say, 'No.' And there were things he could do that I couldn't, so that was fun, too."[39]

Ultimately Bello and Bo were a smash hit.

★ ★ ★

At the same time that the creative team's talks with Bello were proceeding, some of the acts Holst had lined up were unable to join the show for various reasons involving scheduling or financial conflicts. For one particular display he had hired two girls who had previously been trained by Alla Youdina and who had subsequently put together their own double trapeze act. He also had a young man who had left a teeterboard act to develop a solo aerial act on silks. What was needed was a third act to complete the display.[40]

There being no time to find another complementary act, Holst turned once again to Alla Youdina. Feld approached her first, asking if she had any ideas for something new. She suggested an aerial cube with five girls. Her original concept for the act called for four girls to work, one on each side of the cube, while the fifth worked in the middle on silk cords.[41]

Since the show had previously established a good relationship with the circus school in Brazil, it was decided that they would audition the needed girls there. Somehow, between the time of the auditions and June of 2000, when Youdina was expecting the girls at her studio in Vermont, the required immigration paperwork failed to materialize, and the girls were unable to leave Brazil. Both sides claimed the other reneged on their agreement. The girls were especially angry because they had left their jobs and given up their apartments and suddenly found themselves stranded.

Finally when the show decided it really did need the girls and was ready to obtain the necessary papers, the girls refused to have anything further to do with the Americans who had promised and then, according to them, left them high and dry.

At this point, with the clock ticking, Holst was in a mild panic. To resolve the issue, he decided to send Youdina to Brazil to convince the girls to do the act for her. By the time she got to Brazil, however, the original group of five girls had dwindled to four. Youdina talked to those who remained about the act she had planned and how they would be cared for. Because the girls felt they could trust her and wanted to work with her, they were persuaded to come to America. Youdina left Brazil confident that the act would exist. All that remained was for the paperwork to be completed. By the time the four girls were issued the needed visas, however, it was September, and two of them had been coaxed into staying behind by their boyfriends, who could not bear to be separated for two years.

So instead of the anticipated four, just two girls showed up at the end of September. "The cube was done by that time, and everything was ready for five," Youdina recalls. I had been designing everything in my head for five. So when I saw just two at the airport, I didn't know what to do." She appealed to the creative team. "What can I do? The equipment will stay empty. It's not going to work." The reply, "as always," was, "Do something."

Never one to be daunted, Youdina replied, "Okay, but to do something, I need at least one more. That will be the minimum, minimum. Otherwise there is no balance at all. So we started looking for someone who was available and here in this country, because there was no time to obtain a visa. In October, they brought in someone from another show." That gave Youdina about six weeks to train her girls and create an entirely new act with them. "I knew that when we got to Tampa they wouldn't be in my hands any more. They would be in Phil McKinley's hands, so the act had to be finished before then." Youdina knew she had her work cut out for her.

The most stunning disappointment, however, was yet to come. The girls, in Youdina's estimation, were little more than amateurs. "They had no acrobatic training. I talked to Tim, and I said, 'They have no training. What can I do with these people?' I asked him if I could choose somebody else. He says, 'No, they have already signed contracts.' So what to do?"

"Rehearsals" with the cube were held in Youdina's house in Vermont. The first week was spent on conditioning, running up and down the mountains around her home trying to whip them into shape. "And meanwhile we're talking about images and expression and projection and all that."

Even a few months after the opening, Youdina insisted the girls were "still amateurs," who needed at least another year and half to learn to point their toes and keep their knees straight.[42]

★ ★ ★

On another front, the designers' first sketches had been completed by June, at which time they were accepted, rejected, or sent back for further revisions. Sometimes a lot gets thrown out. As designs are finalized, McKinley makes it a practice to personally take them to Kenneth Feld. By the end of June, Feld will have seen everything. "We put all the designs up on the wall and look at them, because you never know until you get them all up together what's going to work." Once approved, the floats will go into blueprints.

At the meeting for the 131st, however, "We threw everything out. We just said, 'Let's start all over.' It wasn't right. It's not an easy gig for a designer," McKinley acknowledges. But he and all the other members of the creative team agree that it is much better to make those kinds of cuts earlier rather than later on. At that point the major players still have the luxury of relying on their gut instincts, and in this case, McKinley said, "It just didn't feel right. It was a hard day."

Some elements of the design did get approved, like Mark Oliver Gebel's Pegasus float. That was a unanimous winner. Feld gave his approval, and construction began almost immediately thereafter. On the other hand, "we held up a long time on the ringmaster's shooting star float. We weren't sure. And if we weren't going to use it that much, why haul it around the country for two years, especially if it is not going to make that big of an impact?"[43]

Throughout this period of creative gestation, McKinley says that he is in the process of creating a film, frame by frame, in his head. It is a document of what the production will finally look like. "Eventually by the time we go into winter quarters the film is complete, and then the film has to become three-dimensional." Along the way various stimuli will have been fed into the raw footage, as for instance in the case of the manège.

Since he knows that each production will have an elephant manège, McKinley confesses to being somewhat preoccupied with it. "What's going to be the theme? Where's it going to happen?"[44] Holst says the Brazilian theme, which McKinley finally settled on, evolved only after he brought the director to Brazil. "I tried to sell him on a Brazilian theme three or four years ago. He couldn't envision it, whereas I was already way ahead in terms of samba schools, and what I could see in the show."[45]

McKinley says he decided to go Latin because it had become such a popular craze. "And then we had this connection to the Brazilians, and he [Holst] was talking about finding girls who really could do samba, legit samba."[46]

Which is what Holst did. For the first time in many, many years, the show was able to boast of having a complement of sixteen girls who were really trained dancers (as opposed, of course, to the so-called Brazilian acrobats with whom Youdina had to work). This was a significant departure from the policy of casting the dancers from the performers' wives or having someone from one of the acts doubling in brass.

The trip to Brazil also inspired the color scheme of vibrant red and yellow for the first half closing. Lurking in the back of McKinley's mind, however, was another incentive for doing the manège in this way: "The first year I was on the show I went to the warehouse and there were these huge feather backpacks. I have wanted them in every single show ever since. They were spectacular." They were originally built at a time the Felds[47] were producing *Beyond Belief* in Las Vegas for Siegfried and Roy. The man who was creating the feather designs for that show was also providing the same service for the circus. Unsure of what exactly was desired in one of the circus designs, he called the designer Don Foote, who told him to make them like *Beyond Belief*, meaning the show, but the designer, failing to make the connection, took the instructions literally and produced a set of feather backpacks so huge, they were indeed beyond belief.

They were three times the intended size, and when the girls who were riding the elephants put them on, Irvin Feld exploded. "What are those things?" he screamed. "Get them off; I can't see the elephants." No further directive was issued or required. The offending backpacks were shipped off to storage.

"I saw them hanging up at the top of the warehouse," McKinley says. "They were incredible. They would probably cost about fifty to seventy-five thousand dollars apiece if you wanted to make them today. I took Gregg Barnes [the costume designer for the 131st] to the warehouse and showed him these costumes, so when we got to the Brazilian thing, 'Carnevale,' I said, 'This is it!' This is where we use them. Gregg designed the rest of the costumes around them."

Once he had bought into the Brazilian theme, McKinley was excited about how the manège developed. "The thing I liked about it was the energy again. And then the dance idea grew to be about teaching everyone to do the Bello and Bo dance."[48]

★ ★ ★

In his efforts to decide on the running order, McKinley says, "I've created the idea that sections of the show are glued together. In the 131st, we started with the trampoline, and the energy was like bamm! I wanted that energy, and I went with it. That's how the opening idea developed, because after the skiers and the motorcycle, we were already at a fever pitch. So the audience is here [he raises his hand above his head to demonstrate the level of excitement to which he has brought the audience], and you've got to meet

that energy, which he eventually did with the somewhat delayed opening production number. And then I always have what Kenneth now jokes about, my
lyrical moment in the show, which is about twenty minutes into the show, depending on what's come before. I've bombarded the audience. Now they need
to stop and breathe, and so I'll put in an aerial act or something that's soft and
beautiful. You've hit them so hard, they're feeling, 'Wait a minute. I've got to
breathe, so I can start over.' So we do the lyrical act to slow down the pace of
the show and allow the audience a moment to relax."

An example of this "gluing" was his decision to encapsulate the manège
within the spec. "I love putting acts in the body of big thematic things. This
is the first year I had performing animals in the middle of every single production. I had horses in opening, elephants in spec, and elephants in finale."
And they were not there merely as part of a parade. "The finale was difficult
because they had to bring the elephants in and down the front and back track
around all the performers. The elephants had to mount their bull tubs and get
ready to do the full floor display that Mark developed with Gunther. And at
the same time we're moving Larry's elephants in with ours. The trainers and
staff thought I was crazy."

The elephants were used in the finale because one of the great challenges
of staging a Ringling performance is keeping the audience in its seats during
the final moments. Feld predicted McKinley would never be able to do it.
"I've said they will never go out the door during a finale of mine, and he
[Feld] taught me a very good lesson the first year. I'd done the whole show and
staged the finale, and I knew there was something not right about it. He knew
the solution, but he just let me work it out. What was wrong was that I didn't
have any elephants in the finale. Nobody walks out on an elephant. Just bring
those elephants out the back door the first thing, and the audience will stay in
their seats. They always do."[49]

In looking for other connections between various elements in the show,
McKinley decided to "glue" the hand balancing and contortionists that appear
in the spec together with the so-called exotics—the camels and the zebras—
using the Arabian nights theme that grew naturally out of the animal display.

In attempting to devise a workable running order that would create an
emotional arc, McKinley takes all the acts that have been booked for the show
and puts their names on index cards. The cards are then laid out on a table and
the shuffling begins. This is a method similar to that used by Michael Christensen and his Grock board on the Big Apple Circus.[50] "If I need a big setup
in ring two and three, [I have to figure out] what I can put in ring one that
people will watch. Like the tigers. If they are taking up rings two and three, I
have got to have something going on either in ring one or on the tracks. And
then you tear down from the tigers. You've got to have another act going on

while that's taking place. In the 131st the cage was already partially down because the end trick involved dropping the cage." In order to clear ring three for the tiger's bottle walk, the transport cages had to get out the back door during the closing trick with the tiger on the swing. So McKinley knew the transition coming out of it was not going to be a big problem because most of the equipment and cages would already have gone. That easy transition made it possible to give Bello his small, solo moment in ring one.

★ ★ ★

By the time McKinley goes into the white model meeting, that film of the show that he carries around in his head needs to be complete. During the summer of 2000, after settling many of the issues concerning Bello's performance, McKinley went out to see the flying act then rehearsing in Las Vegas. "It was so unusual, with the trampoline and the multiple pedestals and trapeze bars we decided to end the show with it." When it came time to decide on music for the act, McKinley suggested "an incredible piece" that the show's composer, Craig Safan, had used in his score for the film *The Last Starfighter*.[51]

In addition to the flying act, Golovko's troupe also had their Russian swing to be considered. Feld was not satisfied with it, insisting that it be more exciting. "We wanted to create this frantic thing instead of some kind of serious swing and acrobatic act, which is what they wanted originally. We said, 'It's going to be fast and furious and Johnathan will be able to create this frantic activity and get people involved with it.'" This new concept for the act was principally developed during the rehearsal period in winter quarters. Johnathan Lee Iverson was given the ball and allowed to run with it. Once the feeling that the creative team wanted was explained to him, he took it and ran, indeed. "There was nothing written for Johnathan. It was all his thing."[52]

Iverson's participation in other elements of the show also had to be considered. This was especially important for the 131st because this time the material would be tailored to his special talents. His first show, the 129th, had been put together before he had been discovered. So its tone was already set. "Now, I had two years to get to know him," McKinley says. "I decided to put him out there and open the doors and see what would happen." When it came to the Cloud Jumpers number, which is what the Russian swing came to be called, Iverson was running all over the arena and screaming at people, because "he wanted to do that."[53]

There was also another bit of tailoring, fitting the music to Iverson's specific vocal talents. The scoring of his first show was incredibly difficult. He was singing high B-flats all evening, which McKinley points out, is "hard to do when you're doing an opera schedule, let alone ten shows a week. We adapted

the music more directly for his voice and then gave him a talk about high powered energy and told him to go for it and just have a good time. So it was a
matter of youth being set loose and taking over."

Also returning was Mark Oliver Gebel, so a decision had to be made as
to where he was going to fit into the overall picture. "I'd gone to a practice,"
McKinley points out, "and he was practicing the liberty horses. He did all the
finish tricks in one ring. I asked him what would happen if we separated all
five of those finish tricks. Put them all in separate rings. I love the energy of
his running from ring to ring because he's so tall. So his finish display was born
out of that [energy thing as well]."[54]

★ ★ ★

When McKinley first began directing the Ringling productions, many of
the performers regarded him with suspicion and skepticism. He had no circus
experience, and some of the things he asked them to do had never been done
in a circus before. "I think a lot of the performers thought, 'this guy is crazy.'
Now they know I've done my research." They have learned to trust that he
will not ask them to do anything that will make them look foolish or awkward, nor will he insist on their doing something that creates a problem. "They
have enough respect for themselves that they'll try to bring off anything I ask
of them. Mark is a perfect example of that with Reno the leopard."

The tricky part of the leopard's ride on the Pegasus float is that he is out
there for a very long time. "When I first asked Mark about it, I didn't really
tell him the whole truth. I just asked him if he could ride in the chariot with
Reno. Reno has been on a float before, but this year his float runs all over the
floor among women with feather fans and men with spears, so there's a lot to
distract him. I did tell Mark his float was the first one out the door and would
be on the floor longer than anybody else. What Mark does is very clever. After I had worked out the pattern of the float's movements, Mark found spots
on the floor where he could have one of the handlers throw him a piece of
meat." The audience doesn't always see it, but Reno is fed at several intervals
throughout the spec, so the animal has been trained to understand that if it be-
haves, there is going to be a piece of meat around the next bend in the road.

McKinley also won the respect of the people at Hagenbeck-Wallace.
The patterns of movement he was able to use in the 131st were made considerably more interesting by what they did for him with the setup of ring
two. "I knew that on the Blue Unit you can't break ring two apart because
the Cossacks need the raised curb. On the Red Unit we have the tiger cage,
which presents a similar problem." He was able to provoke the creativity of
the people at Hagenbeck-Wallace by wondering aloud if there weren't some

way to open up the center ring. A way was eventually found, through the use of ramps. "That allowed me the possibility to create incredible parade patterns. So, God bless Hagenbeck-Wallace. They did it. Now the Blue Unit uses ramps, too, and we go over the curb. You have to look at each obstacle as another challenge to your creativity. Otherwise you would go nuts."[55]

★ ★ ★

Eventually the time came for the much anticipated white model meeting late in the summer. By this time 80 percent of the music had been written, and CDs of it would have been played to give the gathered assemblage a feeling of the mood and tempo of the show. All these elements would be combined with videos of the individual acts. When there was agreement on the feeling and direction a particular element seemed to be taking the show, Kenneth Feld would sign off on it.

In preparation for the white model meeting McKinley went down to Florida, and for several days before he made his presentation, he and Tony Stevens, the choreographer, worked together and in essence staged the entire show. "Then it's done. I show everybody at the white model meeting. 'This is where the parade's going to come in; this is how it's going to be staged.'" His purpose is to give the various technical people a chance to look at it and indicate where the potential problems lie. "They have a chance to give me feedback and say things like, 'when we set this net up, you've got guy lines coming down and you're not going to be able to get under them with a float.' So we basically lay everything out, the grid, everything. Like this year with the flying act, we even hung the [rigging for the] flying act from the grid on the model."[56]

The rigging presented some special problems of its own. "Whenever you create a show like this," Holst explains, "you can't assume that everything's built for Madison Square Garden. That's just a very short part of our tour. You have to build the show and make decisions technically that will work for the most part in every building. And you have to assume that there will be problems in some of the buildings that you go into."

Despite computers and all the methods devised for making precise calculations about such matters, Holst insists that not all potential problems can be solved in advance. "There are some people who want all their problems solved before we get on tour," he says, "and you can't do that." What this means is that the interaction of various points of view at these meetings is going to present some challenges to the creative people. One of these involved the flying act. The technical people wanted Golovko and Holst to make certain decisions about the rigging before it could even be tried out. Holst defended the delay by pointing out that this sort of rigging had never been tried before. "It's still experimental," he reminded everyone, "so you have to allow them to experiment. We experimented with this act right up until we opened in New York. It was only in the last three days [of the Garden run] that the last trick of that act [worked successfully]. Some of our technical people, and rightfully so, wanted to eliminate those swings. I'd been fighting to keep them in, to give them [the artists] the chance to find a way to make it work."

As it turned out the equipment being used in the flying act at the time of its New York engagement was only a temporary compromise. "By the time we got all the engineers and the safety inspectors through the process of agreeing that a particular piece of equipment was safe to go on the road, we had already opened." So there wasn't time to build the rigging that everyone ultimately agreed upon until later in the run.

"It was a little easier with the ski jump ramp because the fellow we had contracted [to build it] had seen the show in the summer, so by the next spring we already knew the exact measurements, what the expectations were, and what we wanted to accomplish and there was nothing to experiment with. The flying act has been totally experimental, and we didn't know how far we could take it. On the other side of the coin, insofar as the flying act is concerned, we have four people who can do triple somersaults. We have five people who do double layouts. There are twelve people in the act. Even if we have three people out for one reason or another, the tricks are still there every single day and that's part of the plan. That's the [mindset] we're in, to cover ourselves so the audience sees exactly the same show every day."[57]

★ ★ ★

It is not just the creative and technical staffs that attend the white model meeting. The transportation department is represented, as are the floor bosses and the unit manager. Everyone needs to know what the new show is going to entail because it affects the work of everyone. To avoid surprises and problems down the road, McKinley tries to be as specific and detailed in his presentation as possible. "I walk in and have a list, a parade order, which I learned from my research at the museum in Baraboo. I saw the parade orders [that are part of the museum's archives]."

In fact, 95 percent of what the show is going to become will be revealed at this meeting. For the 131st, McKinley even indicated the patterns he wanted the floats to follow during the spec. "I had to show them the patterns of the opening because they are very intricate. They're hard to do. I had to show the guys who build them that the floats had to make very sharp turns. We've got a new style of float, which I call 'smart floats.' They can turn on a dime almost. That allows me a lot more access [to various intricate staging patterns]."[58]

After the white model meeting, certain elements were sent into production and certain others were cut. "We design a lot of things that never see the floor," McKinley says, "because of budgetary reasons, because of manpower reasons, because we can't pack it. This year, the girl's backpacks alone took up a huge amount of space. Precedence is always given to the animals, so you've got to designate those train cars first."[59] As more and more space is allocated to the animals, thanks in part to their new and enlarged cages, any remaining space becomes more precious.

By the time production begins at the Hagenbeck-Wallace Co., Mark Freddes, then director of construction, and his staff will have ironed out the technical problems with the floats that had to carry equipment or telescope to get under all the various portals of the arenas in which the show will play. For the Pegasus float, for instance, it was decided to install a Plexiglas hood over the driver to protect him should the leopard get rambunctious.

The birdcage on the Angels of Fire float had to be put on a scissor lift so that it could drop low enough to pack. It was finally decided that if the money was going to be spent on a scissor so that the float could get under any opening, it might as well be able to rise as well. Sometimes surprising benefits come about in strange ways through the technical solutions to what is otherwise seen as a problem.

Following the white model meeting McKinley, as is his practice, took a short breather during September. During that time, when most elements have found their final form, he says "I just sit back, and let it all turn." He uses this time to visit the unit and visit the people who would be appearing in the new show and were currently on the road. They, too, were given a complete preview of the new show with the white model. They were told what they would be doing and what costumes they would be wearing. In this way the returning performers are also made a part of the process.

The work at winter quarters in Tampa got underway about the middle of November, and it concluded with the new show's premiere just before the New Year. McKinley, all his preliminary work not withstanding, went down to winter quarters a week earlier than the start of rehearsals in order to conclude any unfinished preproduction work. He and the choreographer and their assistants set up the white model again and ran through all the numbers once more for themselves to make sure nothing and no one had been forgotten or lost.

It is not unusual for an act to be either gained or lost because of visa or scheduling problems between August and November. "It's always changing," McKinley observes. "For instance, this year I had asked Mark about changing the [tiger] act around a little bit, and he tried. But then he and Gunther came and said it wasn't really worth doing because the cats were pretty irritated about the whole thing." McKinley agreed to return to the act's old routine.[60]

★ ★ ★

Clowning on the show had caused problems for the past several seasons. In an attempt to alleviate them and enhance the level of comedy, Greg and Karen DeSanto, husband and wife, were contracted to serve as directors of clowning for the 131st edition, a position that was created to fill a vacuum created by the closing of Ringling's Clown College. Both were graduates of that program, and Greg had ten years experience teaching there. Their experiences in their new position follow.[61]

For the previous edition Robert Shields of the pantomime duo Shields and Darnell had been installed in this position, but his tenure was short-lived as he had little to no experience in circus clowning and enjoyed no relationship of any kind with the senior members of the show's clown alley.

At first the DeSantos were asked if they would be interested in "mentoring" the clowns on the new show. That designation was chosen in an effort to get away from the idea of there being more than one director on the show. Phil McKinley was solely charged with that responsibility, and the DeSantos soon learned that he had his hand in every element of the show, including the clowning. "Everyone else is a player," Greg DeSanto states unequivocally.

While in winter quarters with the show in Tampa for the first time, the couple's job evolved from mentoring to assisting with the gags, directing some, and providing a voice for the clowns in the process of putting the show together. They quickly learned that McKinley "is very accommodating to the clowns. He wants to know every idea and figure out how he can incorporate it."

The DeSantos, however, did not get involved with writing any of the clowns' material because by the time they arrived on the scene it was too late for them to do so. "We were just going to take the material they had and bring it up to speed."

The fact that Bello was headlining the show took some of the pressure off the members of clown alley, at least insofar as providing the comic relief. "Bello was great," DeSanto says. "He wasn't a threat to the other clowns, which is a whole other story. These clowns that headline shows are nothing but good for clowns. The Ringling clowns, however, tend to take it as an immediate threat to their well being" when a clown is the star of the show.

The DeSantos's involvement in the show began when the Red Unit, which would become the 131st, was in Boston. The purpose of their visit was to sit in, with Kenneth Feld, on the auditions of the new routines planned by the clowns for the new show. It was at this time that Feld canceled a gag spoofing NASCAR racing.

Feld asked the DeSantos if they could have made it funny. Their take was that it was too late to fix it. They suggested getting away from the idea of having to use every member of clown alley in the gags and focusing more on character driven comedy. This last suggestion was based on the DeSantos's recent experience away from Ringling, in situations where they worked more intimately. Good clowning, they had concluded, is character driven, just as it is with all the featured clowns.

"It was a little bit of a letdown for the alley to have its routine cut before winter quarters," Greg DeSanto recalls, "but it also forced them to come up with some different ideas, one of which was the Survivor spoof."

During the production meetings, the DeSantos represented the clown department, which, like the lighting, props, and costume departments, always had an opportunity to discuss its problems with the entire group and keep everyone apprised of its needs. "We would be able to come back to the clowns and say, 'They're happy with this' or 'not happy with this,' and ask where we could help resolve the problem.

"Since the clowns were on call all day, we were able to keep things moving by coordinating what needed to be done by the other departments. That was an element which had been lacking the past year, because that was a job normally done by the director of Clown College."

That meant a lot of paperwork with daily updates. The DeSantos reported directly to McKinley and discussed issues like choice of music with him. "We tried to make everyone's job easier," Greg DeSanto says, summing up. "The main reason it was successful was because they [the clowns] trusted us to handle things for them. Left to their own devices, they would have been overwhelmed by the process. We took the heat off them and were able to tell them, 'Don't worry about that. We'll take care of it. You'll have to deal with it for the rest of the year when this thing gets on the road. For now we'll take care of it. Just worry about your own work.'"

In addition, the couple also directed most of the gags before they were presented before Kenneth Feld. "We didn't iron hand them, but if there was something radically wrong, we gently suggested privately that they should do something because it wasn't working. The few people who really didn't want to listen had their stuff cut."

The night the clown gags were presented, "Mr. Feld, Phil [McKinley], Tim [Holst] and whoever else Mr. Feld wants to have an opinion on it came in, and we presented every piece of material that was going to appear—or we hoped would appear—walk-arounds, gags, production numbers. The material for the 3-Ring Adventure [that portion of the show that occurs before the actual performance begins] was presented in the Adventure format. They came down and sat on the ring curb. Ring gags were presented at the end. Everything had already, more or less, been signed off on by Phil or Tim prior to this, on paper. Then they like to see it, of course, because everything looks different on its feet.

"That's different than when I was on the show," Greg says. "Then they didn't have any idea of what they were going to see. We would just present what we wanted to show them. Now, because of the different restraints of budget and no Clown College to produce props, everything has to be fed through a different system, so Hagenbeck-Wallace has to build all the props, and before they can build them, Phil and Tim have to sign off on them."

Karen DeSanto recalls that she and Greg felt sure that some of the ideas that were being presented that night of so-called Nuremberg Trials would be rejected, but they decided it was better to let the young clowns fail that way, with a try, than to have their ideas vetoed before Feld could get a look at them. "To get them to be productive you have to allow that to happen," she says.

Ultimately, the success of this particular group of clowns, the DeSantos believed, was that they all got something to do in the show and had material to work on for the future. "Previously the alley would become a cesspool of infighting," Karen adds, "which was not conducive to creativity, no less living together day to day."

In the matter of the clowns' participation in the 3-Ring Adventure, Greg DeSanto has had his opinion change after seeing it work. "At first I thought it limited what you could do, but now that I've seen it work and helped put one together, I think it's great. It's one of the clowns' greatest performance opportunities because you can make your connection with your audience right there, and it will carry you through the whole show."

The 3-Ring Adventure includes two eight- or nine-minute clown sets. "We encourage everyone to stay out on the floor as much as possible, if they don't have a costume change, even if they're not working, to do 'meet and greet' and go into the seats. That's another great place to make a connection because prior to this we were hardly ever allowed to go into the seats," Greg points out.

"If you can connect with a few people they're going to watch you the whole show. You really had to work at that in the ring for the people who were forty rows up. Here they're right there. It's a gift. If you're a character down there in the Adventure that they relate to, you've got the show made."

Once the clowns' contributions were approved by Feld, it was the DeSantos' job to lay everything out and make sure everything worked, especially insofar as what was happening when and where. Sometimes, for instance, the matter of a costume change would demand a casting change.

★ ★ ★

The morning of the first day of winter quarters was devoted to the laborious task of introducing everyone through five interpreters. That first afternoon McKinley plunged right in, putting together the first parade. Aside from the actual staging, one of the most important things that McKinley hoped to accomplish with this production in winter quarters was to establish some rapport between the production's two stars, Bello Nock and Johnathan Lee Iverson. They would not only be before the audience more than any other performers in the show, but also they would often be in the arena at the same time, hopefully interacting in a way the audiences would find appealing and entertaining.

Coming in as what he called the "new boy in town," Bello was acutely aware that there might be some resentment from people like Iverson, especially in light of the kind of buildup he had been told he would be getting, not only in the show, but also promotional materials. "He [Iverson] was all it last year," Bello acknowledges. "None of us wanted to put him on the back burner." But there was the nagging worry that the star clown and the ringmaster would not get along. Bello went so far as to tell Feld, "I don't want to work here if the guy hates me, so I wanted to make sure that we got to know each other and could get along. He's a big presence. He's young and . . ." Here words fail him, but Bello understood that Iverson was every bit as ambitious as he himself was.[62]

The problem was that neither man knew how best to approach the other. "He didn't know how to deal with me, and I didn't know how to deal with him," Bello admits. "He's the announcer, and I got to have respect for him, but I want to play. So you want to do something, but you're not sure what because of the respect thing."

Iverson was in something of the same quandary over Bello and the fact that the carrot-topped dynamo was, in his own way, as the star clown, deserving of special treatment as well. "You know you can't be mean," Bello says by way of explaining Iverson's position. "And he can really look mean, especially when he does a certain face. He looks like a young Mohammed Ali."

When Iverson tried a somewhat combative approach, Bello recalls, everyone said, "'No, no, you can't raise a fist to a clown.' They were on him about being mean to me. I said, 'Listen, there has to be some playful mode we can use here.'" Iverson took the criticism and, apparently stymied about what to do, pulled something of pout. "Since I don't know how to react to you, I'm just not going to react at all," Bello remembers him saying. Trying to mediate, Bello offered a suggestion. "Listen," he said. "You can't really hit someone deliberately, but if it's an accident and you say 'I'm sorry,' then that's funny. So when I'm dancing, and I accidentally kick you, you can roll your eyes, and that will be funny."[63]

Bello was, in fact, instructing Iverson on the way a classic comedy team works off each other. If Bello and Bo were the new Laurel and Hardy, Bello and Iverson were about to become the new Abbott and Costello.

After Bello and Bo got to know each other, Iverson was introduced into the act, as well, adding another level of awkwardness at the beginning. Iverson was from New York and a circus innocent who had never worked with an elephant before, and here he was working on rather intimate terms with a very large version of the species. Bello, more than anyone else, was responsible for developing the interaction between the three stars, McKinley acknowledges. "As a director sometimes the best thing you can do is get out of the way. As a director I prefer editing. Throw everything at me and let me trim it down and decide what's going to work."[64]

During rehearsals Bello and Iverson spent some time feeling each other out and dealing with the feedback they were getting, before they did actually become friends once on tour. "In one town," Bello reveals, "we had to share a dressing room, and it was like, 'Okay, I've never shared a dressing room before.' I had a radio, and he had a radio, and he asked, 'Okay, whose gets played?' I said, 'Hey, I'm the youngest of four boys, so if there's something you don't like, let me know, because I'm used to being told what to do.' And he says, 'Me, too; me, too.'"

Then they began playing their CDs for each other, and before they knew it they were sharing their thoughts. "It was amazing how we both lost our dads in the same year and how, at a young age, were expected to do so much. We had a lot of things in common. All of a sudden we started liking each other more and more. So now we have a very, very good relationship. Whenever we come off the float or when we leave somewhere together, and he's in front of me, he'll reach back and put his arm around me and ask how I feel. Then he'll ask me how he sounds, and I'll tell him, 'Great!'"[65]

★ ★ ★

Another of the elements of the 131st edition that had to wait for winter quarters to be developed involved the direct engagement of the audience. "The one thing I love about the circus is that we can talk to the audience, and the audience can talk back to us. They know you know they're there, and they love it," McKinley theorizes. This, of course, is one of the qualities that makes the circus different from the theatre. "And this becomes very exciting for the audience because we spend most of our lives watching film and television and video where we don't participate. I started talking to Bello and Johnathan, telling them to go into the audience, just run up in the audience; just get a burst of energy and go. There's a place at the end of the first half where Johnathan is doing that teaser speech about making sure you come back for the second half, and he grabs somebody in the audience, and he's telling that person personally. The audience just goes crazy because he's right in someone's face. That's the direct contact that was very much in my mind as we were thinking about where Johnathan came into the picture and how we could create relationships with Bello and Bo and Johnathan."[66]

As rehearsals progressed Bello became concerned that there was no moment in the show when he could take some time to let the people get to know a more relaxed and quieter side of his personality. It eventually became apparent that some kind of filler was needed in ring one to cover the final removal of the tiger cage and bottle walk equipment after Mark Oliver Gebel's cat act. It was decided that since wrestling was enjoying enormous popularity at the moment, a comic wrestling match would be just the thing. The creative team came to Bello and asked him to devise such a contest to include audience participation. A similar routine, using boxing, was already being performed by César Aedo elsewhere. Bello agreed to give it a try.[67]

"I did my best," Bello insists. "But there are a lot of limitations when wrestling. You can't get physical with somebody coming out of the audience. And if you don't get violent, it's not wrestling. I tried a lot of different things." But nothing worked to any great degree for the first few weeks of the tour.

"I needed to come up with something that involved just one girl," Bello thought. Frustrated with the wrestling, he asked if he could try something else, and McKinley agreed.[68] Bello worked out the sketch in which he works with one girl whom he takes from the audience. When it was ready, he asked Feld if he could try it out on him. The producer agreed to fly in to see it the very next day. After watching the new act for two performances Feld acknowledged that it was a vast improvement over what they had, and it should be kept in the show. "You know what I like about you?" Bello remembers Feld asking. "It's that you improved just from one show to the next show."

Bello wanted the band to play something he was familiar with during this sketch, but Feld suggested the William Tell Overture and the tango after he gets shot. The only problem was keeping the running time down to five minutes. Bello insisted on six. He didn't want to be frantic even here. He suggested cutting the trampoline by a minute instead, but the creative team vetoed that suggestion.[69] In the end there was a compromise, and the show managed to keep within its allotted time, which was especially important in Madison Square Garden, where the overtime costs would be enormous should the show run long.

Feld, in turn, was pleased with the apple gag, which, he says, "is a nice thing because you've seen this guy who is larger than life, and then you find out he also has a heart and soul, which is what you get to see in that moment."[70]

Bello's performance continued to evolve and became increasingly effective as the tour progressed. Despite having worked in many different venues before coming to Ringling, one of the elements of his performance Bello had to refine was its scale. Bello compares working in arenas to huge theme parks. You are overwhelmed at first, he says, but then "you learn short cuts. I had worked big arenas before, but never in a show on the size and scale of Ringling Bros. I learned to keep turning, to open up, so [in the apple gag] I have to force the girl to open up, too. That's why I'm constantly turning her. It just took getting used to.[71]

"They kept telling me I had to open it up," Bello remembers, but he also believes that although there may be moments when only a couple hundred people see what he's doing, a hundred people here and a hundred people there start to add up, and every one of them has enjoyed an intimate moment he has shared with them exclusively. The effect, he is sure, is cumulative.

And it isn't just Bello who kept evolving and improving. "The show you saw last night," Feld pointed out the day after a stunningly successful New York opening, "was different than the show you would have seen at the Meadowlands[72] because I came in, and I sat through it on Thursday night and was not a happy camper with everything I saw. So we changed a lot when we were in Long Island. We made some cuts and dealt with things. What the audience saw on opening night [in New York] was a product of that. It's an ongoing process even though the show is three months old. I guess an advantage I have is not being here every day. I come in with fresh eyes. When you're here every day little things creep in, and you don't realize where they're going."[73]

McKinley also stays in close touch with the show through its New York engagement, and then somewhat less closely through the entire two-year run. Once the show leaves Florida he visits sporadically. "I have to get out of the way, and they [staff and performers] are glad to have me go. It has to become their show. So I go away for a couple of weeks, and I end up going back, usually when we play Tampa–St. Pete. Then I'll go back in Orlando to check on it again. That's usually when we're doing pictures. I'll catch it again in Knoxville or maybe South Carolina, somewhere in that range. And I go out and check on it in the Meadowlands and at Uniondale [Long Island] and of course we have a rehearsal at the Garden. Once it opens at the Garden I'm on to the next."

The need for changes between the Meadowlands and Madison Square Garden might be attributed to the natural erosion that takes place in many productions, and the director and producer are especially sensitive to that phenomenon. "Kenneth and I both have an uncanny ability to visit on bad days. The nightly reports are great, but then we walk into the building, and something happens—I don't know if people get nervous or we just happen to hit it on an off night, but when I saw the opening at Meadowlands, I thought, 'We have got to get this tight. It's a little out of whack, but its okay.' Kenneth went on Thursday, and he called me late at night, which he never does, and said, 'You've got to get out here. This is not working.' It's difficult to keep it going because we move from building to building. It's very difficult for us to walk in and say, 'The lights are not right,' because they'll say, 'But that's the way they've been.' And I will say, 'That could be, but they're not right.' It just takes tweaking. We also make cuts. The show may be a little long. It was a matter of going to all the acts, saying, 'Just tighten it up; put it on the edge a bit more,' which we almost always do every year. Because lots of times if everyone takes just fifteen seconds off, that's all we need."

That tweaking, McKinley insists, involves more than just keeping the show on a time clock. It gets the acts in and out, while they're still ahead of the audience. "If the audience catches up to you and knows what's going on, it's all over. You just want to be sure you're providing them with a certain forward momentum all the time; otherwise, they are up and out of their seats."[74]

★ ★ ★

McKinley is also responsible for staging the educational show, which is presented to the school audiences at certain early morning midweek performances. That is accomplished about five weeks into the tour. "We don't work on the educational show during winter quarters because we don't want to split the focus. Mine or the performers." One can understand how performers might become confused. The running order is often altered for the student shows in order to work up "a certain momentum." The school shows run about two hours, so what with the addition of the educational material, some things have to be cut. It takes only a few days to stage this version of the show, once the main performance is well set. And then McKinley will be on to next year's production, dreaming up ways to make that show something different while still delivering the expected emotional wallop. He has to be on his toes himself, to keep his colleagues on the creative team from invoking his standing request: "If I ever do anything I've done before, stop me."[75]

NOTES

1. Tim Holst, personal interview with the author, New York, April 1, 2001.

2. Holst interview.

3. Holst interview.

4. Kenneth Feld, personal interview with the author, New York, March 31, 2001.

5. Holst interview.

6. Holst interview.

7. Feld interview.

8. Holst interview.

9. Holst interview.

10. Feld interview.

11. Phil Wm. McKinley, personal interview with the author, Edison, N.J., April 9, 2001.

12. Holst interview.

13. McKinley interview.

14. McKinley interview.

15. Holst interview.

16. Holst interview.

17. McKinley interview.

18. Holst interview.

19. McKinley interview.

20. McKinley interview.

21. Holst interview.

22. Feld interview.

23. Feld interview.

24. Bello Nock, personal interview with the author, New York, April 1, 2001.

25. Holst interview.

26. Nock interview.

27. Nock interview.

28. Nock interview.

29. Nock interview.

30. The manège, in the current parlance of The Greatest Show on Earth, is the elephant act. During the '50s, however, when the show presented an equestrian spectacle, it was referred to as the manège.

31. McKinley interview.

32. Holst interview.

33. Nock interview.

34. Nock interview.

35. McKinley interview.

36. Nock interview.

37. McKinley interview.

38. Nock interview.

39. Nock interview.

40. Holst interview.

41. Alla Youdina, personal interview with the author, New York, April 1, 2001.

42. Youdina interview.

43. McKinley interview.

44. McKinley interview.

45. Holst interview.

46. McKinley interview.

47. Before Feld Entertainment was founded, the family business was headed by Irvin Feld, who died in 1984.

48. McKinley interview.

49. McKinley interview.

50. See Christensen's discussion of the Big Apple Circus creative process in chapter 1.

51. McKinley interview.

52. Feld interview.

53. McKinley interview.

54. McKinley interview.

55. McKinley interview.

56. McKinley interview.

57. Holst interview.

58. McKinley interview.

59. McKinley interview.

60. McKinley interview.

61. Karen and Greg DeSanto, joint personal interview with the author, Baraboo, Wis., July 9, 2001.

62. Nock interview.

63. Nock interview.

64. McKinley interview.

65. Nock interview.

66. McKinley interview.

67. McKinley interview

68. Nock interview.

69. Nock interview.

70. Feld interview.

71. Nock interview.

72. Ringling plays the Meadowlands Arena in New Jersey two weeks before getting to Madison Square Garden in New York. The date just prior to the Garden opening is the arena on Long Island.

73. Feld interview.

74. McKinley interview.

75. McKinley interview.

Guy Laliberté and Lyn Heward at the press conference prior to the opening of Zumanity in Las Vegas. From the author's collection.

Kenneth Feld. Photo by Paul Gutheil.

Steve Smith. Courtesy Steve Smith.

Paul Binder. Photo by Maike Schulz.

Michael Christensen by Scott Thode. Courtesy the Big Apple Circus.

Stanislav Lazarov, David Balding, and general manager Holly Harris (L to R) confer following a performance of Circus Flora. From the author's collection.

Circus Flora's Cecil MacKinnon. From the author's collection.

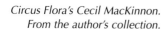

The Kovgar Troupe of teeterboard artists, one of the new style acts. Photo by Bertrand Guay, courtesy the Big Apple Circus.

Pascal Jacob, costume designer Barnum's Kaleidoscape. *From the author's collection.*

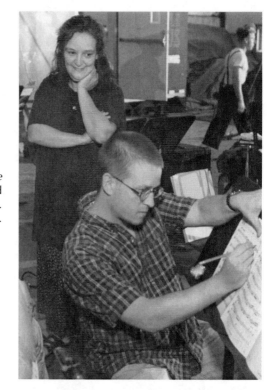

Brigitte Larochelle, composer for the Big Apple Circus's production Bello and Friends, *with conductor Rob Slowik. Photo by Maike Schulz.*

Alla Youdina, independent act creator. From the author's collection.

Composer Miriam Cutler. From the author's collection.

Bello and Bo in Ringling's 131st. Photo by Maike Schulz.

Bello and ringmaster Johnathan Lee Iverson. Photo by Paul Gutheil.

Bello, offstage with his hair down— literally. Photo by Maike Schulz.

Barnum's Kaleidoscape *in New York City's Bryant Park. Photo by Paul Gutheil.*

The Big Apple Circus's Clown Around Town, with Tom Dougherty and friend. Photo by Maike Schulz.

Sylvia Zerbini and her horses, with Ringling Bros. and Barnum & Bailey. Photo by Maike Schulz.

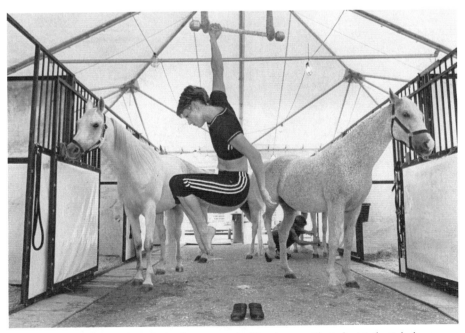

Sylvia Zerbini warms up in the company of her horses. Photo by Maike Schulz.

Slava Polunin. From the author's collection.

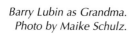
*Barry Lubin as Grandma.
Photo by Maike Schulz.*

David Shiner as the Cat in the Hat in the Broadway musical Seussical. *Photo by Maike Schulz.*

David Larible and his mother as an audience "volunteer." Photo by Maike Schulz.

The performer's lounge backstage at La Nouba *in Orlando, Florida. From the author's collection.*

The warm-up room backstage at La Nouba. *From the author's collection.*

Ringling's Hagenbeck-Wallace scenic studio in Palmetto, Florida. From the author's collection.

Jeff Raz and Barry Lubin, two clowns in
mufti. Photo by Paul Gutheil.

Canada's National Circus School
in Montreal, Quebec. From the
author's collection.

O Notes

$\mathscr{T}$he creative staff of Cirque du Soleil approaches each new creation as an opportunity to grow and develop. They might not be reinventing themselves completely each time out of the gate, but they are never satisfied to repeat a success or stay where they already are, artistically. With *O*, a spectacular water circus, the challenges were especially formidable, thanks largely to the environment in which the show is performed. Now firmly ensconced in the theatre of the Bellagio Hotel and Resort in Las Vegas, *O* took the company one step further than it had gone in any previous effort.

In the matter of advancing its own level of technology and artistry, the company was determined to move forward from *Mystère*, its first venture into a permanent theatre experience. That experience was preparation for both the Bellagio show and what followed in Orlando. "On the human level, *Mystère* provided the new experience of staying in one location, which presented its own set of difficulties for both the artists in residence and the home staff. This was something the company had never done before. It increased the number of performances the artists and technical staff had to be up for each week.

"It also prepared the company from a primitive, technological point of view by demonstrating what technology it could permit itself to have in a theatre, and it prepared it from a human point of view. When *Mystère* moved into Treasure Island, the Mirage people collaborated with the company's set designer so that the theatre could accommodate his set. Since then the company's partners, Steve Wynn and Disney, have had their own requirements for the theatres, so each design has been a collaborative effort."[1]

The result, in the case of *O*, was a classical 1,800-seat proscenium theatre, reminiscent of a 14th-century European opera house, with tiered orchestra seating, side galleries, and balcony seating. Backstage, however, housed the most advanced state-of-the-art technology. Ground breaking took place in February 1996, and construction was completed in January 1998. The height of the theatre, from the bottom of the pool to the ceiling, is 145 feet, the equivalent of a nine-story building. The designers wanted to give the theatre a ceiling worthy of the great theatres of the world. In the center of the ceiling, high above the audience, is a metal meshing surrounded by 4.3330 MR-16 halogen bulbs that can create a variety of lighting effects as the wire mesh reflects and refracts light, producing dramatic changes of mood throughout the production. The wire mesh dome, by the way, acts as a chimney, allowing the warm air to escape the auditorium area and assists, therefore, in the cooling process.[2]

Of the many challenges faced by the artistic and technical staff of Cirque du Soleil in the creation of O, one of the most critical was the design of the theatre in which it is performed. Three years of study and testing went into the 1.5 million-gallon, 25-foot deep pool that measures 140 by 78 feet and is the show's main performance area. "Every aspect of the design of the show and the showroom, itself, whether it is in the water or not, is affected by the fact that there is a pool in the room: the humidity affects the hanging pipes, the ropes, the winches, drapes, everything. It's apparent in every corner of the room," says Anthony G. Ricotta, O's current operations production manager and former technical director.[3]

Something else that had to be taken into consideration is the climate outside the room and how it affected the humidity levels inside. Because of the presence of the pool, the heating, ventilation, and air conditioning staff had to anticipate dealing with the climate in the room by adjusting the humidity, the air conditioning, the heat, and the ventilation. "They are like meteorologists up there, punching buttons and moving vents and closing dampers and doing their magic to make everything, like curtains, hang straight. There are more physical facility issues involved in maintaining this show's integrity than in any other theatre I've worked in. The facility itself plays a huge role in the success of our two shows a night," Ricotta points out.

In addition, at the time of its creation, O represented Cirque du Soleil's greatest exposure to automation. Almost everything moves, the stage and scenery change their shape or form automatically, which, Ricotta says, was a "big learning process for all of us."[4]

Not satisfied with a static performance surface, the show's creative and technical teams combined to outfit the pool with seven hydraulic lifts that can create a conventional stage floor or reshape the surface area of the water. A character may be walking on water one moment and suddenly be underwater the next, thanks to the lifts that are raised and lowered continuously during the show.

Of the seven lifts, four are primary scissors-type and three are auxiliary. The primary lifts are capable of moving nineteen feet up and down at speeds ranging from one to twenty feet per second and have a capacity of 100,000 pounds. The three auxiliary lifts are used to facilitate access to the stage for the performers.[5]

To test the integrity of floor surfaces, costume materials, and other elements of the physical production, two pools located in Montreal, the company's home city, were pressed into service. Samples of surfaces were placed into the water and checked each day to determine if the color or density had changed.

In almost all instances, details anyone might have expected to be very ordinary became extraordinary when mixed with the watery environment. The biggest challenge, according to Lyn Heward, was "taking old things and renewing them with a new perspective."[6]

For instance, considerable research was required merely to decide on optimal water temperature. Since the show included synchronized swimmers, divers, acrobats, and aerialists, all of whom would find themselves in the water at some point in the performance, this was no simple matter. It was a huge departure for Sylvie Fréchette, the swimming coach, who could only provide an answer that applied to her specialty, synchronized swimming. The divers, it turned out, preferred a different temperature. Acrobats who fall from warm temperatures in the air or who intentionally arrive in the water had their own preferences. Each group had its own opinion, and they were all different.

Then, of course, the audience's comfort had to be taken into consideration. If it was decided that 85 degrees was the optimal water temperature, keeping the temperature in the house from reaching the same level was another problem. Heat rises. Mixed with water, hot air gets clammy. The standard for air conditioning in Las Vegas, which audiences expect, is 70–72 degrees.

Another consideration was the chemical base used in the water, bromine or chlorine, and their effect on the lighting and mechanical equipment. The stage's elevators and sliding floors all come into direct contact with the water and the chemicals in it. All of these matters were new to Cirque du Soleil technicians and designers, but they had to be confronted and conquered.[7]

The casting department faced its own set of challenges. For the first time ever Cirque du Soleil was looking for athletes who had no natural connection to the circus. They needed swimmers who could do acrobatics, acrobats who could swim, and divers who could do both. Sylvie Fréchette, who at thirteen became Canada's national junior champion in synchronized swimming and went on to win the gold medal in solo competitions at the 1992 Olympics in Barcelona, came to Cirque du Soleil in 1996 when she heard about the proposed water show and offered her services. She was quickly hired to provide the needed aquatic expertise. She participated in the selection of the artists and, along with choreographer Debra Brown, developed a new vocabulary (there's that word again) of synchronized swimming.

According to Ste-Croix, the problem with hiring athletes was helping them "to find the artist inside themselves." They had to be trained and coached to make them "greater than an acrobat, like a silk worm that becomes a butterfly."[8]

It is worth pointing out here that this problem is not unique to Cirque du Soleil. It is one that is shared by others in the performing arts who are attempting to combine athletics and art. When Daniel Ezralow, Moses Pendleton, and David Parssons undertook the challenge of choreographing *Aeros*, a full-scale theatrical production marrying dance and gymnastics, the *New York Times* reported that audiences responded more enthusiastically than dance critics, prompting Pendleton to observe, "Maybe it should be reviewed by sports writers." The problem was, as the trio of choreographers soon discovered, "athletics and dance don't automatically mesh. Gymnasts do not know how to walk gracefully across a stage or how to make transitions between sequences and reviewers criticized them for not relating to each other onstage."[9]

For the people at Cirque du Soleil, long aware of this problem, the process of turning these former athletes, green in the heady environment of the theatre, into artists became the job of the coaches and trainers at the Montreal studio. Their training in this cocoon, as Ste-Croix, director of creation, might have it, was aimed, according to Patrice Aubertin, training program coordinator, at developing both their ability to do tricks and "having them mean something." To this end, the would-be artists were given classes in movement and scene playing. It was not really acting, Aubertin says, but rather a physical type of role playing, intended to widen their horizons because most came from a very rigid amateur sport background and were trained only in one skill. Not much thought was ever given to emotion. On the contrary, they were trained not to show emotion, to be neutral for the judges. Cirque du Soleil is interested in seeing the exact opposite, Aubertin says, and, as a result, it takes a long time to break down that shell of anonymity and to take away their shyness. That may very well be the essential difference between competitors and artists, the performer's ability to reveal what is inside.[10]

As with all Cirque du Soleil productions the actual training period for the artists began more than a year before the show's opening. This work was accomplished at the Montreal studio and at pools located around the city beginning on September 15, 1997. The artists, of course, faced their own set of challenges. In addition to the problems inherent in learning to combine artistry with athletics, many of them also had to acquire a new skill. In order to be discovered in the pool, they would have to get into the water offstage, behind masking units, and swim, under water, to their locations where they would have to wait for their cue to emerge, as if they had been there all the time. There are eighteen breathing stations underwater for the cast to use during that wait. So in addition to learning their acrobatic moves and how to swim properly, they also had to learn an entirely new skill, adding enormously to a very large workload. Eventually, all the artists, swimmers and acrobats alike, had to become scuba certified.

For some, like Craig Paul Smith, who appears in several numbers and is a featured character, that learning process proved to be an unexpected and unpleasant challenge. "The training that we had in Montreal was really intense," he explains, "because we had a certain amount of time to do it in, basically six months, which sounds like a long time, but we had to learn how to do scuba, and we were also doing experiments while we were learning to do acts."[11]

Actually, the water was something of a surprise for Smith, who did not know he had been hired to work in a water show. After successfully passing his audition, he was brought in for training at the same time as the cast for O. As time passed, he suddenly found himself as part of that show. So Smith, who is originally from Birmingham, England, participated in the water training along with all the others.

"We didn't know if we would be starting an act backstage, up in the air, or underwater. So we were training everything." That included doing things like swimming along the bottom of the pool while holding on to a rope line. Once in position, the swimmers were made to wait for some time before being given the cue to surface. Then to make matters more interesting, and dangerous and demanding as well, the pool was covered with a tarpaulin so no one could see where they were going. This was done to simulate the blackouts during which the performers would be required to move into position underwater.

"It was quite difficult, to the point that if you were a little bit scared, it was quite intimidating." What made it especially discouraging was seeing all the synchronized swimmers who, Smith says "are basically fish," cavorting about as if what they were being asked to do was mere child's play. "And there I was," Smith says with a cringe, "in the corner [shaking]. I wasn't alone, but I was probably the worst one actually.

"Everyone else was donning their scuba gear, diving right to the bottom, and there I was in the corner with a snorkel just getting relaxed about being underwater. I had a few weeks where it was not enjoyable. I was loving the training aspect of it, but as soon as we got on the bus to go to the pool my stomach started churning. But," he admits, "we had amazing trainers.

"When I had my panic attack, I had one instructor with me all the time, going through everything very slowly. It was never dangerous for me, because it never got to the point of my saying, 'I can't do this,' and his saying, 'You have to.' It was more like, 'Okay if you can't do this now, we'll do it another time.'

"We went to the pool every day, and it was everything from, 'Okay, jump in and dive to the bottom,' or 'Jump in and swim to the other side,' to 'We're going to do an exercise and jog so you'll be out of breath and then you're going to jump in.' We did everything. We did dressing under underwater. We did taking clothes off under water. You name it; we did it, and as I think back now, it was fun. Even through my panic attack it was fun. I wouldn't want to do it again, though."

After all that torturous water training, it turned out that Smith never had to use the scuba equipment in the show. "I'm one of the zebras, and originally we tried to start that act under the water, but it was too much of a hassle. It took too much time because we would have to prepare five minutes before the act, and it just didn't work out with the lifts and the costumes. Thank God!"[12]

Like every one of the artists in the show, Smith came into it knowing how to swim. It was one of the requirements. Besides being a zebra, he is the head comet, the group of men in red coats who are the human equivalent of the comets that blaze across the background every so often. He is also one of the catchers on the aerial boat, or bateau.

"Training as catcher was probably the biggest challenge, because I am not good with heights [either]." In all fairness, it should be noted that Smith began his career as a tumbler, at about age seven. "And then I was just upside down the rest of my life, basically," eventually competing in the world championships of tumbling.

He says he is now "totally fine" with the height because "we were on [the rigging] three hours a day in Montreal, and I was able to climb up to the top to get over my fear by getting to know my surroundings, which was fine. Catching, however, was very painful at first because as a tumbler I was used to pressing down, and now as catcher, I'm pulling and so my legs were going numb, and for a month I could barely walk. But your body adapts to what you're doing, so it's fine. But in the beginning it was completely different from what I had been doing before, so my legs, my back, my shoulders, my knees, were like, 'Okay what's going on?'" Despite the rigorous training, some of what he does in the show, particularly the zebra scene, has never gotten easy. "You know if you run a mile every day it's going to get easier, but this never does. It's such a cardio workout. You never come off saying, 'Okay let's do it again.'"[13]

For those who must go underwater, there is a support team of fifteen divers, twelve of whom are underwater during the entire performance. Two of them are fitted with full-face masks with built in microphones that enable them to communicate with the stage personnel. These masks are also equipped with speakers that conduct sounds produced behind the divers' ears, through their skulls, adding another degree of communication, and making it possible to head off problems before they arise. All of the divers are equipped with a personal dive computer to monitor the amount of compressed air used and an alarm to indicate if ascent is too rapid or if they have been underwater too long.

At the end of six and a half months of training in Montreal, the company moved in the beginning of April (prior to an October opening) to Las Vegas to work in their new theatre. That move required everyone, technical staff, designers and artists alike, to adapt what they had learned in the mocked-up facilities in Montreal to the idiosyncrasies of the real thing.[14]

In spite of the watery environment and the unique special effects, O is still very much a circus-based show. "Yes, its theatrical and all of that," Heward agrees, "but it still has the flying act and the acrobatic ground acts. The presence of the water has allowed us to change the perspective of both the aerial acts and what used to be ground acts. All kinds of technologies are being used and have been exploited in one way or another in the context of the show."[15]

★ ★ ★

O was directed by Franco Dragone, who had already brought into port all of the company's previous ten productions. He is credited with the particular integration of circus and theatre that is the trademark of a Cirque du Soleil production. One might think that the challenges of plunging that collaboration into heated water would have been more than enough to satisfy his artistic restlessness. Not so. As with any of his productions, Dragone was determined to go far beyond the mere physical and technical challenges in order to tell us something of what was on his mind.

The show's press kit describes O as "a homage to the theatre."[16] But that only begins to tell the story of O. As with all of Dragone's productions, this one creates numerous, seemingly contradictory, images. Here, for instance, there are many, often brazenly absurd, images of death. Almost no one who sees the show mentions them afterward, because there is so much else to dazzle the eye and excite the pulse in this production, so they are easily overlooked, but they are there nonetheless, and they are there with a purpose that plays to the subconscious.

Pavel Brun, the production's artistic director, was at Dragone's side throughout the creative process. "I had mixed feelings at first," he says of these images, but then he adds by way of defending their presence in the production, "I would say death is interesting. Nobody can avoid it. It's always there.

So let's have some fun with it. We play with it." Dragone treats it with humor, and the result is a depiction of death that is broadly carnivalesque. It is as if he is forcing us to laugh in the face of death.[17]

In paying homage to the theatre, the show begins with a hunchback who hobbles down the auditorium's stairs onto the stage. This character has been identified by Gilles Ste-Croix, Cirque du Soleil, as the "guardian of theatrical tradition." Since we are about to be taken into unfamiliar territory by virtue of this production's special environment, Dragone has provided a welcoming host to keep us from feeling uncomfortable. But it is typical of Dragone's oblique way of looking at things that the guide he provides is deformed.

The performance itself begins when this character draws aside the silk curtain that conceals the stage from view. As soon as he clutches it in his claw-like hand, the curtain is sucked up into a black hole where it disappears in space only to be seen later blazing across the night sky, first in the fleeting flight of a comet and later in the person of four red-coated footman (one of whom is Craig Paul Smith) who also flash across the sky.

Steve Wynn, the mogul who built Bellagio, was particularly enthusiastic about having this effect in the show, sure that it would win over the audience immediately. The technical crew worked for two months getting the curtain to work as Dragone envisioned. The result is every bit as spectacular and awe-inspiring as Wynn had predicted.

Despite its inescapable preoccupation with water, it is not the only element with which we mortals, and therefore the show, must grapple. When it is not taking place in the pool, much of the performance takes place in the air. Fire and ice also spring up or float into spectacular view during the course of the ninety-minute performance.

Perhaps one of the oddest characteristics of the production is that the most exciting acts appear in the middle of the production. The three slowest acts are at the end. When questioned about this, the show's creators say this was done purposefully. It is a realization of Dragone's vision of the show in the shape of a rondo, a circle. This vision spins off the production's title, *O*, which is a play on the French word for water, *eau*, pronounced as the English letter "O." That may have amused the public relations department, but typically Dragone took the pun at face value. He molded his show in the shape of its title. It goes up and then falls away to return to where it started. The order of the show is thus a result of a very serious artistic consideration.[18]

In addition to Dragone, Ste-Croix, Brun, and Fréchette, the creative team also included the director's longtime collaborators Dominique Lemieux (costumes), Benoit Jutras (composer), Debra Brown (choreographer), Michel Crête (sets), Luc Lafortune (lighting), and Jonathan Deans and François Bergeron (sound). André Simard, who came to Cirque du Soleil through École

Nationale de Cirque, created the innovative flying acts that are so much a part of the production.

Unlike most of his colleagues on the creative team, composer Benoit Jutras did not have to concern himself overly with the problems of the watery environment; however, even he used water as a source of inspiration. Jutras's score, he has said, was much influenced by the rhythms, instrumentation, and sounds heard in the great port cities of the world, particularly those in Africa, Eastern Europe, and the Arabic countries. So the show's watery environment played a part in shaping even its music.[19]

Performed by ten musicians, two of whom also provide vocals, the score's instrumentation includes such exotica as an African harp, Uillean (or Irish bagpipes), Chinese violin, ancient woodwinds, and a Colombian guitar. The musicians are stationed in two acoustically isolated booths in an elevated position on either side of the proscenium.

For Dominique Lemieux, who has designed the costumes, the problem, in addition to the concern of durability, was the fact that her costumes had to look as interesting and as beautiful wet as they looked when dry. "We wanted you to see something more than a wet coiffure," Ste-Croix says. What she came up with often looks like a second skin or a fascinating tattoo on their own skin.[20]

In style, Lemieux's designs are reminiscent of several periods ranging across five centuries from the 15th to the 20th, with a special emphasis on the Romantic period. Her designs, she says, were especially influenced by the trends in Venice. (Need I point out the watery connection?) In addition to all their other requirements, the costumes also had to dry quickly. To accomplish this, a silicone application was devised and used on about 40 percent of the costumes. All the shoes are constructed of bull hide, which allows them to be worn in the water without shortening the life of the shoe. Nearly ten different variations of the costumes used in each act were created before a final design was approved.

Both real human and synthetic hair are used in the eight different wig styles used in the show's more than sixty wigs, each of which had to be hand-ventilated and tied. Like the costumes, the makeup used in the show was tested extensively to find the correct waterproof application.[21]

The most complex element of Michel Crête's set, other than the pool itself, is an overhead unit known as a "telepherique." It is an overhead conveyor, positioned sixty feet above the stage. Hanging from the telepherique is the technicians' pride and joy, a carousel unit capable of moving up and downstage at three feet per second and two rpm's in a circular motion. It is equipped with four lifting winches, each with a thousand-pound capacity and the ability to operate at four feet per second. The telepherique itself has been called the theatrical equivalent of a gantry crane with a highly sophisticated computerized control system that synchronizes all movements to create seamless mechanized pictures. It consists of six tracks, each containing two independent winches to transport performers, scenery, and rigging, as needed.[22]

One of the most unusual elements of the set is its rigid "vegetation" curtain made of vapor-resistant plastic. It was manufactured using a technique called "thermoforming," in which Cirque du Soleil has developed considerable expertise.

The stage floor is constructed of steel and fiberglass, combined with PVC and sports matting to achieve a degree of resilience as close as possible to that of the human body. Small holes have been drilled into it to allow water to flow through when the lifts are moving up or down.[23]

Faced with this technological marvel, Dragone approached it as he would one of his performers. When he first arrived in Las Vegas in April of 1998, he spent a long time "shaking the stage," according to operations production manager Anthony Ricotta, to find out what the stage and theatre were capable of doing, in much the same way that he would "shake up" the artists. Its capabilities, he discovered, included producing fountains, fog, and rain. But it was not all trial and error. Because of the technical complexities involved in the show, there were actual sketches and a storyboard prepared before coming into the actual theatre.

Ricotta also recalls the director asking for "a lot of crazy stuff." But such requests, Ricotta feels, were good for everyone. There is usually more than one way of doing anything, and the first thing that comes to mind may not work, so the technicians were challenged to find a way that could work that would be safe and repeatable.[24] All kinds of things failed, but the successes, both technical and artistic, are remarkable.

For Luc Lafortune, the lighting designer, the water presented two great challenges. One was finding ways of changing the color of the water. Because water is highly reflective and filters different frequencies of light, a great deal of experimentation was necessary to discover the correct lighting angles. In order to change the water's color, as they wanted to do, compressed air bubbles had to be blown into the pool at strategic moments. The air bubbles are what reflect the color.

The second challenge, one that dealt with safety rather than aesthetics, was avoiding the introduction of electricity into the water, especially as a great deal of the machinery is powered. A pneumatic control system was created, along with innovative wiring and cabling to ensure the safety of those in the pool. The pool was eventually outfitted with the world's first long-distance ground fault circuit interruption system that protects the 288 dimmers located in the pool.[25]

And then, there was the sheer size of the theater. The proscenium is 55 feet high by 100 feet wide, and the stage, itself, is 100 feet wide, but, Lafortune points out, "the scale of humans remains the same. So trying to focus down on one action versus the larger picture was quite challenging, particularly taking into account that since the scenery was mostly a water surface, light was going to bounce left and right.

"We went to the Olympic stadium in Montreal and worked in that pool. They had Plexiglas windows so that we could look at divers below the surface, and we tried lighting the water from below the surface, and we tried injecting all sorts of solutions in there to give it a certain degree of opacity so it would pick up light and become colorful because the one concern we had was that we didn't want the water to become a prop. If you're going to be doing a show about water called O in the middle of the desert with millions of gallons on a stage, you have to treat it with a certain degree of respect. You can't just go in there and fill the stage with water and have a bunch of jet skis running around, so it was important to us that the water be a character with various facets to its personality, to the same extent that other characters had facets to their personalities. So that was probably the biggest challenge, to be able to take something like water, which is completely translucent, which reflects light, which doesn't react too well to electricity and whatnot, and give it a presence, numerous presences."[26]

The lighting designer first tried working with people who provided fixtures for pools, but more often than not there was little control as far as dimming was concerned and there was very little control in color. It was essentially white light. So that didn't work out as they had hoped. "Then we got in touch with the people who provided all sorts of lighting fixtures for deep sea exploration," Lafortune explains. "These were the people who provided lighting for the exploration of the *Titanic*. They could pretty much do whatever they wanted out there out in the middle of the ocean and a couple of miles down, where there are no rules and regulations about safety, but when you're working in a pool in a showroom in Las Vegas on a stage, there are all sorts of rules and with good reason. We just couldn't use a lot of the stuff we were looking at, although it showed great promise. So essentially what we ended up doing was going back to what we knew worked, conventional theatrical fixtures."

The aforementioned bubbles provided what is known as aquatic masking. The bubbles also hide scenic movement and the coming and going of the performers as well as providing a backing for the lighting. "It's interesting," Lafortune says with satisfaction, "because at some points when you look at the pool, it's like a murky swamp, and in one scene it's black and looks like an oil slick, so there are various personalities to the water and that's exactly what we wanted to achieve."[27]

★ ★ ★

What is unique about many of the acts in the show is that several combine circus (or gymnastic) skills with swimming and diving. One such performance is staged on a movable, floating platform constructed of 3,500 pounds of Styrofoam and fiberglass. Capable of holding up to twenty performers who emerge from underwater, it is maneuvered into position by seven divers. It has fourteen breathing stations on its underside for the artists who are waiting to make their entrances.

The water is also incorporated into the aerial acts as their only safety net or exit. Most impressive is the *bateau* (or boat), a stainless steel apparatus combining parallel bars and a flying rig, with catchers' traps located at both ends. It was designed by André Simard, who was also one of the act's coaches, along with Jacque Paquin.

Didier Antoine, who cocreated the act and was one of the catchers, explains: "I am used to working on the flying trapeze, and on the flying trapeze you use a net to jump into, and you are used to falling on your back."[28]

That technique, of course, does not work in the water. "If you fall on your back in the water, you can really be hurt. So you have to learn how to dive on your head or your feet, so this is a big difference, and we had a lot of problems. Every year when we have new artists, they have a big problem because they have to learn how to fall into the water. So we have, not so much injuries, but a lot of pain. We teach them how to dive. The diving coach can help us explain how to enter the water, but most of the time you cannot plan how you are going to fall, so your reaction has to be a reflex, to avoid your back or your face. It's a risk you have to take and you have to expect some pain."

Some of the aerialists in the show do, however, wear a safety cable or lunge to save them from falling. That is because, according to Antoine, "In certain cases, if you fall into the water, it is going to be very dangerous so you have to use a belt to avoid the fall, as does the solo trapeze at the beginning of the show, in which there is a chance that the artist will miss the water because of the arc of the swing. That's why on the bateau we have also two nets on the sides, in the wings, because on certain swings, in certain falls, you can miss the pool."

Antoine's specialty prior to this show was the aerial cradle, which he performed for fourteen years. The bateau was his idea. "In the beginning it was just a parallel bar with four ropes. Then we tried some things and made some tests and found we could not do so much with that. So we changed it to make it longer, and then we put in a metal bar and said, 'Oh, it looks like a boat.' So, okay, we make it a boat. We trained on that for six months. Since this act has never been performed before, it was difficult for us because we had no history [to rely on]. With the flying trapeze we can watch the Mexicans and Russians, but for this act we had no videos, no books, nothing, so we had to work a lot just to find out what we could do."

One of the greatest challenges is that the entire thousand-kilogram apparatus swings. In the past, Antoine says, everyone avoided this kind of swing, "because it is very bad for the catcher. Usually on the flying trapeze, the swing is like a pendulum. Here, when the boat changes direction, all the weight goes against the catcher. The weight of the flyer is multiplied two or three times. Even for the flyer the impact can be very bad for the shoulders. "So in the beginning we had a lot of injuries. We had a lot of other tricks we decided we couldn't do anymore. They were good for one time, but for five hundred shows, they would cause too much pain."

During the development stage of the act, the bateau was on cables, but rather than swinging in a straight arc, it tended to fishtail, hence the masts that make it look even more like a boat. They help keep the alignment of the swing straight. So they are more than just decoration. "In this kind of act," Antoine says, "we spend so much of our time solving problems. We start something and then we have a problem and then we have to decide what we can do to avoid the problems, so we put in some metal bars, then afterward we put the masts." Sometimes, he says, you may get to the point where you have to say the way to solve the problem is to throw it out.

"That's why when we create a show like this, we spend a lot of money, because we try something for months and then say, 'No.' Sometimes it's not interesting or it is too dangerous. It is too slippery. The water brings lots of problem."

A catcher must stay dry while on the bateau because it is not possible to catch when wet. For the flyers, it is another story. "As soon as one of the flyers falls, it is over for him. We say, 'Bye, bye. We finish without you.' That's why we teach all of the flyers to do the same things as a backup. A backup is always standing by."

Antoine also played the strong man, the character (or *personnage*) who brings everything on stage and who runs through the show. How this character came to be included in the show reveals a great deal of how Dragone goes about creating each new production. "My character was not supposed to be in the show," Antoine says, but he knew that Franco Dragone likes to have ideas come from the cast, and if they show him something he likes, he asks them to develop it further. "So I proposed a lot of things, and he says to me in the end, 'Okay you propose so much that we are going to make a character for you, the strong man.'

"Most of the people come from sport," he points out, echoing sentiments previously expressed by Gilles Ste-Croix and others. "So they don't understand this language, this artistic language. It's not because they are not good; they just don't understand. So it takes a while for them to get it. We teach them how to understand the stage, and then they understand that everything is important, even a simple thing can be very important. You have to have the right timing, be in the right light with the music, and so, after two years, maybe in another creation they are ready to have a character."[29]

This was Antoine's second show with Cirque du Soleil. "That's why I understand [how the newcomers] feel because when I was doing *Nouvelle Expérience*, I came from sport, and I understood nothing Franco asked me. Every time he asked me to do something, he would say, 'No, no, no.' Sometimes he would say, 'Ah, yes,' but I didn't know why he said 'yes.' It took me a year to understand. Usually when you are in front of the public and you try something that may or may not work, you understand much better than with the director telling you 'No, no, no.' With the public you feel the reaction and then you say, 'Ah, that's what he meant!'"

It was during the creation of *Nouvelle Expérience* and later performing in it that Antoine says, "I learned everything: how to respect the public, how to respect your team, how to respect yourself, how to perform on stage, how to put makeup on, how to be there every night, how to share everything, how to know more about yourself because you have to be open to everything. If you are shy, you cannot be shy anymore. You have to learn that what you cannot do in your normal life, you can do on stage. It's like an escape from your daily life. When I was in gymnastics, I used to be very shy and did not trust myself very much, but then you are in front of 1,000 to 2,000 people, and they applaud and give a standing ovation, and it's like a dream, so you learn how to enjoy it."[30]

In addition to the bateau, other pieces of equipment were specifically designed for this show. One such complex unit is a set of three Russian swings, each constructed of stainless steel and partially submerged. The center and largest swing is constructed in two pieces. The top is lowered into place from above, and the base is brought into its submerged position by the ubiquitous divers who also secure the base to the swing. This unit is designed with a church bell on the top of its frame, which is said to have been inspired by the many wedding chapels in Las Vegas. Here it is an invitation to a giant celebration in which eleven divers are projected into the pool in a series of spectacular dives, made all the more spectacular by the motion of the swing. Its movement creates a trajectory that is a challenge even to experienced divers, sending them thirty-two feet into the air. Paquin was also the designer of this unit, and another that resembles a playground jungle gym for the group of artists dressed as zebras, of which Craig Paul Smith is one.

Not all of the show's images are so profound, however. One, perhaps more easily recognizable, was inspired by an Esther Williams film in which she dives off a swinging trapeze. Named the "Garden Swing," it is used in the Russian swing sequence.[31]

★ ★ ★

Almost immediately after the opening of O, the creation team returned to Montreal to conclude their work on *La Nouba* and bring it to Orlando, Florida, for its final rehearsals. That relentless schedule meant that for certain periods after the opening of *Quidam*, the team had been working simultaneously on the two new productions, making this one of the most demanding periods of creativity in Cirque du Soleil history. It is hardly astounding, therefore, that following the premiere of *La Nouba*, almost all of the team elected to take a hiatus from their work with the company, assuming, with justification, that they had reached a creative plateau. Franco Dragone returned to his home in Belgium to found his own production company, taking designers Michel Crête and Dominique Lemieux with him for the Celine Dion project in Las Vegas; Gilles Ste-Croix went off and returned after creating *Cheval Théâtre*, an equestrian spectacle however, both Ste-Croix and Crête returned to the fold to work on another Las Vegas project, *Love*, based on the Beatles' music, while composer Benoit Jutras went off to work on *Le Reve* with Dragone for the new Wynn hotel. Luc Lafortune remained through *Dralion* and then stepped aside to allow his assistant, Nol Van Genuchten, to design *Varekai*. Dominique Lemieux also returned to design *Corteo*.

The exodus also included Laliberté's longtime business partner, Daniel Gauthier, and Jean David, vice president for public relations and marketing. None of them could be blamed for thinking that O had taken them as far as they and Cirque du Soleil could go together.

NOTES

1. Lyn Heward, personal interview with the author, Montreal, Canada, August 20, 1998.
2. Cirque du Soleil, O press packet.
3. Anthony Ricotta, personal interview with the author, Las Vegas, April 19, 2003.
4. Ricotta interview.
5. O press packet.
6. Heward interview.

7. Heward interview.

8. Gilles Ste-Croix, comments made at *O* press conference, Las Vegas, October 21, 1998.

9. Valerie Gladstone. "Everything Is Danceable?" *New York Times* (March 21, 2001): AR 12.

10. Patrice Aubertin, personal interview with the author, Montreal, Canada, August 20, 1998.

11. Craig Paul Smith, personal interview with the author, Las Vegas, April 19, 2003.

12. Smith interview.

13. Smith interview.

14. *O* press packet.

15. Heward interview.

16. *O* press packet.

17. Pavel Brun, personal interview with the author, Las Vegas, October 21, 1998.

18. Brun interview.

19. Benoit Jutras, comments made at *O* press conference, Las Vegas, October 21, 1998.

20. Gilles Ste-Croix.

21. *O* press packet.

22. *O* press packet.

23. *O* press packet.

24. Ricotta interview.

25. *O* press packet.

26. Luc Lafortune, personal interview with the author, Montreal, Canada, May 14, 2003.

27. Lafortune interview.

28. Didier Antoine, personal interview with the author, Las Vegas, April 19, 2003.

29. Antoine interview.

30. Antoine interview.

31. *O* press packet.

·6·

The Making of a
Major New American Spectacle

$\mathcal{W}$hen the Feld organization decided to add a major new American spectacle called *Barnum's Kaleidoscape* to its panoply of entertainment offerings, circus fans hopefully assumed it signaled a return of the big top. Although the show that finally emerged did indeed take place in a tent, it could not, in any way, be construed as a return to the tenting days of Ringling Bros. and Barnum & Bailey prior to 1956. *Barnum's Kaleidoscape* was anything but a backward looking enterprise.

Whenever Kenneth Feld speaks about his motivation to create *Barnum's Kaleidoscape*, he is unvaryingly emphatic on one issue. It was never his intention, he insists, to build another circus. "The last thing we wanted to do was to cannibalize our own market," he says. This was to be an entirely new type of entertainment.[1]

Discussions between Feld and Tim Holst regarding the new show began nearly three years before it became a reality. "We have been dreaming about this for a long time," Holst said at the time of the show's opening in Los Angeles. The reason why it took so long to make it a reality was that, according to Holst, "We kept telling ourselves we should do it for the right reasons."[2]

One of the factors involved that made the decision to go ahead so difficult was that, as Feld pointed out, "Nothing of this magnitude had been created from scratch before. Everything else evolved." He was, of course, speaking of other new wave circuses like the Big Apple Circus and Cirque du Soleil.[3]

Getting the show off the ground, artistically, involved many long discussions between Holst and Feld concerning what should be in the show and what shouldn't. It all came down to a matter of how they wanted the show to affect the audience. And since this show would come onto the scene fully blown, the choice of director was significant.

143

The selection of the director was, no doubt, based on the recommendation of David Larible who was to be the star of the show and its one known quantity. His choice was a young Italian circus historian and director, Raffaele DeRitis.

★ ★ ★

Raffaele DeRitis was thirty-one years old at the time he was tapped to direct *Barnum's Kaleidoscape.* His education, he explains, ran along two different tracks. One, which he set out upon when he was an adult, was directed toward a classical theatre education. The other track began when he was a child. "I ran after all the circuses in Italy. When I was fourteen, I began spending all my summers traveling, visiting circuses. I spent my holidays with circus people all over Europe. And what I began noticing was that the same performers I was seeing in my hometown, I was also finding in Germany and other countries in Europe. This was my way of absorbing the human side of circus culture. I came to know the human side by observing the truth of the daily life of the circus, the backstage life, the traveling life." It was thus that he met a young boy named David Larible. "We used to play football together and see each other at parties."

When it was time to attend to more formal schooling, DeRitis elected to study theatre and the dramatic arts. But that did not deter his other education from continuing as well. "I began to see that circus is the only performing art where the daily life of the performers is strictly connected to the art. I came to understand that the circus is the only performing art that speaks about life and death, because not only is everything at risk in the performance, you don't know if you'll be able to tear down the big top, whether you'll get to the next town, whether you'll have enough to eat.

"Maybe the new circus has cleaned itself up too much," DeRitis thinks now, after seeing what Cirque du Soleil has made of itself. "If you clean it up, you miss the truth. When I was a child and wanted to go to visit the circus, my mother would say to me, 'Don't go there because the gypsies will eat you.'

"The circus is a closed society arriving inside of another society, so there is always suspicion. I agree we have to give back to the circus its artistic dignity, but Zingaro[4] did it [without losing its other essential qualities]. You still feel they [the Zingaro troupe] are gypsies, uncivilized. Yet they have an artistic dignity. So, I think we have to revive the deep side of the circus, the simple side of the circus. It is so beautiful."[5]

After theatre school, DeRitis worked as assistant to Jerome Savery, the pioneer of the French avant-garde in the 1960s. It was Savery who, in 1968, founded the Grand Magic Circus, the first troupe in Europe to mix circus with theatre. Although, like Zingaro's Bartabas, Savery employed many of the aesthetics of the circus, his company remained a theatre ensemble.

While a student at the University of Rome, DeRitis spent as much time as he could with the playwright Dario Fo. "He was a great teacher." Although he had not yet become an international celebrity, Fo's lectures were always crowded. DeRitis recalls that there were often students sitting on the stage and that both Fo and his wife, Franca Rame, were very open, very generous and spontaneous. "Everyone was like his brother," DeRitis says. "When he won the Nobel prize it was like one of us. He was always the same when you would see him in the street."

DeRitis decided to do his master's thesis in film, rather than theatre. "I had done theatre and circus all my life, so I decided I wanted to know more about movies. Not too many theatre historians and directors know very much about movies. I was fascinated with American slapstick comedies like those of Laurel and Hardy and Charlie Chaplin, but I discovered something that nobody had ever paid any attention to in Italy before: the American cartoon comedy. So that is what I did my master's thesis on, specifically Tex Avery. Everybody said I was crazy; nobody had ever heard about this person. But I went ahead, and I analyzed Avery's direction and the gags he used, and the philosophy of comedy in the cartoons. I related what I saw to vaudeville stages and elsewhere. It was something different from circus and theater." In 1994, his thesis was honored by the Italian film critics association.

Like almost everyone who has made a serious study of comedy and comic methods, DeRitis is deeply earnest when he speaks of his work, and rarely smiles. "My biggest influence was the Fellini movie *The Clowns* because this movie was speaking about my life, and the people I knew, and I shared their emotions. It begins with this little boy coming to see the circus. I saw myself in that character.

"When Fellini goes to the big circus of the Orfei family, it is the very same circus I saw in my own life. It was the first circus family I knew. I knew all of them. So the film means something special to me. All the clowns and all the gags you see in the film are the basic type of grotesque clown gags that they really used to do in the small Italian circuses. My childhood is in that film.

"It was the same milieu that David Larible was performing in at that time. When I met David again after many years, I was amazed to discover that we both knew every sentence of this movie. For me [and apparently for David Larible as well] it is not a foreign world. For me it is about me, myself. It is as familiar as my own life.

"While I was at the film school, Fellini was still alive. And sometimes I went to this big square in Rome, Casa del Popula, that is always very crowded. At two o'clock, however, in Italy everything stops. It becomes a desert. I knew that Fellini was sitting every day in this square at a café, Rosatti. His presence was a kind of legend. So I went there, and he was there. I introduced myself, and I said, 'I like the circus.'" So provocative was this opening gambit that Fellini could not resist initiating a conversation.

"Really?" Fellini asked.

"Yes," DeRitis replied, "I worked in the circus with the Togni family and others."

Much to DeRitis's surprise, Fellini exclaimed. "You're very good. You're better than me."

"Why?" DeRitis could not help asking.

"Because I am the biggest liar in the world."

"Why are you a liar?" DeRitis asked, completely taken aback.

"Because I do movies, and in movies you are forced to tell lies. You do circus, and you are better than I am, because in the circus you are forced to tell the truth. How do you tell lies in the circus?"

When they parted, the famous film director shook the young man's hand, and, DeRitis confesses unashamedly, "I didn't wash it for days."

Being a man of great intellectual curiosity, there were other important influences on DeRitis's thinking. One was the actor/writer Eduardo de Filippo, the author of *Filumenia Marturano,* and the so-called Neapolitan plays, which are comparable to the work Arthur Miller had done in the United States. Another was the Italian clown troupe Columbioni. "There are lots of families like the Columbioni," DeRitis explains. "They use a process like commedia dell'arte: no rehearsals. They just play to an audience one day and tomorrow they change. They decide just a few minutes before they go on what they will do, which gags will go which way. Always there are changes, but the work is done very professionally. You can't separate the performance from the life of the show."

Annie Fratellini, the granddaughter of the fabled Paul Fratellini who, with his two brothers, made Cirque Medrano a circus shrine, was another influence on DeRitis, as was Fratellini's musically inclined husband, Pierre Étaix.

After completing his studies and working for a short period with his film teacher, DeRitis became an advisor to a newly formed national commission, created by the new minister of culture in Italy. Its purpose was to encourage the circus arts, and it became DeRitis's responsibility to help the commission decide which circuses should get financial support from the government.

Prior to coming to the Feld organization, DeRitis staged a circus for the Togni family. It was, he says, something similar to what he had hoped to do with *Barnum's Kaleidoscape,* a family circus with characters and transitions between acts without a ringmaster, "but it was not as beautiful a production as I hope the Ringling show will be," he said just prior to beginning rehearsals in Sarasota, Florida, in 1999.[6]

Once DeRitis was hired to direct *Barnum's Kaleidoscape*, discussions regarding the shape of the show began in earnest. All of the participants— Kenneth Feld, Tim Holst, and the director—agree that the process of creation was not an easy journey, in large part because Feld insisted on doing something different than anything already out there.

"Whenever you create something, you don't want to be put into a category with somebody else. You want to stand in front of the marketplace," Holst explained. "On the one hand, whatever we created had to match our overall vision of family entertainment, and on the other hand, we had to make sure it wasn't in conflict with other parts of our business, namely Ringling Bros. and Barnum & Bailey."[7]

DeRitis provided another look at the creation: "This was not updating a show for an established circus, but building, from nothing, an entire new circus identity. We didn't even have a name when I began work in February 1998. In this sense, my work was not just directing a show but helping to develop a whole world, including a one-hour preshow experience and the environment that surrounded it.

"I think that a creation comes from a need. And needs are always different. This project came basically from a business need more than an artistic one. I never saw this as a problem or a frustration, however, because strong artistic results were always requested. I think of *The Lion King*, for example.[8]

"Mr. Feld was always sensitive to the artistic viewpoint. He didn't just invest his money, but also his artistic ideals, his dreams. I had a good feeling from him from the very beginning. We both wanted a crazy, different approach. I started by trying to understand the commercial side of the needs, and I tried to transform them into an artistic need, focusing on four words: intimate, elegant, human, and interactive.

"A big goal was to avoid the style of any circus already in the market. As a European I never had in mind to do a European show. We weren't sure an American audience could appreciate a circus based on European tradition. So we decided to try something different, a direct and human approach that came from my own education, a sensibility that is very close to David Larible's."[9]

Larible was a very strong force during all phases of the process. He and DeRitis had a comfortable working arrangement from the very beginning. Larible, in fact, was more than just the show's star. He functioned in many ways as an uncredited cocreator. During rehearsals Larible exercised an enormous amount of influence over the direction, conferring with DeRitis at every break, making suggestions. It also seems safe to assume that Larible was responsible for the hiring of the white-face clown Pipo, who would have provided the perfect, classic foil, if Larible had done any of the material he had developed before coming to America.

DeRitis readily admits to Larible's influence. "He was basic to my approach. Much of his personal material and many of his suggestions were used as a starting point for a lot of the situations for the other acts as well. After all, he is in the ring about 50 percent of the show, and from his actions almost all the acts are generated."[10]

The first hurdle the new director had to get over was finding a concept that Kenneth Feld would approve. One of the first sources of inspiration came from the corporate office's decision to invoke the name of P. T. Barnum. This came about shortly after *Life* magazine named the showman as one of the 100 most influential people of the 20th century.

As a result, "the first approach," according to DeRitis, "was to consider the universe of P. T. Barnum, relying on the audience's imagination. I didn't want a nostalgic or historical approach, neither a thematic one, but a kind of inspirational one, a living scrapbook or travel journal of Barnum himself. After a few months the approach came to seem too literal and not different enough." That idea, and, over the next three months, three others were also discarded.

The notion of adding the idea of a kaleidoscope to Barnum's name, according to Holst, came out of numerous meetings at a time when the discussions of concept had nearly exhausted themselves. DeRitis admits that by then he could find no way of getting out of a situation in which the concept was becoming "dangerously weak."[11]

In the summer of 1998, Feld proposed the idea of the kaleidoscope. That revitalized all those concerned and forced DeRitis to rethink his various concepts once again. The idea was that a kaleidoscope, as Holst explains it, keeps changing, so there could be a variety of different shows that could come under the banner of *Barnum's Kaleidoscape* that "might or might not be circus oriented, that could be more or less theatrical." Any such future productions could, in other words, have taken any form the organization felt appropriate.[12] "Our intention," Feld said by way of confirmation, "was not to do one unit of *Barnum's Kaleidoscape*. There could be five to seven different units around the world."[13]

While the discussions of concept continued, Holst began scouting acts. In fact, that process had begun even before DeRitis became involved in the project. In the theatre this would be equivalent to casting a play before it was even written. This is one of the major areas in which the modus operandi of circus and theatre diverge. The Big Apple Circus books acts years in advance so that it eventually becomes the job of the director to write a script around acts that were booked long before he came upon the scene. Something of the same was emerging in this situation, with one difference. Before he was ever able to get a concept approved by Kenneth Feld, DeRitis had in mind the kind of show he wanted to create, and so, he says, Holst "was always very sensitive about focusing his search on the needs of the various concepts." DeRitis's role was basically proposing acts. "With my knowledge of the circus world and schools everywhere, I was able to ask Tim for some very specific things to meet my needs. For example, I very much wanted to use the four Bogino boys from the Fratellini school and Fanny[14] as transitions during the show and to build my idea of a charivari for the finale.

"The reason I wanted them was because of their theatrical circus education and their musical sense, which I thought would give a more human approach to their excellent acrobatic skills. The circus is the kind of show where the stagehands' activity is totally visible, so I wanted artists to do this work, not as characters (and certainly not as anonymous stagehands), but as humans, and not be forced into a mechanical choreography. It was very exciting to put them together with the Moroccan boys of the Hassani troupe and the Russians of the Kabanov to produce our charivari and to see their teachers working together.

"Another reason for hiring these boys was that they spoke French, as did others in the cast: David Larible, Pipo, Guy Tell and his partner, Regina, and the company manager, so that helped create a good backstage atmosphere and camaraderie that I think the audience can feel as well."[15]

DeRitis's most controversial request was to use a midget in the show. "The little guy was a surprise," Holst admits. "He was not something we had planned on. I remember bringing him to New York and then to Washington to meet Kenneth. Kenneth had said, 'I don't want to feel sorry for him. I want to show him with dignity, not in the nature of a clown.' And I think that's what we've done with him. There is some humor involved, but he's turned out to be a good little actor, and he does it well."

As for the lady with the geese who was supposed to play the little man's wife, things did not go so smoothly. Her original act was twenty minutes long. "We wanted the softness her act brings," Holst says, "And I had to fight hard for this. This was a hard sell. Nobody wanted those damned geese. But I think her act is charming. After she got over the fact that we were not ruining her act, she got interested and turned out to have a nice acting spot."[16]

The geese, themselves, also provided another unexpected problem when Pascal Jacob decided to design some goose-shaped posts for them to walk around. When the new props appeared in the ring, the geese were terrified and wouldn't go anywhere near them for quite some time.[17]

The one act that caused the director the most concern, however, was a musical group called Nuts & Bolts. Composed of several very old men (one of whom was eighty-seven), the band's performance suggested nothing so much as old-fashioned English music hall. What to do with them? In the initial concept, they were to appear in the reception or lobby tent in a Victorian living room setting that might have belonged to P. T. Barnum, himself. DeRitis did not particularly want the band in the big top, for they seemed so out of keeping with everything else. However, since Feld had discovered them himself, he wanted them in the main show as well.[18]

Of the individual acts engaged for the show, Holst is quick to admit, "There are no absolutely, totally fresh acts here. I can say that as one who has traveled and looked at a lot of circuses. But we have never pretended otherwise. It's like they say: 'It's not what you do, but how you do it that counts.'"[19] And how it is done, of course, is very much a matter for the director.

In the meantime the concept continued to evolve. One of the most critical decisions insofar as helping the show find its final form involved the physical production. "We wanted the tradition of the one-ring circus, but we tried to get rid of the conventional, military aspect of the music and the symmetry of the space," DeRitis explains. *Barnum's Kaleidoscape*, consequently, was studiously asymmetrical and unrealistic. The design of the proscenium frame used fantastic figures that combined the features of many different animals into various bizarre creatures. For Holst this was an important element of the design. "The fact that nothing is symmetrical is significant because we are consciously saying, 'Okay it's not Roncalli; it's not Soleil.' This takes it to a different level."[20]

"As we never adopted a truly historical approach," DeRitis says, "we needed to look at different ways of conceiving a one-ring tent as a performance space. I was lucky to have Pascal Jacob, who is one of the most important circus historians and collectors in the world.

"I think Mr. Feld initially was not totally comfortable with my need for reference because he wanted to see something totally original. To my mind, we were looking at what had been done in the past in order to find ways of doing something different."[21]

After several attempts at arriving at a concept that everyone was happy with, Feld gave the creative team—Holst, DeRitis, and now Jacob as well—what Holst calls the bottom line. "The truth is," Holst recalls, "everything we presented, Kenneth didn't like. He didn't like any of it." Getting Feld to specify what it was he did want, everyone involved agrees, wasn't always easy. He did know, however, what he didn't want.

"We had fallen into the trap of doing everything very traditionally," Holst says, "and Kenneth said, 'This isn't how I see this at all.'

"So I locked them up in a hotel room and said, 'Guys, we've got to do it. Tonight's the night.' We'd been on the brink many times before, asking ourselves should we just stop this whole thing and wait and do it another year."[22]

After a very long night, DeRitis says, "We came back to Kenneth with a rough pencil sketch" and out of that came what eventually evolved into *Barnum's Kaleidoscape*.

DeRitis believes the new approach grew out of a change in the design scheme. That was what took them to the idea of making everything asymmetrical. "I sensed that in this way I could refresh my consideration of the atmosphere, the placement of the acts, the characters, the writing of the music, everything.

"I asked Pascal and his assistant, James Dardenne, to find a way of combining Rodin and Gaudi in the proscenium statues. I wanted to find the metaphors of circus life through the strong contrasts of life and death, the beautiful and the weird, and I went to some primary elements like angels and devils and a mix of mythological creatures. And we carried through this idea of the curved line and stained glass variations into the costumes, too, and even into the lobby tent. It's an interesting approach to the philosophy of art nouveau. You will not find a straight line in any element of the *Kaleidoscape* design. After all, the circus comes from a curve."[23]

In creating the show's numerous design elements, DeRitis and Jacob worked together very closely. Jacob designed not only the décor and costumes for the big top show, but the décor of the lobby tent and its concession stations, as well as the uniforms for the ushers and candy concessionaires. He also designed the show's façade, the wagons, and the external fences and lighting fixtures.

"Just on the external designs alone," DeRitis points out, "we had hundreds of day-long meetings, involving dozens of persons." Those involved included the people from Sells-Floto, the concession people, who kept asking for more and more space for more and more food stations, requiring changes in design and alterations in what could be staged in the remaining space of the lobby tent.

In his own meetings with Jacob and the production staff, DeRitis says he brought in hundreds, "perhaps thousands of inspirational sketches and historical documents from two centuries of European classical one-ring settings and every kind of entertainment from Barnum's time.

"The kaleidoscope idea was also approached in the choice of fabrics for the costumes. If we used red velvet, we used ten different kinds of it in one costume. Dozens of people in the workshops of Parson-Meares and Barbara Matera worked for months on our costumes.

"For the lobby tent I had always been impressed with an old Italian opera house with round sofas around a column and a china flower pot on top. So I asked Pascal to adopt this solution to hide the two lobby poles. I think the result helped to establish the crazy, yet elegant mood of the evening."[24]

In addition to his discussions with Jacob at this time, DeRitis was also conferring with composer Linda Hudes. DeRitis says he had long been a fan of the circus music of Linda Hudes and her husband, Rik Albani, who had, for many years, provided the musical settings for the performances of the Big Apple Circus.

"They are able to do classical circus with unconventional music," DeRitis says. And, he further points out, they had more circus experience than any other composers, and many directors, in America. "So I had no hesitation in choosing them to compose the music for a show that I had always supposed would be based on music."

Nor did they hesitate to accept the composition of the orchestra DeRitis proposed to them. The orchestra he wanted would include a violin, cello, and flute.

"My creative interaction with Linda," DeRitis proclaims, "was simply unbelievable. She has a very conceptual approach, and this was wonderful for me. Whenever I proposed an action, a character, or even just a certain atmosphere, she was able to put it to music in just the way I had imagined it.

"I worked very closely with Linda and Rik, and every month we reviewed whatever part of the music they were working on together. I wanted to guide them with my feelings. I explained even the smallest details of my plot for such things as the opening picture, and the result fitted my vision completely. For Linda it was also important to discuss with Pascal the costumes and his design sketches."[25]

For Linda Hudes, Feld's offer to compose the music for his new show gave her a new level to work at. "The process of doing *Kaleidoscape* was the best experience of my life," she says. "Kenneth Feld said, 'Be creative, be different.' There is nothing a creative person needs to hear more than that. Sometimes he would say, 'Go back, be different.'" Feld agrees that her music was the best he ever had in one of his shows up to that point.[26]

For Hudes, music is the narrator of the performance, just as it is in film and dance scores. Her goal, she says, was to help the audience experience joy. In working on the score for the new show she attempted to follow DeRitis's direction to make the music reflect the characters and what she perceived as the essence of each act. "So for Guy Tell I created this macho, metal music. With the Russians it was this power Russian music. For Sylvia [Zerbini] it is very romantic. Seeing the horses run free was such a vision. I wanted to create a special atmosphere with a percolating conga drum, bell sounds and shaker sounds, ambient vibes. The mysterious melody is carried on the violin and tenor sax. It is ethereal."[27]

Thanks to the violin and flutes that wound up in the orchestra, Hudes believes her score had greater scope and subtlety, none of which would have been possible without the support of Feld and Holst. "Tim played a big part as a facilitator," she says.

One of the women aerialists in the show, billed simply as Vanessa, was also a good cellist. "We wanted to find a way to bring her in, first in a short introduction," Hudes recalls. "But she was so good we wrote her into the whole piece, which is my Chopin prelude in G with Stevie Wonder chord changes." This piece became the musical setting for the show's perch pole act.

In addition to writing the music, Hudes also did her own arrangements, waiting as late as possible "to see if we could get a really good violinist." As it turned out they did. "When Sylvia was on," Hudes says, describing the moment with pleasure, "he was playing right in front of the band. It was like Romeo and Juliet."

One technique she used to get to know the acts better was to study videotapes of their performance. "I watched, in silence, the video of the statue act at least 100 times, so that I came to know every move of their bodies. What I loved about those people was that they were Moroccan. The show was supposed to be, at first, a journey of emotions, traveling all over the world." The artists in the statue act, she felt, were "so exotic, so handsome in their Moroccan way. I wanted to evoke the North African scale and refer to the Tunisian beat. I ended up writing music that matches their performance beat for beat. It is build and release, tension and release. So the whole tent is breathing with the statues. It [the audience] comes to its peak when they [the performers] are at their peak. That's the power of music."

Although Hudes describes her music as classical rock, there are other influences to be found in her score for *Barnum's Kaleidoscape*. "I start the show with the 'P. T. Barnum Rag,'" she says. "It's an historic event and a renowned character, so I've written a tribute to him in rag form. Jelly Roll Morton and Scott Joplin are both influences. I did my take on rag, updated. There is even a Sousa-like trio with a violin melody bringing back a hundred-year-old circus march with a modern feeling."

One of Hudes's greatest challenges was writing music for the show's star, David Larible. His particular heritage seemed at first to clash with Hudes's background. Coming from a traditional European circus family he wanted to use traditional music, the Italian tarantella, specifically. But she took the challenge head-on. She wrote three songs for him on trial. All of them ended up being used. The key, she says, was using the tarantella, updated with a little "ska" (an offshoot of reggae) and some Caribbean festival music, which has the same beat, thrown in. "That contemporized it," she says with obvious satisfaction. For the silly geese and Mother Goose, Hudes used pizzicato plucked on the strings. "It was completely classical."

One problem with composing music for any circus act is deciding what to do about the possibility of misses and repeats. "We make provisions for misses," Hudes explains, "by using what we call RTC or 'Repeat 'til Cue.'" This is similar to a vamp, but, Hudes insists, "I am a firm believer in melody. The Cirque du Soleil people compose in two-bar phrases. I write in eight- to sixteen-bar melodies. We will do a long phrase and then repeat. The conductor must be in sync with performers."[28]

Despite DeRitis's enthusiasm for Hudes's work, things did not go quite as smoothly, even with the music, as he indicates. "We had to decide on how many musicians to use. I didn't want to fall into the trap of saving a few bucks by not having a live band there. I fought very hard for a violin," Holst says. "I fought for the feeling of the show, the emotions of the music. And personally I like the music that was created for the perch pole act," he says, referring to the controversy that arose out of having strings in an American circus orchestra.[29]

As the time to commence rehearsals approached, DeRitis focused his attention on helping the performers create the kind of performance he envisioned. "I started out thinking of every artist as a character who had a backstage life," he points out. "I wanted to establish every artist long before the audience got to see him doing his act.

"This approach came to me as a cross between my own deep feelings about Italian circus life and the creative method I'd learned working with Cirque du Soleil on their production of *Pomp, Duck and Circumstance* in Germany. I was fascinated by the idea of trying to show the relationship of the characters. I wanted to give the audience something, so that they could imagine that maybe one of the artists was in love with the beautiful trapeze artist and another one was jealous of him. So during the transitions between acts you would have glimpses of what was happening backstage during the day. As a child I was so fascinated with the way circus artists lived during the day when not in the ring. This was my idea, to humanize the artists and at the same time create a fascinating world by the costumes and lights and music.

"I drew a very long storyboard with different sections representing the timing, and arrows in different colors to follow the paths of comedy, drama, and the basic character interaction. I used as a fixed point the individual acts and the production numbers. I tried to avoid a true narrative line. Mr. Feld was very comfortable with my approach, and in every meeting (which occurred about monthly) he refreshed my ideas, guided my inspiration, and had an extraordinary sensibility that could reveal the weak points of my work."

The performers, however, turned out to be another matter. They were arriving from France, Siberia, and Hungary with no idea of what DeRitis was about to ask of them. "It was a big risk," he admits. "I imagined their characters just from the pictures and videos that they provided, without ever speaking to them."[30]

In realizing this aspect of the director's concept, the activity inside the reception tent was to have been of vital importance in conveying the character's relationships to each other. It was DeRitis's idea, therefore, to have the various performers appear in the preshow entertainment, performing some action that would help reveal their character. The little man, for instance, would be there as the owner of the show. As the audience entered the world of *Barnum's Kaleidoscape* and wandered about the luxurious tent, it would, moment by moment, soon discover more and more about the lives of the performers whose work they were about to see in the big top. This information would help to explain the way in which the performers interacted between the acts of the main performance.

"One of the acting tools I like to use is a running gag," DeRitis says. "For instance, the little man dreams of being a horse trainer, but he is not able to work with horses, so he works with geese. In that way the goose act can be seen as a parody of the liberty horse act. But I had to set this up."[31] It was DeRitis's idea, therefore, to set up the geese act by having Sylvia Zerbini's liberty horse act appear in the program just before the little man came on with the geese.

Zerbini had been contracted to present both her single trapeze act and the horses. Feld is credited with getting the idea of having her come down from the trapeze and go directly into the liberty act. Zerbini professed no hesitation about this manner of presentation. "I'll be all right," she said, early in rehearsals, "as long as I don't think about the horses while I'm on the trapeze. But," she added, "I've got to remember which horses had misbehaved the last time they were in the ring so I don't let them repeat their mistakes."[32]

On February 1, at the first company meeting, DeRitis unveiled the storyboard to an astonished company. According to DeRitis, everyone was surprised, "but happy and excited. We never had any problem in getting the artists to adapt to the work. I think that was because although we changed their costumes, music, and sometimes their tricks, we never tried to alter their soul or their identity. And everyone appreciated that."

Holst confirms this view of the company. "These performers like to be with each other. They like what they're doing in the context of how they are being presented, treated, and handled. We tried to allow that company feeling to grow. If they're happy, it goes to the audience. And few people understand the passion with which Raffaele, Pascal, and I worked to mold the company, to make them comfortable with the environment and give them the sense that they were free to grow and experiment."

The fly in the ointment, however, was that this approach required some level of acting skill from the performers. Given sufficient time, perhaps, the director could have coaxed the kinds of performances he had hoped for from his cast, but he had just three weeks. In contrast, Cirque du Soleil's workshop period, as we have seen, covers many months.

DeRitis had hoped to have time to work improvisationally in front of an audience as he had learned to do in Europe. "Living with the Togni Circus in the '80s, I had the opportunity to live the true commedia dell'arte system. You never rehearse, but the show is different every day. This was because the audience was different, and the artists were the owners of the show, so they felt free to experiment. After watching the same show thousands of times that was never the same, I developed a feeling and understanding of what works and what doesn't and at what point in the show. Obviously with Kenneth Feld," DeRitis concluded, "you cannot take such a risk because you have to deliver a show at the premiere, and it's not supposed to change for several years.

"Many of the circus performers were not experienced in acting. But they could have been pushed by the others, like David, to play themselves. I didn't want people to try to be funny; I just wanted them to play some kind of situation. I didn't have time to work in a studio the way Cirque du Soleil does, so I just gave the artists a lot of freedom, selecting with them the actions to keep. David was invaluable to me in guiding the characters of the other performers; after all, he was expected to interact with all of them. He was very generous about this."[33]

★ ★ ★

From the very beginning, there were many more problems with the preshow than had originally been anticipated, and as a consequence, just prior to what was to have been a series of hometown previews in Sarasota, Florida, DeRitis was spending most of his energy rehearsing what amounted to the atmosphere that was to establish the party mood for the audience before it went to its seats in the big top for the performance itself. A great deal of time was spent merely creating traffic patterns and finding space for various specialty acts. All of this activity was fueled by the ragtime band Nuts & Bolts, which was the real centerpiece of the preshow performance. There seemed to be little doubt that their infectious musical pieces would send the audience to their seats in a buoyant mood.

There was only one problem with that, one that proved to be unsolvable. After building energy for an hour in the reception tent, the show's momentum was nullified by the twenty- to thirty-minute break required for the audience to find its seats, causing all that excitement to dissipate into something of an anticlimax.

Finally DeRitis had to face the problems with the performance. A major disappointment to DeRitis was the rebellion of the tumblers he had hired to double as ringboys, or *barrier* as they are called in the traditional French circus. "We are artists," they protested. "Why are you treating us this way?" (like stagehands.) They felt exploited. The director explained that they were indeed to act like artists. Their costumes had been specifically designed to remove any suggestion of their being only ringboys. He had a special session with them demonstrating how it is possible to move a chair as a character rather than as a stagehand.

During this period the director also found it necessary to pull back from his idea of incorporating some of the performers, in their character roles, into acts other than their own. The simple fact was that their presence was distracting. Acts like the living statues did not need such embellishments. DeRitis concluded that it was not fair to the acts to have other characters hanging around watching them. With that decision, the possibility of humanizing the performers was considerably dimmed, if not entirely abandoned.

Another problem arose with the white-face clown, Pipo, who was accustomed to using spoken dialogue in his performance. It was determined that the audience would react to speech as an unexpected and, therefore, unwarranted intrusion. Converting him into a silent character proved to be a difficult transformation.

Before long, DeRitis also came to realize that he had a problem with the running order. The first applause didn't occur until twenty minutes into the show. "I wanted it in the first thirty seconds." That lapse occasioned another change in the running order. The first laughs were late in arriving as well, which necessitated moving David Larible's first appearance up in the order. The final blow to any hope of having the planned running gags work, as will be seen later, came from a source beyond anyone's control.[34]

★ ★ ★

At the same time that DeRitis began working with the performers, the physical show was being put together, and then the difficulties were no longer conceptual but physical. One of the reasons why so many things suddenly became nagging problems was simply because no one in the Feld organization had had much experience in dealing with such things as lot supervision, sanitation and housekeeping, ushers, box office staff, food, and the front-of-house management. All these areas were, as Feld says, "things we had taken for granted for years." They were areas for which the Feld organization did not formerly have to take any responsibility. Suddenly now they did. "We were responsible for every single aspect," Feld says.[35]

And since, as Feld insists, "this show is about customer service and this philosophy had to be exemplified by every single employee in all aspects," every detail of the operation had to be considered very seriously and considered anew, because as Feld further points out, "there was no infrastructure. We started with a blank canvas."

To help fill it in, the Feld organization turned to focus groups for suggestions. "The more we talked to people through focus groups, the more we found there were certain expectations that had to be met. One of the big concerns was bathrooms," Holst recalls from those early days of exploration.[36]

Despite what they had learned from the focus groups and all the design work Pascal Jacob had done, the restrooms had somehow gotten lost in the shuffle. Nobody thought about designing them. Peggy Williams and Holst, himself, were frantically decorating the interiors of the public toilets just before the aborted Sarasota opening.

The restrooms, of course, were an important element in the overall scheme of things because it had always been intended that the show would be upscale. "I don't mean that in an arrogant way," Holst insists. "But our marketing strategy was to put us in places like Century City. We wanted to be in Beverly Hills, one of the most exclusive parts of town, because this is the vision of the show."[37]

Even the selection of the garbage cans had to be carefully considered. In fact, they created a minor crisis. At one point, the show had cornered the market on trash cans in the Sarasota area before they were able to decide which to use. Then they had to decide whether to have benches or not. "If people are coming an hour before the show, they may need to sit," Holst explains. "All these little decisions were part of the process of deciding how we would want to be treated going to such an event ourselves." Then there were the potted palms and the other living trees spotted around the front door. The lighting fixtures and the fences ended up being made in Europe.

As far as the seating was concerned, "We didn't want to have ordinary seating," Holst says. "Comfort was a big concern." The seating system came from a manufacturer other than the one that provided the tent. "It didn't come in exactly as we wanted," Holst recalls. "I liken it to when you buy a home; inevitably, any new home owner is going to experience some surprises." The surprise here was that the seating didn't fit into the tent, causing a considerable delay in getting the venue ready for the proposed Sarasota opening.

Then there were the wooden floors, which were planned for the entire area of both tents and the passageway between. "Little things turned out to be huge," Holst says by way of understatement. For one thing it took a very long time to put down the wooden floor and get it level. Then the kind of wood used in both the frames and the decking had to be changed. All new plywood had to be installed because "the humidity did something we hadn't anticipated to the wood."[38]

All of these unexpected difficulties necessitated canceling the planned preview performances in Sarasota in late February. Instead, management invited those who had bought tickets in advance to two dress rehearsals. Tryout dates in Texas were also scrubbed, and the show moved directly to Irvine, California, on no fewer than fifty trucks.

Another problem that added to the prevalent feeling of chaos at this time was the matter of the lighting design. Because of his own busy schedule, the designer, LeRoy Bennett, was very late in coming aboard the project and consequently late in delivering the design. "I wanted a feeling of totally natural light," DeRitis says by way of explaining the thinking that eventually led to the absence of followspots. He [Bennett] immediately understood my vision," DeRitis says, "and so he chose to use nothing but vari-lite." These are lighting instruments that can be automatically adjusted and refocused.[39]

Bennett recalls that the idea of eliminating followspots came to him through Kenneth Feld, although he agrees that it may have been the director who planted the idea in the producer's mind. "We wanted this to be a more theatrical show than a circus," Bennett suggests. "We were just trying to be a little different." There were, he concedes, moments when followspots could definitely have filled in spaces where the area lighting was inadequate. "There was a resistance from some (but not all) the performers, because they were used to working within a spotlight, and now they had to be a little more precise in what they were doing" so they could hit their marks and be illuminated.[40]

The major problem, however, was that programming the vari-lites took a very long time and the process had to be completed at a time that should have been dedicated to other matters, like the performers, who found their own involvement in this process painfully uncomfortable. Anyone who has ever endured a technical rehearsal in the theatre will easily understand this. The situation here was made even more difficult than it normally is because of the pressure of time and the fact that circus performers are not used to working under such conditions. "In the circus you can't ask performers to follow the lights," DeRitis explains. "But this is what we tried to do, and I think the result is something different from what has been done before." But the victory was won at a great cost to nerves and tempers. It added another element of tension when the performers should have been thinking about their performances, and when the producer was nervous about seeing a finished performance.

In defending the idea of natural light, DeRitis says he wanted the feeling of stepping into a church or some strange, mystical place. Kenneth Feld,

DeRitis explains, wanted the audience, upon walking into the big top, to say, "Oh, my god, how beautiful."[41]

★ ★ ★

All these problems created the delays and distractions that kept the show from staging the series of previews in which DeRitis had hoped to hone the performance in front of an audience. "In a one-ring show you never know what you have until you have an audience," he insists. But he was not to have that opportunity. By the time the show got to California, he, as well as some other prominently placed management personnel, was no longer with the show.

The departure of a director is hardly an uncommon event in the world of commercial theatre. It happens with Broadway-bound shows fairly frequently as they struggle to find themselves. Prior to producing *Barnum's Kaleidoscape*, Kenneth Feld had been involved in just such a creative endeavor, the Broadway musical *Big*. As its coproducer he had inserted himself rather deeply into the creative process. So DeRitis's removal, at least in the theatrical world, was not without precedence. Neither was the hiring of a so-called uncredited "play doctor."

"Raffaele had a particular vision, and we gave him some guidance, and he took it as far as we felt he could take it," Holst explained once the show was in California. "Kenneth and I both felt there wasn't any more that he could bring to the table, but we knew we needed something more, and it wasn't a lot, and Kenneth and I felt we were too close to do it ourselves." Phil McKinley, the director-choreographer of Ringling's three-ring circuses, was brought in to do the tweaking.

"According to our program, and I honestly feel this is deserved, Raffaele gets credit for the directorial part of the show," Holst insists. Once performances began in Los Angeles, however, there was almost no discernible attempt being made, either in the lobby tent or the big top, to convey the subtext DeRitis had tried to give the performers. But the discussions, the previous character work, must have had some impact on the company and on the final product as Holst confirms by pointing out, "Raffaele did a good job in developing some characters that maybe in most circuses would not have been developed."[42]

In addition to all the problems normally attendant on the opening of a new production, it was fate that stepped in and delivered the final revision that, as it turned out, changed the production in a way that would never be reversed. Sylvia Zerbini fell from her trapeze during the show's opening engagement in Irvine, just days prior to its official debut in Los Angeles. Although not seriously hurt, she did stay off the trapeze for a few weeks while recuperating and presented only her horses at the premiere performance.

That necessitated another change in the program order, and instead of opening the show as originally planned, she came on late in the first half, long after the goose down had floated from the ring. Her place in the running order did not revert to its original position even after resuming the trapeze act because it was Kenneth Feld's feeling that her appearance made a greater impact coming later in the program.

In the new running order, the geese appeared before the horses, and any possibility of establishing the gag DeRitis had intended was lost. But losing that bit of very subtle humor was more than compensated for, Feld believed, by bringing Zerbini on much later in the program when the audience was fully ready to appreciate her remarkable performance.

DeRitis dismissed the changes, saying that 90 percent of the show that opened in Los Angeles was his. "We never wanted to tell a story or create a theme," he insists. "The result of our work was a very, very logical approach to the show. I'm happy about the result with one act going into the next with the character relationships providing the rationale and replacing the speaking ringmaster in the classic circus."[43]

He further defended his work by insisting that employing a concept did not necessarily turn a circus performance into Cirque du Soleil. Arriving at a concept, he pointed out, means "you have found your identity. Working on a concept means you are trying to find your identity. Finally the concept tells the audience who you are. It is a way of looking at everything so there is harmony in all elements of the production. The concept brings harmony to all the acts. It's not something that is so clear, but you feel it."

"There are two ways of doing a circus," DeRitis points out. "One way is to set a mood and tell about something in the spirit, in the manner of Cirque du Soleil. The other, the way, which is also the way the Big Apple Circus does it, is simply to present the acts in the best way, connecting them in the best way, because the focus and structure is really the acts."

So while the subtext of the characters may be undecipherable, the acts did move from one to the next without any pauses or breaks or any announcements from the ringmaster. "Here there is nothing between the acts and the audience. I was always telling the artists to remember the audience. You're playing for them, not yourselves. Don't look down at your feet when you leave the ring; look at the audience. They are following you, even when you leave, because you have created a great energy."[44]

Feld, himself, kept close tabs on the show during the end of its time in Florida, and he spent the bulk of his time in Los Angeles while the show was in Century City. Of the producer's involvement, Holst says, "What I find interesting from all my years of working with him is how close he is to this project, how involved he is in so many details. I found myself backing off and allowing Kenneth to be more involved in some of the decisions, because he wanted to be."[45]

Ultimately, one must conclude that Kenneth Feld was the most powerful force involved in *Barnum's Kaleidoscape*, both in its creation as well as in its demise. It was his decision to close the show after a very successful run during the holiday season in New York City. The reviews and audience reaction had validated the artistic merit of the show. So had its location in Bryant Park behind the main public library on Fifth Avenue, in the very heart of the city's most affluent shopping district. None of that, however, could make up for the financial losses it had incurred before coming to Manhattan and those that loomed ahead given the inescapable numbers of its operating expenses.

NOTES

1. Kenneth Feld, telephone interview with the author, May 10, 1999.

2. Tim Holst, personal interview with the author, Los Angeles, May 1, 1999.

3. Feld interview.

4. Zingaro is an equestrian ensemble, which, despite DeRitis's admiration for its artistic integrity, has decided it is not a circus at all, but a theatre company, albeit an equestrian one, literally a horse opera. The work of Bartabas, Zingaro's founder, is discussed in chapter 8.

5. Raffaele DeRitis, personal interview with the author, Sarasota, Fla., March 6–7, 1999.

6. DeRitis interview, March 1999.

7. Holst interview.

8. Julie Taymore, the director of the stage version of *The Lion King*, was given complete artistic freedom by the Disney people who produced the show, proving that even a giant corporation with very set ideas on how its products should look could back off and not interfere with a creative artist or try to mold that artist's work in its own image.

9. DeRitis interview, March 1999.

10. DeRitis interview, March 1999.

11. DeRitis interview, March 1999.

12. Holst interview.

13. Feld interview.

14. In DeRitis's concept, Fanny Kervich's character was to provide one of the threads that tied the various moments of the show together. She played the role of a starstruck groupie who wanted to join the circus and in the finale does. This role was eventually dropped from the show.

15. DeRitis interview, March 1999.

16. Holst interview.

17. Pascal Jacob, personal interview with the author, Los Angeles, May 2, 1999.

18. DeRitis interview, March 1999.

19. Holst interview.

20. Holst interview.

21. DeRitis e-mail to author, June 4, 1999.

22. Holst interview.

23. DeRitis interview, March 1999.

24. DeRitis e-mail.

25. DeRitis e-mail.

26. Kenneth Feld, telephone interview with the author, April 5, 2000.

27. Linda Hudes, telephone interview with the author, March 16, 2000.

28. Linda Hudes interview.

29. Holst interview.

30. DeRitis e-mail.

31. DeRitis interview, March 1999.

32. Sylvia Zerbini, personal interview with the author, Sarasota, Fla., March 6, 1999.

33. DeRitis interview, Los Angeles, May 1, 1999.

34. DeRitis interview, May 1999.

35. Feld interview.

36. Holst interview.

37. Holst interview.

38. Holst interview.

39. DeRitis interview, March 1999.

40. LeRoy Bennett, personal interview with the author, Atlantic City, N.J., September 15, 2003.

41. DeRitis interview, March 1999.

42. Holst interview.

43. DeRitis interview, May 1999.

44. DeRitis interview, May 1999.

45. Holst interview.

· 7 ·

The Big Apple Circus's *Clown Around Town*

$\mathscr{D}$uring the course of the fourteen-month gestation period that each of the Big Apple Circus's productions goes through, meetings are held periodically, involving the various members of the creative staff. The first of these might be informal meetings between Paul Binder (artistic director) and Michael Christensen (creative director). Out of these discussions a theme for the new show is agreed upon. Christensen and the director would then conduct a series of meetings over a period of months, formulating the show. Once ready, the director and Christensen would describe the show to Dominique Jando (then the Big Apple's associate artistic director). From this Jando would produce the first written script, which was then presented to Binder for his input. The script was then presented to the entire creative team, which included at various times Binder, Christensen, the director of clowning (now Barry Lubin, formerly Michael Christensen), the scenic and costume designers, the composer, and possibly the past equestrian director, Katja Schumann. Jando would take notes, and after each meeting, publish an updated version of what amounted to a working script. This would then be distributed to each member of the creative staff. Over the course of those aforementioned fourteen months, as many as eleven versions of the script might emerge before the first rehearsal began one month prior the new production's first previews.[1]

The changes that were recorded in the various scripts for the production slated for the 2000–2001 season reflect revisions in everything including the show's title, the running order of the acts, the nature of the clown reprises, transitions, and various details of the narrative. While that production was in development, its working title changed from *Urban Show* to *In the City* before settling on the final version, *Clown Around Town*, eight months later.

Insofar as the running order is concerned, the positioning on the program of the fast-change artists David and Dana, the flying return act of the Flying Pages, and the juggler Serge Percelly is a fascinating look at creative vacillation. The flying act at first seemed a good choice for the closing act, given the fact that it required the erection of a safety net, which, if the act were in last place, would not need to be removed. But the closing act does not really conclude the performance. There is still the traditional finale featuring the entire cast, quite a contingent to maneuver around the guylines of the flying net.

The Flying Pages were, by the fourth revision dated December 21, 1999, put into the position of first act closing, and the prestigious closing slot henceforth went back and forth between the juggler and the quick-change artists, with Percelly apparently taking firm hold of that position from February 2000 onward and into rehearsals and previews.

The first articulation of the show's theme or concept appears in the draft dated November 11, 1999:

> The show is loosely inspired by the tale of *The City Mouse and the Country Mouse*, which would be in this case, *The City Clown and the Country Clown*: the country clown (Jeff Gordon) comes to visit his city cousin (Tom Dougherty), who, in reality, has never completely adapted to the city (as the good clown he is). The third main character is the city slicker (Dinny McGuire), who can be their guide, mentor, or nemesis, and, in any case, their straight man.

The narration then went on to describe the tone and style it was hoped the production would achieve through its physical setting:

> The show will open on a definitely urban look. Geometrical, with shades of grays, chromes, asphalt, cement, and violent contrasting lights and people living in general uniformity. Gradually, softer, more varied colors will creep in, as well as flowers and trees, and a more joyous, free-and-easy atmosphere. Tentatively the first part will cover a full day, from dawn to night. The second half is the second day, although no day progression is intended there, just a gradual change of look, leading to the finale.
>
> Although the locale is defined (a big American city) the period is not. Each act may be placed in the period that fits it best, as long as it is a classic urban period: the Thirties, the Fifties, the Seventies. This will inform the costuming and the musical surroundings.
>
> The set, at the opening of the show, is definitely urban. Each side of the bandstand evokes city streets, with high rises and also Broadway-style running and blinking lights (light streamers may also define a skyline). The look is sleek, with silver and chrome. Gradually this look will give place to

sneaking in trees, flowers and more silly/happy elements. A full moon which can become a sun (according to need) is behind the band. Projections (or rear projections) can be made on it (the Big Apple Circus logo, for instance). The ring entrance could represent an old subway entrance. (There could even be a turnstile at times, where the artists leaving the ring should put a token; if they have no tokens, they have to take another bow!) There is an electric tickertape where messages (such as thanks to our sponsors, "The Show will start in five minutes," or "Intermission," etc.) can be displayed.

On February 10, the sentence "The look is colorful, very 'Toon-City,'" was added to the description of the set, indicating a significant change in thinking from the previous "grays, asphalt, and cement" intended to guide the set designer, and thus pointed the style of the physical production in an entirely new direction.

Reality did not entirely set in until the version dated May 1, 2000, at which time budgets and projected costs would have begun to impinge on creativity. At that time the "electric tickertape" (or zipper light as the Times Square electronic message came to be known) was dropped, no doubt due to considerations of cost.

Throughout this period of creative development, the role of the ring crew also underwent significant revisions. They were first seen, in the November 11, 1999, narrative, as "delivery people for various companies (their costumes in the same style but different colors)." To further integrate their movements into the narrative, it was suggested that "each time they deliver some props they are tipped by the Ringmaster."

The ring crew was recast as bellhops, now from various hotels, in the February 7, 2000, version, "costumed in the same style, but in different colors." This change may have been inspired by the fact that the Mike and Pascale Sanger dog act was to be set up by two bellhops. Sanger himself worked in bellhop costumes and used suitcases as props. Since the ring crew would need costumes, it would have seemed a logical and amusing move to make all members of the ring crew bellhops as well.

On February 10, the idea of augmenting the ring crew with "a composite tumbling troupe" surfaced for the first time, with the note that they should "be used as often as possible in bits that require moving props while *acting*."

Ultimately, the bellhops appeared only once in the production, as a transition into the aforementioned Sanger dog act. Their appearance involved more than merely moving props. A parade of half a dozen or more of them marched around the ring curb walking "dogs" that were nothing more than fluffy balls of fur. This gambit also allowed the two star clowns to get into the act as well.

The narrative describing the action of the show's opening moments reveals the kind of detailed thinking that goes into the creative planning that takes place long before the first rehearsal. The following is taken from the November 11, 1999, script:

> Opening: A city at dawn. We hear a radio news station (traffic, weather, etc.). A jogger passes by; a cop is on his beat. Then, an elegant lady rider on a horse enters (Katja Schumann), perhaps accompanied by a child rider on a miniature horse (Tito). She is doing her morning ride in the park, which can give an opportunity for a glimpse at a high school passage.
>
> The park image slowly disappears. As the city wakes up, city noises slowly take over, until the city imagery comes in focus, and a highly energetic charivari of city characters fills the ring. Possible characters: a group of Wall-Streeters with briefcases and cell-phones (doing, among other things, a briefcase drill), a street vendor, cabbies, Con Ed personnel, delivery man, elegant lady with a dog (and cell-phone), dog walker, newsie, mime, cops, three-card monte con-artist, more cops.
>
> Dinny McGuire has been in the crowd all along. [*Note that his character is unspecified at this point.*] Eventually Tom Dougherty enters, and they both spot each other in the crowd. As they go towards each other the charivari fades away. Dinny asks Tom where he has been. Tom explains that he is expecting his country cousin, Gordoon, who has "Broadway" ambitions, but he couldn't find him at the station. There is a big commotion, and Gordoon enters on a horse-driven old cart covered with trunks, suitcases, bird cages, etc, driven by either Katja or Mike Sanger, wearing straw hat and overalls over an old Union Suit. Tom and Gordoon are now ready for a tour of the Big City.

Note next the significant changes in thinking that took place by the February 7, 2000, version, including a reversal of roles. At that point Gordoon became the city clown, and Tom, the country bumpkin:

> A city park at dawn. A couple (man/woman) with sweat-bands and ear-phones jog through the ring, followed immediately by a lone jogger, followed by another jogger, acrobatics-minded and carrying a boom-box; he tunes it in, and we hear a local traffic report. Then he stretches a little, does a standing somersault and exits as Katja and companion (Maxie on a pony?) enter on horseback for an early morning ride in the park. The riders and joggers wave and greet each other, but they remain in their own little bubbles of privacy. There is a low-key, gentle control of horse and pony and one feels that the horses would like to "jog" and the joggers would like to "trot."
>
> As they exit, Mr. Paul (or Dinny) enters and acknowledges them with a nod or a gesture. Mr. Paul [speaks] *Welcome to the Big Apple Circus!* . . .

(Maybe a couple of other joggers go by) *An early morning jog or horseback ride through Central Park* (in New York; another name or the term "a city park" for other locations). *The city is waking up.*

Gordoon enters wearing a long sleeping cap and rubbing his eyes.

Mr. Paul [speaks]: *Oh, hi, Mr. Gordoon! Ladies and Gentlemen, this is Mr. Gordoon. . . . Good morning! What's up?* (Gordoon whispers) *Oh, your cousin Tom, from the country, is coming to visit you here? Wonderful! Where are you meeting him? . . . Right here? Well, what's he look like?* (Gordoon dashes out and reappears with a life-sized stand-up photograph of Tom.) *Hmmmm. . . . Definite family resemblance! And when is he supposed to arrive? . . . Oh, right now?!* (The screech of a subway train coming to a stop is heard.) *Hey, maybe that's him!*

It is interesting that the dialogue, noted above, actually made it into the final version and was performed without cuts or revisions.

The subway doors open (sound effects) and the entire company spews into the ring, along with Tom. The ring teems with people, everyone is there: pizza delivery (speaks to spectator: Did you order this?) Newsie (Regina) gives audience member a newspaper. There is constant motion, and participants make passing contact with the audience. Mr. Paul and Gordoon are totally comfortable in this, but Tom is being buffeted about like a pinball (as much comic action as possible). In this mess Gordoon sees Tom when Tom doesn't see him and vice-versa. Gordoon loses his life-sized picture of Tom, enabling Tom to disappear in the crowd. Meanwhile Paul has exited. A subway turnstile has been set up at the ring entrance. All exit except for a group of Wall-Streeters and the joggers. A long line forms as people leave the ring, stylistically passing through the turnstile. The charivari begins.

Dinny is also in the ring, wearing an apron and cap over his costume, pushing a hot dog cart with a folded (closed) umbrella (Gordoon is hidden in the folds of the umbrella) . . .

The charivari, like the dialogue, also made it into the actual performance, but in a position much later than the one suggested above. At that point it included the tumbling troupe alluded to earlier, along with the ring crew and the three members of the Slipchenko act, and is next described in some detail:

Into this madness rides a mounted cop (Sasha) who blows a whistle to re-assert law and order. The horse is followed by two members of the ring crew with a wheeled trashcan and a shovel. (It would be nice here if the horse could do a short routine of some "side-steps" which the cast can also do, as if the horse were leading them.) Everyone is friendly again, and this gives Dinny a chance to come forward and sell his drinks and hot dogs. We soon realize that every time someone buys something from Dinny, they are served by two hands coming out from the folded umbrella. (Must find an exit for cop and horse, but leave the wheeled trash-can in the ring.)

We can see from this that the entrance of the country clown was considerably changed. The above version of the narrative remained more or less intact, with the addition of specific performers assigned to certain roles, until the beginning of rehearsals. The only change involved that folded umbrella on the hot dog cart. By May 1, 2000, when the script designates which artists are to be used in which scenes, the mysterious umbrella person was to be played by a character "to be announced."

One piece of business that remained in the narrative from almost the beginning, until rehearsals, involved Tom Dougherty's entrance. Different versions have him arriving by subway, taxi, or both. How to represent the taxi in a circus ring was solved early on. During a blackout the audience would see the headlights and roof sign of a taxi and hear the screech of brakes before the lights were restored to discover . . .

Dinny and Gordoon alone in the ring looking at Tom's waving legs (wearing roller-blades) which stick out of the wheeled trash-can. They lift him out of the can and set him on his feet. He is rather the worse for his ordeal and keeps folding back into the trash-can. The second time he is lifted upright, he has a bunch of flowers which he presents to Gordoon. Tom folds into the trash-can again. This time when he is lifted out, he presents Dinny with a bunch of carrots.

It is, of course, considerably easier to imagine such comic action than it is to turn it into a physical reality, especially with real people in real time, as opposed to the cuts that could make such a gag work on film. This little comic exchange was never performed.

A couple of other clown interludes imagined for the time needed to rig the flying net were also jettisoned before they were ever tested in front of an audience. The following was included in the December 21, 1999, narrative:

Gordoon and Tom have found a job as high-rise window washers. One of them (Gordoon) is taken up on a bosun chair, which gets stuck half-way to the top of the "building." In order for Gordoon to get down, a net is needed. During net set-up Gordoon interacts with pigeons.

This was amended on February 7, 2000, to the following action, which was to function as a transition from the acrobatic parody in which either Tom or Gordoon was to become attached to a bungee cord, sending him floating high above the ring:

Immediately pandemonium reigns in the circus. The air is filled with the screaming sirens and hooters, etc, of every city emergency service. Dinny (in a Fire Chief's hard hat) directs the rescue. The pedestal [from the acrobatic act that proceeded] is taken out. The ring crew race in with a red fire wagon complete with flashing lights and sirens. It unfolds to reveal the net, which is quickly hooked up. Meanwhile the three Slipchenkos, wearing hard-hats and carrying a ladder are doing a fall about routine.

Tom (or Gordoon) floating in the air, now spreads his cloak and becomes a Kite with Gordoon (or Tom) playing the other end of the string.

Instantly three or four UV [ultra violet] kites join Tom floating in the air. People in the ring hold them on long flexible poles. Three more kites join the spectacle (worked from the bandstand). It is a spectacle in UV, very beautiful. (Tom needs to be lowered and unhooked during all this.)

It was Dougherty who was ultimately sent aloft, hooked up to a body harness that he had used in a parody of one of the featured acts, a highly dramatic adagio, and the UV effect was saved for Gordoon's reprise in which he sent rolls of toilet paper skyward, from whence it floated earthward in fascinating, abstract patterns. Neither pigeons nor kites became a reality, although a single pigeon did appear early in the show during the prelude in which Gordoon first appears.

While studying the various versions of the narrative provides a fascinating glimpse into the thinking of the creators as they grappled with the problems inherent in this kind of circus production, what is most interesting to note are the changes that took place once the show got on its feet in rehearsals and the directors began moving real people, props, and animals around the circus ring.

It is obvious from reviewing the performance videotapes that some ideas were jettisoned entirely. Others provided the inspiration for moments in which they were used in a different context and in a different way.

The entrances of the two main characters and the opening sequence that was actually performed were much simplified. The trash can, hot dog cart, the mounted policeman, numerous characters who were to provide atmosphere were all abandoned, and the action was made to move forward without complication, rather expeditiously.

Regina Dobrovitskaya is discovered in the silhouette of the moon as the lights come up to discover Gordoon seated on a park bench, when a single pigeon flies over head. He tries to feed the bird from his sandwich, but it will have nothing to do with him. Gordoon runs off in pursuit of the bird, so that he can have a wire, which will be used later, hooked to his harness. A few joggers and a businessman pass through the ring and Gordoon returns, still chasing the pigeon, which now takes him up in the air for a quick circling of the ring.

Juggler Serge Percelly enters, dressed in warm-up clothes, bats a few imaginary balls with his tennis racket and exits. A horseback rider enters the ring as Gordoon returns joined by Paul Binder. They proceed to have the exchange noted earlier. At the conclusion of Binder's speech, the screeching sound of a subway car coming to a halt is heard and the curtains of the entrance portal are parted as the male members of the company enter, dressed in business suits. They are joined by Regina Dobrovitskaya, who is tossed about by the men in an acrobatic routine.

Gordoon returns reading what we assume is a telegram. The charivari segues to the Slipchenko Russian barre troupe. They are dressed as workers from the garment district, and their barre is hung with clothing about to be shipped to retail stores. The Slipchenkos do a few comic tricks and exit, as Dinny McGuire, dressed as a cop on a bike, enters. Gordoon shows him the message he had been reading, and we are told by McGuire that cousin Orville is on his way in a taxi.

The previously noted taxi business then takes place, and Gordoon and Orville are discovered in separate spotlights as the lights are restored. Eventually they back into each other, embrace, and McGuire says, "Welcome to the city," as Dana Kaseeva of David and Dana enters for her hula-hoop act.

This is considerably less complicated and faster moving than anything that had been previously contemplated when the performance was still on paper.

One of the most gnawing problems throughout the early stages of the creative process was what to do with Regina Dobrovitskaya, the one female member of the company who had no specialty in this production and whose role remained vague and her function in the narrative amorphous.

She is imagined, at various stages of the planning, to be, at different times during the performance, a newspaper boy, a telegraph delivery boy, a fireman, and a cheerleader, a bat girl. In one version she is identified as "a Jackie Coogan" type kid. In another the fireman has changed to a cop. In a move that may have been motivated by frustration more than anything else, she is finally made "the circus sprite," a role that reflects the production team's inability to find anything that really provided a legitimate rationale for her turning up every so often.

As "the circus sprite," she was dressed in a "circusy," white, spangled leotard, which never changed. When she was needed, as for instance in the charivari, she simply appeared with no purpose other than to take part in the act. In a move intended, presumably, to make her more an integral part of the performance, she opens the show posed in the set's sun-moon orb, as if presiding over the entire affair. (Whether anyone in the audience arrived at that interpretation, or even gave any consideration to her presence is another matter altogether.)

In comparing the actual performance with the various versions of the written narrative, it is clear that while working on paper, the Big Apple's creative team tended to overcomplicate, whereas the rehearsals moved in the opposite direction toward simplification. In deciding whether all those hours, the energy, and creative thinking that go into the narrative are anything more than a waste of time, one must consider the possibility that although much of the preplanning is abandoned in rehearsals, all that preparation may actually be useful, during the rehearsal process, in arriving at the final product more effectively.

The Big Apple Circus's narrative is the equivalent of Cirque du Soleil's period of research and development, although the methods used by each are diametrically opposed. Whereas the Big Apple creative team starts with complex ideas and then moves toward simplification, Franco Dragone, in his work with Cirque du Soleil, proceeds from "a vague premonition" that is very simple. In the case of *Quidam*, Dragone wanted to investigate the sense of isolation most human beings have from each other. Working outward from that idea, Dragone continually added complexity, image by image and moment by moment, creating what ultimately amounted to a complex mosaic as he moved with his cast through a long series of workshops.

Ringling's Phil McKinley approaches rehearsal in yet another way. The preparation he does with the model makes it possible for him to walk into the first day of rehearsals and begin immediately, with little or no deviation or further exploration, to create the circus that he has already mapped out or "filmed," in advance, in his head.

What these case studies illustrate is that there is no one way of arriving at a finished circus production. The approaches vary according to the temperaments of the people involved, the technical limitations each must consider, their budget restraints, and, of course, their innate talent.

NOTE

1. Dominque Jando. Productions notes, Big Apple Circus, *Clown Around Town*, 1999–2000. All the dated excerpts in this chapter are taken from this single source.

III

THE PERFORMERS

• 8 •

Circus Stars

$\mathcal{I}$t is not, of course, merely the directors, designers, and composers who are the artists of the circus. Many individual performers are every bit as creative as the men and women whose work we have already examined. The way in which they present their remarkable skills is as carefully considered and refined as the work of any of the artists already noted, or, for that matter, any other performing artist.

Perhaps the most notable circus performer of our time is the late Gunther Gebel-Williams, who trained and presented a variety of animals with Ringling Bros. and Barnum & Bailey for more than twenty years. Circus fans usually attribute Gunther Gebel-Williams's greatness to his way with animals, but it was his way with audiences that made him the circus's only true superstar.

A female journalist writing for the *New York Times*, in April of 1999, well into Gunther's retirement, still couldn't help wondering what was the secret of his appeal. Was it "charisma? courage? sex? The contented smile of a tiger who has so much to eat he simply cannot take another bite?"[1]

It was, of course, all of these things, but first and foremost (let's be honest) it was sex appeal. Of Gunther's debut, I wrote, "One can almost hear every feminine heart in the arena palpitating. Blond, bearded and Nordic, he has certainly replaced the daring young man on the flying trapeze as the circus's sex symbol."[2] That was a theme that swirled around Gunther for his entire career.

Pursuing her query further, the aforementioned female reporter wrote, "There was always the air of an animal in rut when he starred in the center ring of the Ringling show, and it didn't all come from the tigers. Strutting around the ring with his unnatural white-blond hair, his beloved leopard Kenny in a signature sling around his shoulders, Gunther Gebel-Williams had something that was not touted in the posters, though the ladies didn't need a program to figure it out."[3]

Nor did Gunther. His wife, Sigrid, confirms that he was very much aware of his status as a sex symbol, "and loved every minute of it."[4] But there was even more to Gunther's appeal than simple sex. Both sexes and all ages responded to him. A great deal of it had to do with the way he carried himself in the arena.

"Although he does no end of truly remarkable things, it isn't so much what he does as how he does them," I wrote, back in 1975, at the time of his third appearance in New York. "There is," the review continued, "an air of nonchalant showmanship" that was undeniably appealing.[5] Unlike so many circus performers, he had a way of bringing audiences into his work, instead of shutting them out. Whereas other circus performers often seemed sullen or uncommunicative, he wore an immutable smile that told audiences how much fun he was having and invited them to share his joy.

Gunther would invariably joke with the cage boys and elephant men during his act, which only added to that feeling of nonchalance and made each performance seem as if he were improvising the entire thing on the spot. And yet despite the casual air with which it was all carried off, his performance was simply extraordinary.

The informal relationship he seemed to have with the people who worked for him, at least while he was in the ring, projected a sense of humor and charm that managed to reach every seat in the house. Every move he made, no matter how small or offhand, added to the impact this consummate performer registered in the arena. So awe inspiring was the effect he created I could hardly believe that the 5-foot, 4-inch man who showed up for my first interview with Gunther Gebel-Williams was actually the man himself. In the arena, instead of being dwarfed by its size, he grew in stature and gave the impression of being nearly seven feet tall.

Even in his retirement, it was a commonly held belief, with a good deal of truth behind it, that Gunther could walk into the arena wearing a black jump suit and every eye would go to him. He had the special charisma of a person who knew he was good at what he did, or as his boss Kenneth Feld put it, "When he walked into a room, even if you didn't know who he was, you knew he was somebody."

Reviewing a filmed tribute he had made to honor his retired star, Feld observed, "He always had a smile. You couldn't capture him in a bad look because he didn't have one. He had so much joy when he was out there performing. That's what came across. It was honest."[6]

The effect Gunther had on audiences is somewhat surprising given his own admission of preferring the company of animals to people. But the truth is he wasn't nearly as inept at dealing with people as he tried to make others believe. He just didn't give himself credit for the innumerable acts of kindness and patience he showed toward fans and individual members of the audience.

"I think Gunther was a guy searching for love," Feld says. His personal history is something of a classic Freudian casebook. More or less abandoned by both parents who showed little or no interest or affection toward him, he attempted to compensate with a string of surrogate father figures and animals. "The purest love is from animals," Feld points out. "You give and you get. There's nothing else. No ulterior motives. He knew that. So that was one thing. The other thing was he wanted that adoration from an audience. He made you love him. When you sat in the audience and watched him, you loved him. It wasn't like, 'Oh, this guy is great.' It was that you fell in love with him."[7]

Gunther gave 12,000 performances, never missing a show. In Madison Square Garden he posted a record 1,191. To compile such numbers meant not only did the show have to go on, so did he, no matter what. This single-mindedness is amply illustrated by a story told by Kenneth Feld:

"In the late '70s I was in Lima, Peru, with my father, and we got a call from the show, which was coming into Memphis, Tennessee. At the time Gunther was training some lions, actually, young lions, and he went to check on them when the train was stopped just outside of Memphis. After checking on the animals he ran back to his own car and as he jumped on the train, he stepped on the coupling, and his foot got caught in it as the train started to move. Someone must have yelled, because they stopped the train, and they pulled his foot out. The doctors actually thought at first that they might have to take the foot off. It was totally smashed.

"We were to open in Memphis the next day, and by the time we got to the show—I couldn't believe it—he was all bandaged up in this huge bandage, so he couldn't do the tiger act. There was no way he could do that. But he did the elephant act. He sat in a folding chair right in front of ring two on the other side of the track behind the footlights. The spotlights hit him, and he was in a tuxedo, and his foot was propped up, and he had a microphone, and he was yelling commands to the elephants. They came in, all nineteen or twenty of them and did the whole routine. And all the while they were looking around to see where he was, knowing that his presence was there in his voice. He worked the elephant act for the next couple of weeks like that, and he was able to recover.

"His work ethic was just extraordinary. He never missed a performance even though sometimes he was sick as a dog. Sometimes he would come out of the cage just shaking with the flu or something. And then to think about what this guy did—to train an act with twenty leopards while you're on the road, in your spare time, that was something."[8]

But it wasn't just the animals that took precedence in Gunther's life. The circus and the animals were really one entity. "As far as the circus was concerned," Sigrid affirms, "we [his family] always had to step back. The circus came first. If it wasn't the animals, it was interviews or a film; anything for the show came first. We never made a fuss over it. We all stood by him and around him to make him happy."[9]

Gunther Gebel-Williams's legacy, however, amounts to far more than all the performances he racked up, the stardom and celebrity he achieved. He changed the way the public thinks about the circus and the way the profession thinks about animal training.

★ ★ ★

In America, the few circus families that have prevailed, have tended, like the Ringlings, to be entrepreneurs rather than performers, and few have been successful over successive generations. In Europe, however, the most prominent circus families are usually both artists and entrepreneurs, and they have long histories spread over many generations.

One of France's renowned circus dynasties is the family Gruss. Its patriarch, Alexis Gruss Jr., is credited with having revitalized the circus in France in 1974 with the founding of Conservatoire National des Arts du Cirque, which he created with Silvia Montfort. It was the first circus school in the western world. To celebrate two hundred years of circus in France, he also created *Cirque Gruss à l'ancienne* (the old-fashioned circus). Its success was based on a unity of style that grew out of the simple fact that most of the people in the show were members of the Gruss family.

Alexis's elder son, Stephan Gruss, explains the family's continued success by pointing out that the traditions of circus are passed on from generation to generation, and one of the most important traditions is that the circus is made up of families. The family Gruss is driven by an especially strong esprit de corps. One doesn't have to be a Gruss to be part of the family. The spirit exists in all members of the troupe. It is this spirit that explains why the troupe works so well together and produces such good material.

The family consists of Alexis Gruss Jr. and his wife, Gipsy, who are great circus artists, and who have passed on their knowledge and their skill to others in the family. Alexis is especially good with horses. He has taught his children how to work with horses so that they are free, but at the same time anxious to perform. He has also trained all members of the troupe to do acrobatics on horses.

Gipsy is the director of the performances and is teaching that skill to her daughter, Maude. The younger brother, Firmin, is a jockey; he works on the freestanding ladder and juggles in many numbers and works the family's elephant. Stephan's wife, Nathalie, is also involved and becoming more accomplished in some numbers such as her foot juggling feature.[10]

Basically Cirque Gruss is an equestrian show. For the family Gruss, Stephan points out, the circus means especially horses. They have no exotic animals, but for one elephant and a camel. There are no hippos or giraffes. Ninety percent of what the family does is with horses. At present there are more than fifty horses of various breeds in the Gruss stables at Piolenc, in the south of France.

In their off-season home in the Provence region, the family has built a combination training facility, recreation center, and circus museum. They are here, in this semitropical retreat in the south of France, from April until September, offering tours, daily demonstrations, and weekend performances. It is the place where the family has put down roots. Stephan explains that his father wanted such a place for two reasons. First he wanted a permanent home, where he could raise the consciousness of the public about the circus because there is not much time to establish such a relationship when they are traveling. And it is here that the special spirit is nurtured among the members of the troupe and the animals and all the ancillary members of the company. It is the perfect setting to live together as a family. It is also beneficial for the horses. It is wonderful not to have to pick up the family and move all the time. Being in a stable environment for six months allows the Gruss family to perfect their acts.[11]

Although the family's circus carries the phrase "old-fashioned" in its title, Stephan is quick to point out that a traditional circus doesn't mean that it keeps only to archaic ideas. The Gruss circus builds on traditions and continually keeps evolving for the times. It uses the traditions of the past to build a life in the present times. Having to create a new performance every year forces the family to be more creative, to keep up-to-date with costuming, music, and more exciting presentations.[12]

★ ★ ★

One of America's greatest native-born aerialists is Dolly Jacobs, daughter of Lou Jacobs, the Ringling clown whose face became synonymous with American clowning.[13] She has been called a goddess thanks to the beauty of her aerial act. But her circus career did not start out so heavenly. She made her show business debut at the age of four, appearing as the rear end of a giant dachshund. It was a disaster. She tripped and fell, losing her costume and any hope of following in her father's famous footsteps.

Although it was quite a few years before she felt confident enough to show her face in public again, that humiliation was not the end of her performing career. Far from it. All it proved, Dolly says now, "was that I was born with wings and feathers rather than a funny bone."[14]

The wings, it turns out, ironically came from her mother, Jean, who joined the Ringling show in 1948, putting aside a promising career as a professional model with the Conover Agency. On May 5, 1948, in Madison Square Garden, however, Jean fell during the Monte Carlo aerial ballet and never returned to the show as a performer. It would be up to her daughter to wear the feathers of flight.

But over the years Dolly learned a thing or two about winning and holding an arena's attention from her dad. "I learned from him, watching him, how he stood out. He was incomparable. I wanted to be the same," she says, thinking back to the time when she first joined the same circus in which her dad had become a star clown. "After spending five years as a showgirl, I knew I wanted to be a solo artist and be different. Instead of blending in, I wanted to be unique."[15]

In the year 2000, she was at something of a crossroads in her career. She believed she might still have a few good years left as a performer, depending on her recovery from back surgery. In addition to her signature piece on the Roman rings, which made her famous, she had also developed a pas de deux on the straps, originally with Pedro Reis, her partner in the founding of Circus Sarasota, and currently with Yuri Rijov. That act, since it is less demanding physically, may extend her performing life a bit. But more important to her is the project she has undertaken with Pedro. Together they are hoping to preserve the circus heritage of Sarasota, Florida, both by bringing the city's unique history to new prominence and by training the circus performers of the future. In so doing, looking backward and ahead simultaneously, she hopes to preserve her father's place in circus history, honoring not only the profession he so enriched, but his place in that history.

"When you lose your heritage you become less rich," Dolly believes. "So we are striving to get the general public to appreciate the history that is here and to preserve it through the education of future performers."

Dolly knows firsthand what Sarasota once was. She grew up there, attending public schools, rather than traveling with her father. "I had a normal life and education growing up," she recalls. "Both my sister and I swam competitively. I studied ballet and gymnastics. The majority of the kids in my circle of friends were circus kids. So I enjoyed both worlds. I was in Sailor Circus, an after-school program, when I was very young in the tumbling and group aerial displays."

She joined Ringling as a showgirl when she was fourteen years old. "At the time the Flying Gaonas were on the same unit, and Chela Gaona talked to me about filling in for her at some performances." That arrangement did not work out at the time, but, as Dolly points out, "I always had my eye on flying, only I wanted to do it solo."

In addition to her desire to be a soloist, there was also an independent streak that made her determined to be a star. "I always did everything on my own," she says. "I worked on my act on my own, and I had to start from scratch." In her first effort at achieving her goal, she bought the rigging for a low-wire act, but she had no one to teach her the required skills.

When Dolly graduated from high school, her godmother, Margie Geiger, who had performed on the Roman rings, started training Dolly on the single trap. Eventually Margie convinced her to try the rings.

"Once I found the swinging rings, I found the freedom I was looking for. I practiced for three or four months, two sessions a day, three to four hours in the morning and another two to three in the afternoon. By the time Margie arrived for practice I was already warmed up, so it was intensive work for those several hours. I was nineteen years old, and whenever I worked without having anyone else around, I kept a clown horn handy to use as an alarm if I needed help."[16]

Dolly did her own act on the show for the first time in 1976. A few years later, she joined the Farfans' flying act, appearing in both at the same time. "I did a two and a half, a one-and-a-half layout, the shoot-over in the passing leap, and a triple to the net. It was quite rigorous doing both acts and practicing between shows," but she had truly taken wing and loved it.

To earn the center ring she was determined to accomplish a trick she had read about, but had never seen anyone else do. "It took a long time to convince people to help me learn to do the somersault to the web (a full flyaway somersault.) Everyone thought it was too dangerous. I learned mostly by trial and error. When I auditioned it for the Felds, everyone in the show came out to watch. They were all very supportive. I was a solo act from that time on. It was a big step in my career."

Dolly says she is now at the point in her career where she doesn't have to think about what she's doing, and "I can totally enjoy it." So what does she think about when she in the air? "I imagine myself in the ballet. It taught me the ABCs of grace and poise and form. I continue using that. And I imagine things that have moved me the most."

After achieving center ring solo status, Dolly stayed on with the Ringling show, in part to look after her parents. She left after the 1984 tour when her father semiretired from clowning. "I needed to grow and taste other places. I stayed a few extra years to take care of my dad, but by '84 I needed to be my own person."[17]

She next went to the Big Apple Circus. "They were doing a kind of 1890s show. I had never been in a one-ring show before. I could see the faces of people in the audience; it was a chance for me to become more in touch with them as individuals." That intimacy gave her the opportunity to be less exaggerated and more refined as an artist. "I had to tone down my makeup, for one thing," she remembers. She also enjoyed being on her own, having grass under her feet and having the privacy of her own trailer. "I thought I had died and gone to heaven." As it turned out the Flying Gaonas were also on the Big Apple at that time, and Dolly finally got a chance to fly with them, filling in for Chela in the morning shows.

Next it was off to Europe for the winter shows in London and Munich among other major cities. "That was another form of growth. They have a different perception of the circus there," Dolly emphasizes. "I found a new respect as a circus artist, not only from the audience, but from the people I was working for as well.

"I was in Germany in '87. I loved Germany. My roots are there. I went back to Monte Carlo in '88. Jeannette Williams, acting as my agent, contracted me there."[18]

Except for Williams's efforts on her behalf, Dolly was doing her own bookings. She had no exclusive agent. "I was shy at first, but learned to speak up. As a woman in the circus, you do everything. You have many roles besides performer and wife and mother or caregiver. You do your music, costumes, rigging, negotiate. My dad was very soft-spoken; I had to speak up for him. So I learned."

She is still learning new skills. "I'm a born student," she says. She has become the spokesperson for Circus Sarasota, whose goal is "to put the circus back on the artistic level where it was meant to be." Her partner, Pedro Reis, had joined the Ringling Blue Unit for the '84–'85 tour. Reis was with an act called the Survivors, an aerial act that originated in South Africa. "I really admired the act," Dolly recalls. "I was in awe of what they did. I thought it really took guts to do those things over a concrete floor, especially for Pedro. In between seasons we were both practicing at the Sailor Circus facility, and we became friends."[19]

Pedro, she points out, has been thinking about starting a school for many years. He is not from a circus family, but learned his flying skills at a YMCA in Cape Town, South Africa. An accident eventually forced him to stop performing. "It was an opportunity," as Dolly sees it, "to start pursuing his dream at a younger age. I support him and believe in him in every way. I let him do the business; you can't have two bosses." But she shares his dream of preserving the artistry of the circus and the passion that artists like her father had for it.

Many opportunities seem to lie ahead. "Sometimes things fall into your lap and change you," she observes. "For me it's been a pleasure because I'm able to talk to strangers about the people who enriched my life and the lives of others. I don't know where my road is leading, but it is in the right direction. It's what you leave in the hearts of others that counts, not how much money you made."[20]

★ ★ ★

Sylvia Zerbini also grew up in the circus, but it was her appearance in Kenneth Feld's *Barnum's Kaleidoscape* that made her a true star. Prior to that engagement she had always presented her two acts, the trapeze and the liberty horses, as separate entities. When she combined them, it was as if she were finally integrating the two aspects of her personality that had formerly run parallel.

"You belong in the air," her father, Tarzan Zerbini, insisted whenever Sylvia, still a youngster, begged for a horse of her own.

It was always her sister Pat who got to work with the elephants and horses. This was not, however, a simple case of sibling rivalry. Sylvia just had a thing for horses. "I always wanted horses," she confesses. "I've got pictures of when I was six years old leading Johnny Herriott's ponies into the ring. But my father was always saying, 'You don't belong with animals.'"

Sylvia spent her childhood watching her father train and present lions and tigers, while her mother, Jacqueline Zerbini, worked a spectacular trapeze act. "So I grew up around both," Sylvia recalls. "My backyard had animals and a trapeze hanging from a crane bar, so I always played around on the trapeze like all circus kids do. You know, playing flying act off the ladders and so on, and I always helped with the animals."

But sister Pat was considered the tough one of the girls. She went into the cage with her father and was given animals of her own, like a Lipizzaner, to train. "They kept giving me costumes and a web and a trapeze, and I kept practicing my aerial work."

The practice obviously paid off. Sylvia has been performing on the trapeze, in front of an audience, since she was fourteen. "My dad decided he wanted eight girls on single trapezes. He put all these trapezes up, and I begged him, 'Please let me work.'"

She got the usual parental brush-off. "Okay, okay," he finally agreed just so she'd stop pestering him. Everybody in the act did a similar routine, but Sylvia finished on her own. Once in the show she began adding new tricks every year, creating the aerial routines for the girls and devising their choreography.

Finally, when she was sixteen, Sylvia got a horse of her own and taught it everything that she could think of having it do. "I didn't present it in the show or anything, but I brought it on the road. It was like a pleasure horse."

When she was not on the road, the horse was boarded at a local stable, and "I was your typical horse girl; I would go there after school and take riding lessons."[21]

Today Sylvia Zerbini takes her stable on the road, but she is as much in love with her horses as when she was in school. She tends to their grooming, bathing, and feeding, braiding their tails every night. "Horses have always been my love, so I'm pretty fortunate to be calling this a job because it's something I've always wanted to do."

Eventually her dad purchased a troupe of liberty horses and brought Daniel Suskow in from France to break the act and hopefully present it on her dad's show. One thing was sure. They were not going to be presented by Sylvia. "My dad just absolutely did not want me on that side of the circus." But there was no way he could keep her from those horses. "I was there helping Daniel with the lunges and everything. That's how I got introduced to the basics of horse training. I was the only one who knew them other than Daniel and his daughter, Sandrine."

Suskow started the act, and then, as fate would have it, he got a contract with Ringling. It was agreed that he would go off for a short period of time, and then return to finish training the horses. In the midst of all this, however, he was called back to France and unable to return.

"He called me from France," Sylvia remembers, "and he explained that he was no longer in the States. But he assured me that I would be able to finish with the horses. He promised to talk me through whatever problems I might have." At this point Tarzan had little choice but to turn the horses over to his daughter, "and then," she says with a laugh, "I had to prove that I was capable of doing all this."

Today she says that it was Suskow who taught her horse sense. "I actually finished breaking the horses over the phone. I'd run into a problem, and I'd be on the phone hysterically calling France. And this was before cell phones. We had a pay phone in my dad's winter quarters in the barn, and I was on my own. I had one groom and six green horses that were very young and frisky. I'd call him and explain the problems I was having with number two or three, and he would tell me how to correct it over the phone."

Since the horses had been trained by the French-speaking Suskow, Sylvia continued speaking to them in their "native tongue." Today, even though the original horses are gone, she still talks to her horses in French.

Suskow may have taught her the basics of horse training, but, she adds, "My lead horse, Oran, taught me how to train the rest of the horses. I was twenty-two years old at the time." Prior to that she had only worked with her own riding horse and never in the ring.[22]

Now, Sylvia Zerbini presents two beautiful acts, one in the air and one in the ring with eight horses. When she first found out that Feld wanted her to do her two acts back-to-back, starting in the air, she began practicing her aerial work and then jumping directly into the ring to work the horses to build her stamina. "That seemed to help me quite a bit," she says, "but the hardest thing was the mental part. It still is."

A half-hour to forty-five minutes before going up on the single trap, she prepares herself in the same manner as many stage actresses. "I don't like to talk to anybody and just prepare myself for the act. I want the feeling to come across that I'm really enjoying myself, and that I love what I'm doing. And in order to feel this I have to block everything out, so I need thirty minutes where I don't talk to anybody and just listen to music and stretch. That's my little thing. And with the horses coming in right afterwards, I had a hard time blocking everything out and relaxing during the trap act because I was thinking, 'Okay number two did this and number three did that.' I had a hard time blocking them out, but now I got it down pat, so I'm set."[23]

"Horses are tough animals to work with," she continues. "I don't work with harnesses. I wanted to do The Big E [before moving on to the Ringling arena show] because I needed to use harnesses on the horses. They were new. They'd never been exposed to lights and music; they're a new bunch together. I knew there was going to be kicking and biting, and that little bit of restraint was going to help tremendously in getting them to focus on me and getting their cues instead of watching each other.

"During the first week I worked them with harnesses, and then they were doing really well, so I started taking the harnesses off and since everything was still new they were really focused on me. By the third week there was still a problem with number four, so I had eight horses in the ring and one of them had a harness on him. He's three years old, and he's a little stud, and so human-like. He is so smart; it is unreal. I had to put a muzzle on him as well as a harness. With horses if you just once let them get away with something, [you're going to have a problem]. They get ring smart instantly. You practice them, and they'll do everything fine. Then you go in front of the audience, and they're like, 'No, we're not going to do it.'

"If you give up and let it go because you're presenting a show, it will be very difficult to get it back. So you want to make sure that you have it 100 percent before presenting it."

Much of her own movement in the ring seems highly choreographed. "I compare what I do to the difference between classical ballet and jazz dance. I'm probably not doing it right according to the experts, not handling the whips right. I move around a lot when I train, and I use my body to give a lot of cues, besides the verbal cues," she says describing her somewhat unorthodox style of presentation.[24]

In her debut with the big Ringling show, she was once again presenting her two specialties as one brilliant act. "I was hoping we would do something completely different. But they feel the aerial work and coming down into the horses is such a beautiful transition that Kenneth didn't want to lose it," she said prior to her first tour with Ringling. "At first I wanted to combine the whole thing. I wanted horses running in the ring and be swinging in the air at the same time. It was hard for me to get them to leave that aerial into the horse thing. I'm assuming it's because they feel people are not expecting me to come off my trapeze and start working with horses. So there is that element of surprise. Originally I wanted to come swinging in on my lyre and have all my liberty horses roaming around in all three rings and then come down and get to it. I have a creative imagination.[25]

"The thing about the lyre is you can take it a lot higher in the coliseums than you can a single trapeze. I don't work very high on the trapeze, about twenty-five feet and that's it. The lyre I'll take up higher. I'm looking forward to being able to do that because if you work thirty-five or forty-five feet in the air, it's more impressive."[26]

Riding and aerial work, she points out, actually work against each other insofar as conditioning her body is concerned. On horseback her muscles are contracted and tight, whereas on trapeze she has to get the muscles stretched out. So there is a conflict between the two acts in their physical demands. Although her formal dance training is limited to jazz, her stretching exercises are reminiscent of a ballet dancer's workout. Much of the work is done at a dance barre. Other exercises require the use of weights.

After falling from the trapeze during the previews of *Kaleidoscape*, she was afforded the luxury of a masseuse for a few months during her recovery. It was wonderful, she says somewhat dreamily. "To be able to work without pain is wonderful and a rarity."[27]

★ ★ ★

Undoubtedly the most heralded flying act of our time and arguably the best such act of all time, the Flying Cranes was created by the Russian Vilen Golovko.[28]

Watching this act in performance, however, one has little sense of the dogged determination, sacrifice, and pain it took to achieve such perfection. Each movement has the beauty, grace, and ease of the inevitable. But that, after all, is what art is supposed to be all about—making what we are seeing look effortless, as if it had come to the artist in one magnificent burst of inspiration. In the case of the Flying Cranes nothing could be further from the truth.

Although his father, after whom Vilen is named, was one of the most important men in the Soviet circus (he staged the opening ceremonies for the 1980 Olympics and the 1986 Goodwill Games), the young Golovko did not begin his circus training until he was thirteen years old. Prior to that he had been a wrestler.

He has subsequently followed that tradition with his own son, who did not begin taking gymnastic lessons from one of the men in his father's act until he was thirteen. "Children should have time to be children," he says.[29]

After attending Russia's circus school, where he was trained as a performer, Golovko entered The National Institute for Theatre Arts, roughly the equivalent of America's Juilliard, where, in addition to working on advanced degrees in music, theatre, ballet, and opera, one could also earn a degree in the production of circus and theatre spectacles. It was a very elite program, and during the period of the '70s when Golovko attended, a tremendous creative energy prevailed. Among Vilen's classmates at the time were Valentin Gneushev, whose work is featured in chapter 1, and Pavel Brun, who worked for Cirque du Soleil in Las Vegas and is the cocreator of the aerial high bar act in *Mystère*. He now works for Franco Dragone in his studio in Belgium.

Of the school's three star pupils at that time, Golovko is generally conceded to have been the most gifted. He remained in school until he was nineteen and then entered the Soviet army. He was discharged in 1979, at the age of twenty-one. Upon his return to civilian life he first created a trapeze act, which he sent out on tour while he stayed home to create the Flying Cranes with his father and Piotr Maestrenko.

As it turned out, this remarkable act was to be the last great artistic achievement of the Soviet circus into which the government and circus bureaucracy poured all of its best resources unstintingly. Specialists in every field were brought in as consultants. More than 300 drawings were used in the design of the rigging.

The rigging ultimately devised by Maestrenko is vital to the act's success. Whereas the standard flying frame has room for one flyer and one catcher at a time, the Flying Cranes' rig uses two catchers and several positions from which flyers may leap. In addition there are several electronic winches that pull the flyers aloft. This allows for an uninterrupted series of flights, many of them overlapping, and all of them completely choreographed and breathtakingly exciting, both visually and technically.

There are some who criticize the use of winches, as if they were somehow comparable to the mechanical advantage gained by mechanics (or lunges), but since the winches simply substitute for climbing rope ladders, they hardly seem like a form of cheating. It's the difference between climbing stairs and taking an elevator. There's no trick involved in either case. One just happens to get you where you're going faster and is accomplished a great deal more artfully.

The flyers, mainly recruited from the field of gymnastics, trained and rehearsed for more than four years at government expense. The act made its debut on May 25, 1988. Eventually it came to America that same year and won the attention and kudos of the world, thanks to the exposure it was afforded by the American media.

After the breakup of the Soviet Union, the government simply withdrew its support of all performing artists, and many circus acts fell apart, unable to support themselves. Having absolutely no concept of marketing, being unfamiliar with contract negotiations, and desperate for work in order to survive, Russian circus performers found themselves at the mercy of producers and many acts disbanded. The period from 1992–1994 was a particularly trying time for Golovko as well, but he was determined to keep the Flying Cranes together, whatever the cost. He took what work he could find and paid the ten artists and various technicians in his company out of his own earnings.

One of his assignments was staging the stunts for the Police Academy show in the Soviet Union. Because of his international renown, he also had many offers from outside the Soviet Union. He was invited to work for Cirque du Soleil, and did so for a short period. He was invited to teach at the circus school in Montreal, but declined. He staged a water show in Soviet Union, and when there was no work he borrowed money at usury rates just so the Flying Cranes would be able to stay together and survive. "Freedom is expensive," he says rather dryly. "Especially in Russia."[30]

By 1998, only six of the original ten artists remained with the act. One of these was no longer able to fly, having sustained permanent injuries from a fall. One more, fifteen-year-old Tanya Klepatsky, who has been described as the Tara Lipinsky of the flying trapeze, was added as an understudy for Golovko's ex-wife, Elena, who was still with the act but married to catcher Michael Iliushkin. She will always be in the act, Golovko explains, because "the artistic marriage remains, and art is higher than personal relationships." The artists are supported by four technicians, and by 1998, when the troupe was appearing in *Aireus* at the Hilton Hotel in Reno, Nevada, the extended family of dependents had grown to thirty-one persons of various ages.

While at the Reno Hilton, all fifteen members of the troupe worked out for three hours each afternoon, from two to five, on stage before their evening performance. Most of their time was spent limbering up and staying in shape. Toward the end of their session, they worked on the Russian swing in preparation for a new act that Golovko was developing and eventually ended up on The Greatest Show on Earth. Here, too, the pain and personal commitment it has taken, not only to keep the act together, but also to maintain its level of artistry, are fully evident. At least three members of the troupe were then working out minor injuries. At the time Golovko participated in this interview, he was to have arthroscopic surgery on his knee the next morning. He predicted that he would be back in the act in ten days.[31] And so he was.

As a result of this kind of devotion to their work, the troupe's performance was virtually flawless. All the same moves and tricks were still there, but the music had changed somewhat. What was most amazing is how well they all knew and used the music. They knew when to enter in order to catch the musical phrasing at just the right moment so that it would carry them through each climax.

Golovko has no permanent residence. He lived in Reno for two years while the Cranes appeared in the Reno Hilton. He lives where he works, he says, although he is anxious to get his green card so that he will be able to continue working in America. To win this status he must be designated an "extraordinary talent." It would seem that the creation and survival of the Flying Cranes are triumphs of determination and artistic integrity that more than amply demonstrate the required talent for such status.[32]

Time and economics, however, eventually forced the temporary dissolution of the Flying Cranes. There was not enough work to keep the aging company together. Working on his own, Golovko was hired to create a flying act for the 132nd edition of Ringling Bros. and Barnum & Bailey Circus. His experience in this new milieu is documented in the case study of that production.

In 2005 Golovko reconstituted the Flying Cranes with an all-new company that debuted in Moscow. The new troupe consistently throws a quadruple somersault.

★ ★ ★

One of the latest trends in the new circus movement is the creation of specialized spectacle—exclusively equestrian, acrobatic, or juggling. The newest outcropping of this trend is the all-aerial performance of the French company known as Les Arts Sauts.[33] Its first production, entitled *Kayassine*, appeared in New York in 1999, as part of the Lincoln Center Summer Festival, at the same site occupied by the Big Apple Circus's big top when it is in residence at the art center.

Founded in 1993, Les Arts Sauts grew from the original troupe of six to a company of twenty-five, including twelve "trapezists" and thirteen others, which includes musicians, a vocalist, and technicians. Together, the twenty-five function as a collective. That means they all have an equal voice in what they do and how they do it. There is, to quote the program notes, "no hierarchy." Pressed on the issue, however, the group will admit that a director, Hervé Lelardoux, came in to provide "an outside eye" and to suggest the order in which events might be placed, but presumably his suggestions had to be agreed to by all the members of the collective. That may be why the performance sometimes seems so difficult to follow.

The first section of the group's performance is exceedingly studied. Here the only woman in the company languorously entwines herself in a silk ribbon that may seem more like a birth sling than a piece of drapery or cloud swing, taking a great deal of time between moves and positions. That goes on for quite some time as several male bodies, scrunched over into fetal balls, descend from the ceiling and hang, more or less motionlessly, in place. In the meantime, the soprano, whose voice has a lovely haunting quality, is vocalizing. Although the sounds she produces have no relationship to any human language, the effect is certainly not unpleasant, even if it does tend to sound like vocal doodling.

Perhaps the most exciting moment of the performance comes when the steel structure that supports the flying rig is raised from the ground to the aerial position. The rig contains a fly board, a fly bar with a cradle above it, a swinging cradle for the catcher, a second cradle seldom used, and places for the musicians. Those waiting their turns to fly skitter above the rig into various holding or resting positions.

While the flying is technically demanding, there seems to have been no thought given to building the level of skill as the performance progresses. There are exciting moments every so often, but the arrangement of the flights, despite the "outside eye," seems rather random. The flyers also incorporate various styles in their individual performances, from crabbed to extended. In all cases the emphasis seems to be on expressing the joy of flight. Even when a flyer misses and lands in the net, he acts as if he is having great fun.

All of this brings to mind the inevitable comparison with the Flying Cranes. In their fifteen-minute performance, the Cranes manage to use their extraordinary skill, daring, and theatricality to bring drama, poetry, and true excitement to their performance. In contrast the performance of Les Arts Sauts is slow and more considered.

What is truly unique about the performance is the manner in which the spectators are treated. There is only one entrance, and because of the physics of the structure, each member of the audience must force his way through a blast of air by squeezing through two pieces of inflated rubber that resemble two giant inner tubes. The same procedure must be followed on the way out.

Once again the birth image comes to mind. Once inside, the audience is seated in reclining lounge chairs with a headrest, putting one into a posture that is comfortable enough to remain looking upward for the eighty minutes of the performance.

The space in which the performance takes place is also fascinating, if not very cheerful. It is an inflatable dome that is anchored in place by thousands of gallons of water that are placed in several continuous tubes that run around the base of the dome.

Whatever the effect of its performance, Les Arts Sauts has taken the circus into a new realm where the exploration of a new means of presentation makes important contributions to the future development of circus.

★ ★ ★

We have heard much of late about horse whisperers. Bartabas, the man who is the founder and director of the French equestrian theatre known as Zingaro, however, says he is a horse listener. Prior to the New York opening of his production of *Chimère* in 1998, the then 41-year-old artist spoke to the *New York Times* of his fourteen years association with his unique equestrian spectacle.

"The more I plunge into the relationship of humans with horses, the more it seems to resemble the relationship between human beings. That's the universal side of our work," he told the interviewer. "The horse for me is like a mirror."[34]

Bartabas, who is known simply by the single name, says that his inspiration springs from working with the nearly three dozen horses stabled at the theatre's home in Aubervilliers on the outskirts of Paris, where the humans and horses of the troupe live together in an almost bohemian existence.

Bartabas's sometimes controversial methods of training are not in the tradition of the classical schools of dressage like the Spanish Riding School in Vienna. To begin with he does not select horses for their breeding or looks, but rather for their personality (much like Valentin Gneushev selects his human pupils). Nor does he look for horses of a certain age. And, although Zingaro is a theatre, the horses are not selected for particular roles that must be filled in a particular show.

Despite such protestations, however, Bartabas had at that time already acquired six horses of a particular look—cream-colored Portuguese horses with distinctive blue eyes—for his show, which opened in the fall of 1999.

In contrasting his methods with those of dressage, Bartabas explains that in classical training, horses are under permanent control. "They are taught mechanically to do something very specific." That is the opposite of how he works. "We're not there to show how well we ride the horses. My aim is to bring out the personality of the horses as you might with people, to let the horses express themselves. Movements are proposed," he says, "never imposed."

In terms of training, therefore, Bartabas would best be described as a listener rather than a whisperer. "My work is to learn to hear them and what they want to say."

In attempting to explain his methods further, he says, "A dancer or a musician can suffer for hours on end because he knows why he is suffering. But a horse cannot suffer. When you work a horse, you have to go in stages until he finally gives you the movement. If the movement involves pain, he will resist and remember. You have to listen to each horse because what works for one does not work for another. There is no single method."[35]

Despite the criticism of his methods in some equestrian quarters, Bartabas was named the director of the Academy of Equestrian Arts housed in the stables of Versailles when it reopened in February of 2003 after having been closed for nearly 200 years. Zingaro's twenty Portuguese Lusitanian horses have taken up residence here, and ten hand-picked students have begun training in the equestrian arts as well as music, drawing, dance, and fencing.[36]

★ ★ ★

Each of the performers in the above discussion represents a distinguished level of artistic achievement. If their work has proven to be provocative and stimulating, it is because they have all pursued their art through a creative process that is every bit as demanding, imaginative, and thoughtful as those of their fellow artists in the other performing arts.

NOTES

1. Joyce Wadler. "Still Bringing Out the Animal, and Animals," *New York Times* (April 9, 1999): B2.

2. Ernest Albrecht. "Splashy Circus Spectacular a Treat for One, All," *Home News* (April 2, 1969): 23.

3. Wadler.

4. Sigrid Gebel, telephone interview with the author, September 21, 2001.

5. Ernest Albrecht. "Gebel-Williams Makes a Circus a CIRCUS," *Home News* (March 27, 1975): 16.

6. Kenneth Feld, personal interview with the author, Vienna, Va., September 17, 2001.

7. Feld interview.

8. Feld interview.

9. Gebel interview.

10. Stephan Gruss, personal interview with the author, Piolenc, France, July 8, 1999, translated by Dominique Jando.

11. Gruss interview.

12. Gruss interview.

13. Dolly Jacobs, personal interview with the author, Sarasota, Fla., August 5, 2000.

14. Jacobs interview.

15. Jacobs interview.

16. Jacobs interview.

17. Jacobs interview.

18. Dolly Jacobs appeared in the Monte Carlo festival twice. Her first engagement there was in 1977. She is here speaking of her second appearance. On both occasions she won the "*le dame du cirque*" award. She also won a silver clown in 1988, presented to her by Prince Albert.

19. Jacobs interview.

20. Jacobs interview.

21. Sylvia Zerbini, personal interview with the author, West Springfield, Mass., September 29, 2001.

22. Zerbini interview, September 29, 2001.

23. Sylvia Zerbini, personal interview with the author, Williston, Fla., November 12, 2001.

24. Zerbini interview, September 29, 2001.

25. Zerbini finally achieved her ambition and presented her new act as she envisioned it here in her second Ringling tour.

26. Zerbini interview, November 12, 2001.

27. Zerbini interview, November 12, 2001.

28. Vilen Golovko, personal interview with the author, Reno, Nev., November 14, 1998.

29. Golovko interview.

30. Golovko interview.

31. Golovko interview.

32. Golovko interview.

33. Ernest Albrecht. "Can an All-Aerial Circus Fly?" *Spectacle* (Summer 1999): 34.

34. Alan Riding. "Using the Horse to Hold a Mirror to the Human," *New York Times* (September 6, 1998): 20.

35. Riding.

36. Corrine LaBalme. "The Dancing Horses of Versailles," *New York Times* (March 2, 2003): TR 3.

· *9* ·

Clowns on Clowning

$\mathcal{N}$ot content merely with producing pratfalls, the clowns of the contemporary circus are quite possibly the most thoughtful of all circus artists; after all, being funny doesn't just happen. As a result, clowning in the contemporary circus has changed more radically than any other of the circus arts.

When Larry Pisoni, the cofounder of the Pickle Family Circus, first joined the San Francisco Mime Troupe, that most influential group of street performers, he sat down with Joan Holden, the troupe's resident playwright and announced, "All I want to do is make people laugh."

"Fine," Holden replied, unimpressed, "but what about your politics?"

What indeed?! Politics or, to put it another way, one's view of the world, may be the one quality that separates great clowning from good clowning, and good clowning from making a clown of oneself.

By the time Pisoni had reached the half-century mark, he had come to the conclusion that "making people laugh is no longer my number one motivation. If that is all there is to it, then I ought to look elsewhere [for work]." Now, he says, his purpose is to "inspire." A circus, he adds, "like a good meal, should be complete, not just dessert. The circus ought to be working toward inspiring that ecstatic experience. It is a joyful experience. A clown should add to that." He should add something more than providing a distraction when the rigging needs to be changed.[1]

In attempting to make the distinction between the three levels of clowning, the Russian clown Slava Polunin, interviewed while he was appearing with Cirque du Soleil's *Alegria*, had the following to say about his profession: "Basically there are three types of clowns. The first is the [contemporary] Ringling style clown who is nothing more than a mask. He has no character. Then there are the older style clowns like Emmett Kelly, Lou Jacobs, and Coco

[Nikolai Poliakov]. They were much deeper. The third is characterized by the San Francisco Mime Troupe. They moved into the theatre. This type of clown wanted to leave the circus because it was behind the times. This type wanted to go forward."[2]

And what was it that made Emmett Kelly and Lou Jacobs deep? Both portrayed highly individualized, but recognizable, reactions to the human condition. Dressed in his tramp's rags, Kelly was the perpetual victim, who, no matter how he tried, could never win. One can find in Kelly's autobiography, *Clown*, a catalogue of the various "gags" he used throughout his career. In all instances, he ended up a loser, and his face always told us that he knew it.[3] Lou Jacobs, on the other, was often a victim of his own hubris. Judging from his makeup he always seemed triumphant. But what was it he was so proud of? Shooting a defenseless rabbit with a double-barreled shotgun at close range? Eventually even the rabbit got the best of him, escaping unscathed. Another tramp clown, Otto Griebling, knew he was a victim, too. How could he not? Just look at him: another bum. But rather than meekly submitting as Kelly did, he raged against his fate. He was loud and aggressive and in your face. What good did it do him? He ended up a loser just like Kelly.

In a society that worships youth, beauty, and strength, Barry Lubin's Grandma is old and weak and female. We may love her, but she is definitely one of society's underdogs. So when she takes on a starchy authority figure like a self-important ringmaster and wins a temporary victory by making him (or her, as it was in a recent instance) look foolish, we can share in the victory, because in our heart of hearts we all know we are losers, too, simply by virtue of the fact that we are human.

It would seem, then, that the secret of great clowning is that the clowns must remind us of ourselves. The clown must, in other words, be human. "In America, clowns are just beginning to make themselves human," Slava says. They are only just beginning to develop "a personality with problems and a psychology." He points to such people as Ronlin Forman, Bill Irwin, Avner the Eccentric, Geoff Hoyle, Bob Berky. "These are the people who make ideas."

Slava points out that the clowning in Russia has undergone a radical change in recent years. "There has been a long tradition of clowning and a lot of good clowns in the past," he says. "But in 1970, everything stopped. The old style didn't match what was going on in the other arts and the world. The clowns had not yet found a new style. The first one to do this was Leonid Yengibarov. He has shown the direction. He was the innovator. He began to do clown gags that were not funny, but very sad. They ended sadly. He felt that life was not funny any more. It was filled with pathos. He began doing what Buster Keaton and Charlie Chaplin had done in the movies. But he couldn't go too far because the circus was not ready for this kind of clowning. The audiences liked it, but the government didn't." *Politics* again!

When Slava decided to be a clown, he says, he couldn't watch anyone but Leonid Yengibarov. "He gave food for the brain. He understood how clowns were supposed to be now." What Slava came to understand is that people wanted to identify and become emotionally involved with their clowns. "They wanted to be able to live the situation the clown created. It was very symbolic for the time. Clowns tried to be a mirror of the political times. For example, there was a routine of a man talking to himself on the telephone, and the character he created was very lonely, very rigid, and very lost. Because of perestroika, people did not know what to do, how to live, which way to go. People were lost and confused. The public understood they were seeing themselves. They were living in their fantasy because they couldn't live in the real world, so they go and live in the fantasy world, just like the man on the telephone.

"In another very popular routine two men are standing in line and every time the first tries to do something, the man behind him says, 'No, you can't do that.' Clowns had rediscovered their voice, creating a new world of symbolic protest. The audience began to like it because it was like a mirror."

In the '70s, clowns left the circus. Now they are going back to circuses like Cirque du Soleil, and Éloize internationally; the Big Apple, the Pickles, Flora in America; Archaos, Plume, Roncalli, in Europe; and Oz in Australia. "There are," according to Slava's estimation, "about ten modern circuses where the clown can find his place and an audience."[4]

Although its potential is only now being fully explored, the circus, it would seem, provides a fertile field for comedy. The reason for that is circus clowns are surrounded by one display after another of complete and unambiguous triumph. Almost every act in the circus is a symbolic display of human achievement and victory over the human condition. In contrast there are the clowns. Unfortunately they have rarely been allowed to take advantage of this inescapable incongruity with its unlimited potential for comedy. This surely accounts for the great success of the parodies of the major acts offered by the clowns in Cirque du Soleil's *Dralion* and the Big Apple Circus's *Clowns Around Town*. Only one clown comes to mind who was consistently allowed to capitalize on that incongruity. And that, of course, was Emmett Kelly.

Kelly talks about how he had to convince John Murray Anderson, who was then staging the Ringling show, to allow him to work, as Pat Valdo, then Ringling's performance director, put it, "freelance," throughout the performance. Kelly also asked to be excused from any costume changes so as to afford himself a greater opportunity of establishing his "character."[5]

This failure to take advantage of the incongruity inherent in a circus performance is found all over the world. Slava points out that for the past twenty years, European clowns have been leaving the circus to work on the stage because there are more opportunities and possibilities for work where they have found a new philosophy.

In Europe, it should be noted, there is not the division between clowns and comedians that there is in America. That is why Slava started his clowning career working in small experimental theatres akin to New York's off-Broadway model La Mama. He had a troupe of about fifteen clowns who worked as an ensemble, much like the San Francisco Mime Troupe. "Audiences liked our spirit very much," he recalls. "At the time the people needed this form of social protest. Gorbachev was in power. The people were tired. They wanted to fight, but couldn't. Who was there to fight? And how?" So they turned to their clowns in whose performances they could find relief for their frustrations.

In 1982, Slava organized a festival, Mime Parade, which he likens to Woodstock. Eight hundred performers showed up. When they saw what Slava was doing, "it was like an explosion. They understood that abstract mime was very limited."

When he decided to work in the circus, he locked himself up in a small village and created a one-man show. His performance in Cirque du Soleil's *Alegria* was a small piece of work that came out of that self-imposed exile.

When asked what inspires him, Slava smiles and shrugs. "Life's experiences," he says. And then to satisfy his questioner, he adds, "Thinking, observing, art, philosophy, music, painting, the plays of other people. My favorite director is the American Robert Wilson. I enjoy the work of the German choreographer Pina Bausch, the Buto Dance Co., Japanese art, Fellini, Buster Keaton and Charlie Chaplin. I am just a person of art." To the question, "How long have you been working on your present act?" he replies quickly, "All my life."[6]

The more traditional approach to clowning was, for thirty years, represented by Ringling Bros. and Barnum & Bailey's Clown College. It sent approximately 1,000 graduates out into the world, the majority of them working, at one time or another, as circus clowns. Despite such apparent success the school and its graduates were often held in low regard by an older generation of clowns. Since the Ringling management seemed to prefer a particular type of clown face, the criticism was that the school was more interested in cloning than clowning.

Such criticism tended to overlook the enormous benefits the school brought to the field of clowning. If nothing else, Ringling's Clown College established the fact that clowning was an art, and like any art could be taught. It also established the criteria for other programs that professed to train clowns that proliferated after its closing.

One of the problems young clowns face, whether they wish to become traditional clowns or the contemporary circus comedians, is the lack of opportunity for artistic advancement within the circus. Those who left the circus invariably say they did so because they felt they had gone as far as they could go artistically in that venue.

All the talk about the "art" of clowning, the nobility of the profession's heritage and the comic spirit that they encountered in the school instilled, perhaps more than anyone realized, an ambition to be something more than another face in a crowded clown alley. It ignited a spark that invariably burst into flame, but the traditional circus, they soon discovered, could not provide the oxygen needed to keep it alive.

While Clown College promoted the idea that anyone could become a clown, its students soon figured out pretty quickly that you can't be taught to be funny. "Your sense of humor is yours alone, and you need to find that spot in yourself that takes the information you're given and translates it into an action or reaction that creates laughter."[7]

At various times during its history the students at Clown College were fed conflicting approaches to clowning. On the one hand they were inspired to be creative, and, on the other hand, they were taught a series of standard tried-and-true gags. Robin Eurich, who attended the school in 1975, has identified these gags as the "Book of Knowledge" that any journeyman clown needed to be both familiar with and could rely on as a living. There was real comfort in the traditional gags. They required no thinking, just remembering. The people who invented these gags did them very well because they were designed to play to their individual strengths, which may not have been the strengths of those who followed. So the circus owners wanted something new. This one change has led to the variation that we have seen in the past twenty-five years or so and has favored a "new" kind of clown: loose, character based, improvisational. The unlikely crucible of street performing, improvisation, mime, theatrical clowning, and other venues provided the necessary spark for this change to happen. Eurich also notes, in a telling aside, that "every modern innovation in the circus has come from an outside source."

In pursuing this change in clowning, Eurich continues, "Folks who were forced to perform in a constant trial and error situation, learning from their mistakes and living by their wits, unaware of the traditional gags, became sought after because they could be counted upon to come up with something 'new.' This is why we have Bill Irwin, Denis Le Comb, David Shiner, and many others. David Larible's act in the days of traditional clowning would have been seen as simple and unworthy. Things have changed."[8]

There have also been other changes. One of them is the trend away from white face. "Even those that do put on whiteface are not truly traditional white face clowns," Jackie LeClaire, a spokesman for the "Old School," points out. "They don't wear the starched collars, the stocking cap. Most clowns wear wigs, and if they are in whiteface, it is a character white." That trend seems easily traceable to what was happening in Clown College. Every year fewer and fewer white face clowns were given Ringling contracts. It didn't take long for the hungry youngsters to catch on.[9]

Many changes may also be a result of Ringling's 3-Ring Adventure, which precedes the performance and gives the audience a chance to get up close and personal with the performers. This calls for a one-on-one sensibility that Steve Smith, once the dean of Clown College, insists is a "whole new mode of operation. You can't scare people to death." The new style of makeup, or lack of it, is not, according to LeClaire, "as overwhelming to the children."

Clown College must also be credited with bringing women into the profession. Female clowns still have a certain prejudice to overcome, however. Amy Gordon, who works strictly in the comic vein but is not a traditional clown, says that people are not prepared to laugh at women. "People still tend to put women up on a pedestal, and you don't laugh at people on a pedestal. So the trick is to make them look funny. Costuming helps, but you don't have to be gross. Just silly."

Another problem facing contemporary clowns is the growing sophistication among audiences. As a result the trend is away from traditional clowns in favor of circus comedians who, instead of relying on a smile or a giggle, can draw big laughs and carry a show.

One such clown is David Shiner. As a boy growing up in Boulder, Colorado, he remembers always being in love with acting. In college he studied theater. After completing his formal education, however, there was a period of about ten years when he was rather aimless, wandering about, doing community theatre at night, building houses during the day.

★ ★ ★

In 1980, a new walking mall opened in Boulder, and it quickly became a magnet for itinerant street performers. During that summer Shiner encountered his first mime troupe, Samuel Avital, from Israel. "I fell in love with it immediately. I understood everything they were doing, even though they weren't speaking. I was enchanted. I never saw that before other than Red Skelton," Shiner recalls of his epiphany. "And I thought, 'This is something I can do.'"

The very next day he was out on the street, himself, in whiteface, doing what he hoped was a passable imitation of Marcel Marceau. "I was terrible," he says now. However, he persisted, and during the course of the summer met many street artists who were passing through, on their way to one coast or the other. A juggling duo, Dr. Hot and Neon, told him about Europe and advised him to check out the streets there. The summer of 1981, he was in Paris.

"I started working the street in front of the Georges Pompidou Museum and St. Germain-des-Prés doing my clown stuff. I just went and did it." By that time he had already learned one of the tricks that would ultimately make him famous among street performers. One day in Boulder he went out in the middle of the street and stopped a police car and got a huge crowd, and he instantly realized, "Oh, that's the trick. Do something crazy. Guerrilla theatre. The reason I started involving the audience was because my mime was so bad nobody would watch. In Europe I would just accost people in the street and involve them in improvisations, and it became the sensation of Paris."[10]

Shiner spent three years working the Parisian streets. In the summer he would go to Avignon and spend four weeks there working the festival. "I learned how to do a character. I learned what's funny and what's not, mostly through improvisation. That's where my mean clown started to develop, on the streets. The nasty clown. No one had ever seen that before. They'd always seen the nice clown with the balloons and the toy animals. I was mean, so it was new." At this point in his career, however, he had not yet abandoned the white face.

In the summer of 1983 he got a job with a little one-ring circus, Le Puits aux Imates, which toured the outskirts of Paris. During the course of that season he was seen by Dominique Mauclair, who invited him to do the Festival Mondial du Cirque de Demain in 1983. There he caught the eye of Bernard Paul, the director of Circus Roncalli, who engaged him for the show's 1984 season.

"It was a big challenge for me, to take my street material and develop it as a real act for a live show. I had already developed my car routine with Le Puits aux Imates. I had that number, and I took one of my old street bits where a man breaks my camera and I threaten to break his. I learned to improvise in the ring in that piece. I did the car and the camera for one year with Roncalli."[11]

In comparing working before a street audience and a circus audience, Shiner says, "It's easier to work an audience that has bought a ticket. On the street I had to work very hard to keep them there. I had to be very brash. I would never recommend it as a place of learning—at least not for too long. It's a very hard way to learn. It's very stressful.

"I got arrested many times and was taken away. Sometimes they also took my money, especially in Switzerland; they always took your money there. 'Throw him out of the country and take his money,' they'd say. And you'd come back in a week. You always had to keep one eye out for the cops. The thing about the Swiss is that you'd never know when they'd haul you away. If they'd seen enough of you, they'd send you away."[12] Tough critics.

After a season with Roncalli, Shiner decided to strike out on his own again, teaming up with René Bazinet (who later became a principal clown with Cirque du Soleil), and then it was back to Switzerland, this time under the legitimate auspices of the Swiss National Circus, Circus Knie. "It was a great experience being with a traditional circus, with all the animals." And then it was on to Cirque du Soleil, where he gained international exposure. "That is where I invented the cinema number from an old street routine. It was the best thing I ever did."

After Soleil, Shiner worked on a Sam Shepard film, along with Bill Irwin and the Red Clay Ramblers. "When I was invited to do the Lincoln Center Fun Festival, I asked Bill if he wanted to do it with me, and I also asked the Ramblers." That was how *Fool Moon*, his Broadway show with Bill Irwin, was born.

That show, Shiner explains, "took the environment of the theater and used elements of both vaudeville and circus. Bill's spaghetti number [from that show] goes back to the Pickles; my cinema number goes to the streets and Cirque du Soleil; the car goes back to the circus, too, but I involved Bill in that so it became something totally different."

Shiner says he would like to direct a circus sometime, perhaps Germany's Roncalli. (His wife is a German horsewoman, and he has, for the past sixteen years, maintained a home in Germany.) Roncalli's founder and director, Bernard Paul, Shiner points out, has been directing his circus for twenty years, and the show needs to be revitalized. "It's still a great show," Shiner says, "and I see great possibilities in it."

To be great, he thinks, a circus needs three essential ingredients: a great lighting designer, a great composer, and a great director. It is his ambition to create something that combines the elements of theatre, street, and circus. He would, he says, "bring in acts that don't traditionally fit into the circus. They can work, if you present them in the right way. There's no limit to what the circus can be. Look at Cirque du Soleil. No one ever thought it could be that. They took it to a whole new level through a combination of elements that resulted in a show that was deeply poetic and very symbolic. Circus ultimately to me is very symbolic and spiritual. You're dealing with high-wire walkers, men who fly, animals, clowns; it has deep psychological symbolism in it. I think that's what is so attractive about the circus. If it's done well, we see very deep profound elements of our own lives in the structure of the circus.

"The clown is usually the central figure because he is so symbolic of the dilemma of man; he's the rebel. The clown is dealing with our struggle in overcoming pain and sorrow. For me, the clown has always shown us our deepest pains through laughter. The clown is ultimately a healing character, a cathartic figure. He demonstrates the pain. It's all there. With that kind of awareness, you should be able to create a really incredible show.

"So I would make my circus with a troupe of about thirteen people. For me, it's always about human feelings, creating deep felt feelings in the audience that they can follow, something that they relate to in their own life. I would use the acts, being very aware of what each act meant symbolically, what it elicits on the emotional level, and then delve into that experimentally and creatively to find the deepest, most powerful way of presenting it so that it elicited the deepest emotional response in the audience. That's what I would experiment with, a troupe of great performers that have acts but can also be developed as actors.

"Then you can create a poetic event that utilizes all the skills of the performers and the environment of the circus to create poetry, a show that's very healing. I would use elements of mysticism, elements of sound. Music would be very important because sound elicits very profound emotions. I would use different types of sounds and music and experiment with all of that."

When it comes to the future development of his own clown character he says, "I don't think my clown will ever have a voice. It's just too powerful in silence. I do mime words. But there's something about the laughter of comedy, when you're not speaking, that goes much deeper than a joke. It's much more profound. A pratfall, a great pratfall, has deep symbolic meaning. Symbolically it represents every mistake we've ever made, our struggling, trying to make things work. It's not specific, and it's universal. Bill Irwin has a piece in which he is running in a circle, and he trips twice at the same place, so to avoid tripping again he steps over that spot and ends up falling flat on his face. That's hysterical, because it's your life. That one routine represents life. It's symbolic; that's why we laugh so. We're not consciously thinking, 'Oh, this is what life is about,' but we recognize it in the subconscious, so it provokes deep laughter that you can't get from a joke."[13]

Cirque du Soleil has had a number of clowns like David Shiner whose work has greatly enhanced the productions with which they have been a part. But since clowns play so prominent a role in its productions, the company has discovered that clowns require special handling. "The first problem associated with clowning," Lyn Heward points out, "is that it is influenced by culture. The Russian style of clowning was appropriate to *Alegría* because it is, like the show, more poetic. The purpose of the clowning in *Quidam* is not the same as it is in *Alegría*. In *Alegría* the clowns are a part of the thread of the story. In *Quidam* they represent the underworld. They are the folks that got left behind. So the context of the clowns in *Quidam* is quite different than it is in *Alegría* where they are part of the theme. In *Mystère*, Benny LeGrand is that obnoxious interjection. He prides himself on that to a certain extent.

"Another problem is that clowning is also the one element in the show that takes the longest to adapt within the context of the show. Even Slava took about six months to become fully comfortable within the context of the show. Other clowning styles are integrated with more or less facility.

"The other thing to take into consideration is that we build house troupes here. Our shows are not a collection of independent acts. We bring the people here and make the acts here. But still the clowns are coming from the outside. We have not tried to train clowns here. We take the clowns for what they are, and we try to fit them into the context of the show, but they haven't benefited from the six to nine months of integration and working with the rest of the team.

"So they tend to be fairly marginal, on their own. They also tend to be a little older than the rest of the cast. They are more experienced with life and, therefore, their integration into a group that has been together for nine months before we open the show can be more complex. It's difficult because it's not just a pasting together of unrelated acts. They have got to fit.

"The young clowns are not as experienced. In *Quidam* the new clowns are young, in their twenties, the same age roughly as the rest of the company. They meld well, but their acts have not evolved as the more mature clowns' work tends to do. Nor have these clowns worked together before, so in a sense they were developing their acts on the spot, whereas Slava arrived with a repertoire, which he adjusted for Cirque du Soleil. In *Mystère* Benny [LeGrand] and François Dupuis [Baby] had their persona developed, and they had the concept.

"It all depends upon your expectation for the show and how you want to put them into it. You could go to shows where clowns are an unrelated segment—comic relief—or whatever. If you want to knit your clowns into the fabric of the show then that's a lot more work because you're taking experienced people with their own material and very well defined persona. With *Quidam* the comedy is more identified to the moment than to the persona or the characters that the clowns have developed.

"So I really do see us as having a problem with clowns. It's a question of integration and how we choose to integrate them into the show.[14]

"Slava knew he didn't want to do ten shows a week for the rest of his life at his age. So we both knew he would only be with us for a limited time. Others of our clowns have gone from show to show. Slava still works with us in helping to choose replacements and checks up on the replacements periodically. Other performers are content to stay and develop in their roles. Some have been with us five years or more. Sometimes we feel they need a change of context. Some changes are selected on our part. Others are theirs. René Bazinet [the featured clown of *Saltimbanco*] did the entire run and is still involved in training a lot of replacements.

"Gilles Ste-Croix is very experienced in working with clowns. He gets the job of working with the clowns on all of our shows regardless of the artistic director. He understands that he can guide but not impose."[15]

It should be noted here that Cirque du Soleil makes a very sharp distinction between clowns and characters, or what they call *personnage*. The latter are often grotesque, but they are not expected to deliver the kind of response required of the clowns. John [Gilkey], the master of ceremonies of *Quidam*, who arrived with his persona and some sketches of acts, is an example of a character rather than a clown, per se.

And speaking of Gilkey's experience within the company, Lyn Heward says, "We are beginning to realize that clowns need a little more latitude [in the length of their contracts]. Clowns need rejuvenation. They need the space to go out and do their own thing and grow a little more [before they return]. Clowns are very sensitive people, and often, in spite of what they do on stage, they are very introverted people. So we have to accept the fact that there will be changes in our clowns" [during the run of any one of our productions].[16] Gilkey, however, wanted to create something new and not be stuck within a single character. He left that show for a time, then returned to the Cirque du Soleil fold in *Dralion* and *Varekai* briefly before joining Franco Dragone's production company in Belgium.

But a single, enduring character that runs through an entire career is the norm in the clowning profession, and the more recognizable and identifiable that character, the more success the clown is likely to be. Certainly that is true of Barry Lubin, who is one of perhaps a half dozen clowns working in American circuses today who are truly distinguished artists. Like the others in that very small fraternity, he has the unique gift of being able to make an audience love him.

While in Clown College, he decided he wanted to be different than his fellow fledgling funsters. But how? He graduated without having found the answer. He did, however, emerge with a contract to clown with Ringling Bros. and Barnum & Bailey. On the first day of rehearsals with The Greatest Show on Earth, he decided to try out a new character, one that was the opposite in just about every way from all the other clowns in the show.

His character, he decided, would be the one and only human being he could think of who was universally loved. He called this new creature "Grandma." Without changing his basic makeup, he turned himself into that little old lady by pulling on a wigful of gray curls, adding a pair of steel-rimmed spectacles, and trading his baggy pants and floppy shoes for a straight red dress and a pair of wedgies.

The character, however, was not an instant success. It was obvious to Lubin that the character drew lots of attention, but the way in which he had chosen to present her didn't quite go over. Nonetheless, he knew he had something worth developing. In Grandma, Lubin had a clown character that was neither physically threatening nor actively confrontational, a character, in other words, who could appeal to all those children and adults who were terrified or simply put off by most other clowns.

During Lubin's three years with The Greatest Show on Earth, "trying to please the audience instead of myself," the Felds [Irvin and Kenneth] were patient and allowed Lubin lots of latitude to find a way to make Grandma work on all levels.[17]

They next sent Lubin and Grandma to Europe to appear in The International Circus Festival of Monte Carlo. As it turned out, Europe and Grandma did not understand each other at all. The Felds, on the other hand, continued to believe in the character, and brought Lubin back to the states to appear in another one-ring show they were then producing at the now defunct Circus World in Florida. It was here that Lubin finally found a way to make the character work in a focused situation.

Eventually Lubin and the Big Apple Circus discovered each other. That was in 1982, and Grandma has been an endearing and enduring fixture (but for a few brief sabbaticals) ever since. Of his position there he says, "The audiences know me very well. Basically everything is set up for me, so when I walk in there, when I make my first appearance, it seems like at least half of the audience knows who I am. It's not that I can do no wrong, but I don't have to break the ice anymore.

"Every time I do an engagement for a different producer, where I've never worked before, I have to prove myself. It takes a certain amount of time, and it takes a different effort to do that."

One of his pet gripes is the idea that the circus is for kids. "It's for everybody," he insists. "That's what I've been striving for my entire career. My feeling has always been that the parents have to be laughing, too. I'm aiming for material that's going to work across the board. I like to call it family entertainment, rather than children's entertainment.

"My greatest satisfaction comes from making an audience of all ages and ethnic backgrounds laugh at the same thing. That's the joy of the circus. It's like Bugs Bunny versus Barney. Barney is not for adults. But Bugs Bunny appeals to all ages because of the multileveled humor.

"To me, everything is character based. The success that I've had is 100 percent character based. My material is secondary to the character. If you buy the character across the board, then I'm ahead of the game. I've learned early in my career that as long as I go in there with a commitment to the character, I'm home free. If you go into the audience with love in your heart, it tends to come back to you. When I'm at my best I feel like I'm a conduit for an energy that passes through me. I see it in a very spiritual way. When things are incredible, it's not in my control. It just happens through me, this energy.

"The best lesson I got when first learning about clowning came from David Nicksay, my clowning teacher at Clown College. He said, 'The clown is in you already. It's not an acting role you step into. The clown should come out of who you are. It's basically finding the clown within you and letting him out.' That's my job.

"The reason I started doing arena shows again was because I was given an opportunity to do spot dates, not an entire season, and because I saw David Larible succeed as a solo in a way I hadn't really seen before. Even though I had been exposed to Lou Jacobs and other clowns who really held their own, David was able to do something that didn't appear to be traditional American clowning and yet really hit the American audience. I don't think I'm a traditional American clown by any means, so I started working for the Royal Hanneford Circus, and I tried to adapt what I had to a three-ring circus, and it was successful. My attraction to the three-ring circus is the energy. The amount of energy you can get out of 15,000 people is phenomenally exciting."

But, he insists, "I can't be one of three acts going on at the same time. I need to work with very strong ringmasters. On the Royal Hanneford show, the ringmaster represents the authoritarian figure that is juxtaposed to my character. And with eight spotlights on you, even in a gigantic arena, people are forced to focus on you. It's easier to get everyone's attention in a ninety-five seat theatre, but it can work in an arena. I got their attention by interacting with the ringmaster before I did my bit. I would have had a much more difficult time without that setup.

"I found I needed interaction when I first started my career, so I went directly into the audience. I worked in ways that couldn't possibly have worked in a three-ring circus for the entire audience. It was my third season on Ringling before I developed anything that I could actually put on the arena floor that was appropriate and wasn't using the audience. All those small things I did on Ringling translated into what I did on the Big Apple and are also applicable in that ninety-five seat theater or any theatrical setting."[18]

★ ★ ★

So what is there about David Larible that makes him so successful? It's almost too predictable, the story David Larible tells of how he came to be a world famous clown:

"When I was in school I was in a lot of trouble, because anytime I could do something funny to make everybody laugh, I would. I was the class clown, and it felt sooooo good," he says with appropriate emphasis. "I didn't care about the punishment, and sometimes it was pretty bad. I didn't care because I had made everyone laugh, and everyone liked me because I made them laugh.

"When you grow up in a circus like me and my child right now, you are thrown into this world, this court of miracles, where you are surrounded by many different artists, and I think you naturally choose what you want," he says by way of explaining his evolution from class clown to star.

"My son is only four," this clown of clowns continues. "I don't think he's going to be a clown. He's around the animals all day long. The animal trainers tell me he knows the names of all the elephants, so I think that's what happens to the circus kid. Certain things attract him. I was attracted by the clowns. I used to sneak in their dressing room and watch them put their makeup on, and I was fascinated by them.

"My father used to tell me that clowning is the end of the process, not the beginning. All the greatest clowns of the past, Otto Griebling, Lou Jacobs, were not clowns at first. Everyone gets into clowning later on when they know what they are doing. You have to have the experience of the arena. But I always wanted to be a clown, so my father says, 'David, okay you want to be a clown, first be a good acrobat, study music, learn everything you can about show business and circus.' So I started and worked hard, even when I was young, and I didn't understand why I needed to. I used to ask my father, 'Why do you make me go to music school? I don't want to be in a band. I want to be a clown.' 'A good clown has to be a good musician,' he answered. So I play five or six instruments. The trumpet is my major. The others I play because I love music, and I use them in some of my routines.

"He also made me study classical ballet. And I would say, 'Dad, I don't want to be a dancer.' He says, 'A good clown has to move nicely and have harmony of movement, and ballet gives you control of your body and all your movement is nice and graceful.' So when I started, I was a dancer in a show; I was an acrobat on the trapeze. And finally I started clowning, understudying other clowns. I was encouraged because everyone was telling me 'David, I think you have talent for that.' So you go—Boom! Boom! Boom! [He is musical even in conversation.]

"I grew up in a real circus family, where I used to help put up and tear down the tent. I drove a semi to the next town. I worked until everything was up, and then I would go to my trailer, have a shower and shave. My aftershave was my makeup. Literally. My father used to tell me, 'Are you breathing? Then you go and do the show.' I don't know if that is right or not, but he taught me to respect the audience and the work. The twelve and a half-meter diameter circle is not only a place I go to pay my bills. It is a temple for me. And I think whoever enters that temple should be prepared.

"That is the way I was raised. I never missed any performances. In eleven years [with Ringling], I never missed a show. I worked with pneumonia, with a broken nose. In Detroit I had surgery at noon, woke up from anesthesia at 4, and at 7:30 I did a performance with *Kaleidoscape*. I am crazy.

"When you do comedy you depend on the reaction of the audience. The timing is being given to you by the reaction of the audience. You do the job. Boom! There's the reaction. Boom! You go to the next one. Here [in a large arena] for example the reaction arrives very late. Sometimes it messes up your timing. So you have to be very attentive to what you're doing. You have to listen. I think a good circus performer always has to understand that there is audience."

Here he launches into an intriguing digression. "There's a difference between a good acrobat and a performer," he observes. "Sometimes there are people who can do amazing things, but they don't have that special thing. We are always talking about Gunther. But Gunther was Gunther because he had something different. Over my career I have performed with many great performers and great stars, and every one of them has this quality. When they get in the ring, something happens. You can tell from the audience. They change, and it happens in a moment. Maybe somebody was eating popcorn and in that moment they turn and watch. Why? It's difficult to explain, but I think there are some people who are born with what we call star quality. And people fall in love with this performer."

That brief side excursion does not cause him to lose his train of thought. "Sometimes it is a mistake to wait too much for the reaction [in an arena like this]. Because the big risk is that the rhythm is gone. So sometimes you overlap the reaction. You don't wait. The next joke is arriving, and the reaction [from the last one] is coming back at the same time. But it can screw up the rhythm that every comedy act should have. A comedian should have a good sense of rhythm, absolutely, and a good ear.

"Comedy is like music. In music when you have a concert, every single element has to be played at the precise moment." Here he demonstrates the sounds produced by the various sections of the orchestra. "And that is the same with comedy. Sometimes it is difficult, and we don't get it right. Sometimes people say, 'Oh, that was great tonight,' but you're not happy with yourself. Because you know it was not right. You know that concert that was supposed to happen where every element comes in at the right moment didn't happen, and this is frustrating."

Coming back to the big show after *Barnum's Kaleidoscape* the problem was not having to readjust to the larger space. "The problem was that I was doing one totally new routine. That takes time. Now the routine is starting to be good. At first it was okay. It was not good at first because a routine needs to be performed. An act or trick you can practice into perfection and when you do it, that's it. How are you going to practice comedy? To practice comedy you need an audience. And you see this works. I keep it. This I take out. You move on.

"A new routine, I think, is a risk you have to take. And I think that's why there are few, if any, clowns that have a big repertoire. Normally clowns have two or three routines, and they go with that their whole career. I'm the only one that I can think of—the only idiot—that takes that risk. Every two years I come out with something new. But it's great. You put yourself in question all the time, and I love to do that."

If you can't practice a comedy routine without an audience, is there anything that can be done before you go out there and put yourself on the line?

Yes, he agreed, there is some preparation, but it involves conceiving the new routine. "I start out writing down ideas. Boom! An idea comes, and I write it down. What I write down, I take and put it in a drawer and don't look at it for another two or three months. One day I go back and take it out. If, for me, I have the same strong feeling at that moment as I had when I first had the idea, in that case I'm going to start working. So that's what I did this year. I had this idea of doing a routine about rap because rap is everywhere. It's a form of communication that is very strong right now.

"I started thinking about it at the beginning of last year, when *Kaleidoscope* closed, so I had a full year to work on it. I knew I was going to come back here to Ringling last February. Kenneth told me, 'David, I want the knife routine back.' I was not very crazy about that because that was the first routine that I did here and that routine was copied all over the world. Every single little circus everywhere, but Kenneth says, 'David, there are a lot of people that sing "My Way," but when Frank Sinatra was in concert, everybody was asking him to sing that song because the way he sings "My Way" is not the same way others sing it. I think it is a great routine, and a lot of people ask me to bring back the knife routine. And I say, 'Okay, you're the producer. If you want me to do it, okay, but the other one has to be new.' And he says, 'Of course.'

"So I started working. And at the first production meeting I say, 'Look, I want to do a routine about rap.' And everybody thinks that's a great idea. It's contemporary, and I explained what I thought I saw.

"Because I couldn't use my mom in the knife routine, I started to develop and create the routine always having in mind to use my mom. She has been performing with me for eight years now. She's like my partner. I say, 'Mom, it's up to you. Do you want to perform the next two years?' And she was like, 'What do you mean? Of course I have to perform.' And I think it is important for her to perform. It keeps her involved. She is seventy-one, and it is important for me to have her there. It is wonderful."[19]

All Larible's preparation is cerebral. He never, he insists, works physically without an audience. To emphasize the seriousness of this point, his voice becomes deeper, the volume drops. "Because what I do involves a lot of spontaneity. When a clown starts working too much in a studio in front of a mirror, he becomes an actor. We are not actors. We are clowns. There's a big difference between an actor and a clown. A clown doesn't play a character. I don't play David, the clown. I am David, the clown. There's a big difference."

An actor, he suggests, has to be ready to play Hamlet today and somebody else the next day. And everything he says and does is predetermined in advance by someone else. "[On the other hand] if you're a good clown," he says with a slightly sardonic chuckle, "you should create your own routine and not take it from other people and direct it yourself. Only in this way can you own the routine. The routine is yours. It is a long process. You have to begin from scratch. And even after when I finally do it in the ring, after eight or nine months of thinking about it, there is another two or three months in the ring cutting angles and just . . ." Here words fail him, for the first time, but it is clear he is talking about the process of refinement that makes an act uniquely his own.

In that early stage of development, he videotapes his performances so he can step back and watch what he is doing as if he were in the audience. But mostly the refinements occur to him in the ring during a performance. "Sometimes, if you are around circus and clowning as long as I have been, you start to visualize things because you have everything in your mind, the ring, the positions, and you know where things should be and when. Once you start to do it a couple of times you realize that something may be out of place in one position, so you move it somewhere else. It is a work of research, a work of doing. You have to do it. There is no other way. There is no routine that you can rehearse in the studio by yourself and say, 'Okay, tonight I am going to do it in front of an audience, and it's going to be a success.'" He is, he says, still in the discovery process of his latest creation. "And of course it's going to be like that for all the two years, because normally after the two years, I still am changing little things because I am never happy with what I have.

"In this routine there was some misjudgment on my part. I thought I could play much more with the costumes, and I could take much more time and get more laughs than what I actually do. What I discovered was the costume was going to get a laugh, and boom its going to be finished right there, and I have to move on. And that's probably because of the dimension of the ring and the arena. People cannot really tell what a guy is wearing. It registers, and afterwards you have to move on. So that misjudgment was quickly fixed.

"You have to have the humility to say I was wrong. If you stick with something that is wrong, it doesn't matter how much you like it. It's the audience that has to like it. If they don't like it, you have to take it out. You cannot be in love with what you do. You have to go [into the ring] to give and not to receive. That's a mistake that so many performers make. I see performers, before they even begin their act they are asking for applause. The applause has to be something that comes to you. You don't ever have to ask for it."[20]

Because Larible's performance involves audience participation to a very large extent, choosing the people whom he takes into the ring with him is critical. Selecting them has been complicated somewhat by the 3-Ring Adventure that has in recent years come to proceed the actual performance. There is, consequently, no opportunity to look the audience over and identify likely candidates the way someone like David Shiner does. So Larible goes, he says, pretty much on instinct. "If someone pulls back or has his eyes down," they are easily passed over as he approaches the audience, his fingers itching to take hold of a likely candidate. He is not, he says, looking for someone who might be funny. That's his job, to make whatever they do seem funny. He just needs someone willing.

Sometimes, however, inspiration comes from the people he takes out of the audience into the ring. "I will see things that were not in my mind when I conceived the act. And that's the secret. When something funny happens, I try to make it happen every night. In one way what you have to do—and here I have to use a word that I hate because I don't think it reflects what I do—but sometimes you have to 'manipulate.'

"It's not like you take advantage. But you have to have such a strong presence that without realizing it they do what you want. I receive letters from people that were in the ring with me, and they say, 'David, we didn't know it, but we were doing exactly what you were telling us to do.' You should never let them control the routine or you're going to be in deep trouble. They should be spontaneous, of course, because you don't want to keep saying, 'Don't do that; don't do that.' You have to let them be themselves, but don't let them be in control of the routine. I have little tricks that I will do to encourage or discourage people from doing certain things.

"There are certain tricks, and they are something that you have to do. You may have some guy who is trying to do too much or is moving too much [trying to be too much of a showoff] so what you do is throw focus to somebody else right away and throw your shoulder to [the showoff]. And so he feels left out and slowly he calms down. Little things like that you discover."[21]

Larible started doing audience participation in 1982, with Circus Krone, in Germany. "In twenty years you start developing little tricks and discovering little secrets," he says. "Sometimes without even realizing, night by night, we get information. We are like a sponge. Nothing is said because in the next show you have a totally different audience, and you have to start all over again, but I think that is one of the things I love most about what I am doing. When you do a routine by yourself in the ring, even if you try to keep it fresh and you try to change little things every night, after a while you become almost automatic. You find yourself moving automatically to do this—Boom! Then this—Boom!

"Right now there are a lot of clowns that follow my form of clowning. But, as far as I know, only four or five do it right. All the rest transform themselves into something like social directors. They bring people into the ring and make them do something funny, and you laugh at them, but the secret is not to laugh at them, but to make the audience laugh at my reaction. I am the clown. I am the one that is supposed to make you laugh."[22]

Occasionally this "clown of clowns" takes a brief sabbatical from the circus to work in the theatre. "It is much easier to do theatre than circus. You don't have people with cotton candy. When you're on stage everybody's in the dark and everybody's silent. That's easy. You don't have people all around you. You don't have to be funny with your back, because it doesn't matter where I'm turned. I'm always going to have somebody looking over my shoulder, so you have to be funny or expressive with your shoulder.

"Whenever I am not working here, I go do theatre. I go all around the world to festivals, just like a guy with a piano, and it refreshes me. Every time you get a new experience and can do something different, it makes you richer, not only as a performer but also as a person, because you have to put yourself in question all the time. It's too easy to say, 'Well, I'm David Larible, and I am the star of Ringling Bros., and that's it.' Being a performer is not about that. Being a performer is to take risks and to have a flop once in a while. Why not? Like when I went to Monte Carlo everyone said, 'David, why do you want to go to Monte Carlo? It's a big risk. If you don't win the Golden Clown everyone will say, 'You see, he went there, and he didn't win.' And if you do win everyone will say, 'Well, we knew it; it was because he is David Larible.' It was a big risk, but then I take a risk every night."[23]

★ ★ ★

Ringling has increasingly relied on a star clown like David Larible or Bello Nock to carry the show, and the traditional clown alley is less and less prominent, in part because trained and seasoned clowns are increasingly difficult to find. When Ringling closed its Clown College, several individuals and programs attempted to leap into the breach. The most successful of these, and certainly the most encompassing, is the Clown Conservatory program run by San Francisco's Circus Center and headed by Jeff Raz.

Author, actor, play director, and circus clown, Jeff Raz is the director of the school's clown training program, which started in 2000 with support from the National Endowment for the Arts. Before beginning his training program, Raz performed for many years with the New Pickle Circus. He previously taught classes at the Ringling Clown College, San Francisco's High School of the Arts, and the California State University's Summer Arts Circus Workshop.

Originally Raz's program was titled Clowning for the New Circus. This was, he says, "because of all the talk about the new circus movement that began with Make-a-Circus and the Pickles here in the mid-'70s, and flourished with Cirque du Soleil, the Big Apple, and Cirque Éloize. In Make-a-Circus and the Pickles, clowns have always been central to the show. With Cirque du Soleil, the clowns still hold a prominent place; performers like John Gilkey, Benny Le Grande, and David Shiner have been very central to the show. So in this sense the new circus does bring clowning to the center. Earlier in the past century, the possibilities for clowning in this country were more limited and lost some of the heart and political thought that clowns once brought to circuses.

"I start with the body, and how to be eloquent and multicultural and multidisciplined with the body," Raz says of his approach to training clowns. "My own path started with skills. I learned to juggle when I was fourteen; then acrobatics came a little later. The new circus is using the incredible acrobatic skills developed by Chinese and Russian performers and directors; that has raised the skill level of the circus in this country. So I emphasize skills with my students. Clowns always use skills as ways to speak. You need to have such control of the skill that your audience hears what you're saying without noticing the amount of skill. For a clown it's the heart and the mind and the soul that you're going for, but in a circus setting, skills are part of your language."

There are eighteen hours of instruction each week, one of which is devoted to body awareness, dance, and mime. Two hours are given over to learning circus skills, four hours to acrobatics, and six hours to clowning. A three-hour slot is reserved for guest teachers in everything from makeup to Japanese and Balinese theatre.

A good part of the instruction deals with structuring a clown routine. Raz explains: "Tandy Beal, who directed the Pickles in the past, went on a search for clowns when Diane Wasnak [Raz's partner in the ring] and I retired; and she came back and said: 'I saw all these wonderful people, but no one knows how to put an act together.' I've seen that many times, too, and get very frustrated, partly because I also have a theatre and playwriting background. A clown entrée or a clown routine is a little play, but it is not an easy construction. You could have the greatest character in the world, be totally connected with your inner clown and with every culture in the world and have a million skills, but if the act is not shaped, the audience isn't going to fly with you. That's why, after we briefly consider character in our class, we go right to structure, and I teach old clown entrées, pulling from different cultures.

"These old entrees often include dialogue. I have not focused on dialogue, although we did some when we worked on the French entrée, and then last week Joan Mankin [former Pickle Circus clown] brought in a Shakespeare monologue from *Two Gentlemen of Verona*. I also use words in stories to enrich the material. I feel very strongly that good clowning addresses difficult issues, and you need all the tools you can get, including words, to explore these issues.

"I am in the business of sending people out to get the clown jobs in circuses around the world. It takes a long time to train clowns, but I want our clown students to be able in the near future to audition for any kind of show." Graduates have worked for Ringling, Cirque du Soleil, the Pickles, Cirque Éloize, and many other circuses, theatres, and puppet troupes around the world. "I want them to be able to hold their own with a couple of solid entrées and to improvise within a given format, to do what's needed to be a professional clown both in the ring and on stage.

"I am also interested in the students performing in the community, in hospitals, senior centers, universities. Clowning can be used to help make a community, help change a community. So we are exploring that as well. I think there are new ways, which none of us has conceived of yet, for clowns to work within society."

The Clown Conservatory now has formed a partnership with San Francisco General Hospital, which gives the young clowns experience of working in the community. In addition, the conservatory has a relationship with New College, which allows students to work toward their MFA by taking the Clown Conservatory program in conjunction with additional academic classes at the college, thus making the conservatory a two-year program. Plans are being formulated to create a third year that will come before the current two. Three years, Raz believes, is a more reasonable amount of time for training clowns.

"I try to give my students the tools they need to fill out a freelance career," Raz concludes. "They'll have some teaching opportunities later in local schools and summer camps. We're trying to be very pragmatic in terms of what is involved in a clown's professional life, but also to be dreamers and agents of social change."[24]

Certainly that is the breadth of preparation required of any clown who hopes to work in the contemporary circus.

NOTES

1. Larry Pisoni, personal interview with the author, Charleston, S.C., June 2, 1995.

2. Slava Polunin, personal interview with the author, translator Nina Krasavina, New York, April 12, 1995.

3. Emmett Kelly. *Clown, My Life in Tatters and Smiles* (New York: Prentice Hall, 1954).

4. Polunin interview.

5. Kelly, 196.

6. Polunin interview.

7. Ernest Albrecht. "A Bunch of Clowns Get Serious," *Spectacle* (Summer 2001): 8.

8. Albrecht, 8.

9. Albrecht, 9–10.

10. David Shiner, personal interview with the author, New York, N.Y., December 6, 2000.

11. Shiner interview.

12. Shiner interview.

13. Shiner interview.

14. Lyn Heward, personal interview with the author, Montreal, Canada, August 20, 1998.

15. Heward interview.

16. Heward interview.

17. Barry Lubin, personal interview with the author, New York, N.Y., November 8, 1998.

18. Lubin interview.

19. David Larible, personal interview with the author, East Rutherford, N.J., March 7, 2002.

20. Larible interview.

21. Larible interview.

22. Larible interview.

23. Larible interview.

24. Joel Schechter. "Training Clowns for a New Circus," *Spectacle* (Summer 2001): 38–39.

• 10 •

Training the Artists and Building
and Maintaining the Performance

$\mathcal{A}$mong the most important elements in maintaining the standard of artistic excellence that is the hallmark of the productions of Cirque du Soleil are the facilities it enjoys at its home base in Montreal, Canada. Designated the Creation Studio by the company, it opened in 1997, built at a cost of nearly $60 million Canadian dollars and covering, after several expansion programs, an area of approximately 32,000 sq. meters. In addition to providing the administrative and artistic support for its numerous far-flung activities, the building is also a striking symbol of the company's brilliant success at joining art and business. Neither function dominates the other. Business and art have equal status in the building, as they flow in and out of each other's space in ways that are both natural and exciting.

Some of the interior windows in the administrative area overlook the studios where the artists work. The artists, themselves, must pass through the central open court that connects all the various departments that work in the building on their way to rehearsals, training sessions, and classes. Even the elevators, with their glass doors, promote this sense of being a part of something larger than oneself. As a result of the floor plan and the design of the partitions that feature an almost total lack of opaque physical divisions between any of the 1,600 people who work in the building, there is constant interaction. The building's central foyer features a broad staircase that can be turned into stadium seating for large meetings involving the entire staff.

The costume shop, expanded before the building was even open, was then enlarged again. The vast amount of space devoted to the costume department is essential to maintaining, replacing, and building the costumes, wigs, hats, masks, and shoes for an ever-multiplying number of productions, all running simultaneously around the world. Eighty percent of the fabric used in the costumes is custom dyed on the premises. Many of the costumes are also hand painted or use silk screen printing.

To facilitate the repair or replacement of costumes, each piece of wardrobe is catalogued in a register that includes the required pattern, information on construction techniques, and samples of every piece of fabric, thread, button, fastener, and decoration used in that particular item.

One of the techniques that the costume department has developed is the direct application onto the performer's leotard of patterns and designs, sometimes including musculature, that allow the costumer to "correct" slight imperfections or highlight a performer's outstanding features. Because so many of the costumes include hats and masks, plaster casts are made of every performer's head when he or she first joins the company. These are used, instead of the actual performer, to fit the masks, wigs and hats, which are so much a part of the characteristic look of Cirque du Soleil productions.

Each plaster head takes three technicians about two hours to make. All are stored for future use, when replacement costume parts are needed. The head casts are also used to make bald caps, which require between three and six coats of rubber. With performers coming from thirty different nationalities, approximately thirty shades of rubber are needed to match the various skin tones of the people for whom bald heads are a design requirement.

Rehearsal and training facilities include a 70-ft.-high studio covering more than 4,400 sq. ft. of floor space. It is equipped with a trampoline-like grid made of braided metal cable, 38 km. thick, which is stretched about 60 ft. above the floor. Technicians work off the grid in complete safety while hanging acrobatic and aerial equipment.

A training floor covers 2,400 sq. ft. and contains a fast track and a pit filled with 25,000 styromouse cubes rather than the conventional safety net. Another room is large enough to simultaneously accommodate a mockup of the set for the next production in one corner, a flying rig above another, and still have room for the rehearsal of individual and ensemble acts in the remaining open space.

In addition to the main studio, there is a dance studio, about 1,100 sq. ft. in size, and a music studio.[1]

All of these facilities come into play when the performers, who are recruited by Cirque du Soleil, begin their training program, which is designed to ensure that they will be well prepared for the physical and artistic demands that will be placed upon them once they become a part of one of the company's productions.

The training element in the Cirque du Soleil program has two functions: to train replacements who will assume roles in existing productions and to research ways in which those artists cast in a new production can best realize the vision of the "conceptors" for that production. Until 2005, the general conditions of the training involved in both functions were overseen by Patrice Aubertin, then training program coordinator, in the Montreal headquarters. Since that time the mandate of the creation studio has been extended.

Aubertin, whose work is at the juncture of science and art, came to Cirque du Soleil with a varied background that included eleven years of gymnastics, both as a coach and an athlete. In his early twenties, he pursued a career in music as sound engineer and show producer. He then went back to school and earned a degree in physiology and exercise physiology at Simon Frazer University in British Columbia. His field of expertise, he explains, is different from physical education in that it is more scientific. It is concerned with the ways in which the body reacts to certain types of environment and training.[2]

He and his staff are always busy, even when a new show is not being prepared. Injuries to acrobats are almost inevitable. How the organization and he decide to deal with the injury depends on its type and its implications for the production in which the injured artist is cast. If it is known that a person will be out for a long time, and there is someone who is trained and capable of jumping in, the company will send him or her to the production temporarily until he or she can be replaced either by the rehabilitated artist or a fully trained replacement.

The casting department keeps a backup list of people who would be able to do a specific number, but such a practice doesn't always work out, as for instance in the banquine number in *Quidam*. It is so intricate and the level of skill is so extreme that replacing a person is very difficult.

What is done in such an instance is the number will be built so that if one or two people are out, the number can still be performed and the audience will not see the difference. So if fourteen people are on stage, only ten may be actively taking part in the number. They will try to perform it all as much as possible. If they feel it will compromise the security of the artist, certain elements will be changed or eliminated. If the base porter doesn't feel good or is having a back problem, then it would be better to do only a three high that day. As a general rule, however, the artists try to do the complete number.

The artists are also trained so that when they miss a trick, they should attempt it a second time. This is a standard and accepted convention. In a number where the likelihood of mistakes is great, as in the rope skipping number of *Quidam*, which is so complex and involves so many people, the musical director knows that if there is a mistake, they will start again. A high degree of complicity exists between artist and bandleader, and the music is designed for such contingencies.

Aubertin's responsibilities included escorting replacements to a production already out on tour. This is done to help the replacement become integrated into the existing framework as painlessly as possible. After all, as Aubertin has observed, life in the studio is very different than it is on the road. In the studio the artist is pampered during a training period that can last as long as four months. During that period the would-be replacement is catered to in the extreme. A physical preparation specialist, coach, choreographer, and physiotherapist, and perhaps one or two others, will all work with him or her, to ensure that the replacement is completely prepared. That is a ratio of five to one. On the road it will be the exact opposite. He or she will be one of many, all of whom must rely on the services of two coaches and two physiotherapists. Some artists are not immediately equipped to deal with that kind of thing and are somewhat lost. They come from training five hours a day to having an hour on stage a day. They suddenly have so many new things to learn about working under a big top. The kitchen is outside. They don't know anyone in the cast, so they are under a lot of stress, emotionally and physically.

So it has been found to be a lot easier to integrate replacements if they come with someone who will stay with them for a short time. This strategy allows Aubertin the opportunity to meet the coaches, physiotherapists, and artistic coordinator on tour and show them what techniques the replacement had been trained in and to alert them to any personal abilities and problems.

Injured performers, by the way, are not left to their own devices, either. They are sent back to Montreal for rehabilitation. With so many productions on the road and so many roles to fill in them, Cirque du Soleil can little afford to abandon an artist just because of an injury.

In addition to training replacements, most of which is accomplished in periodic general training sessions, the studio and its staff are also profoundly involved in the creation of new productions. During that phase of production, known here as research and development, new acts will be created using apparatus designed and built to the specifications of the coaches and trainers.

Aubertin, for instance, was very much involved in the design of what the company has come to call the power track. In addition to taking part in its design work, Aubertin did the original testing of the apparatus.

Prior to the power track, there was the fast track. The design and concept are a little different, Aubertin explains, but both are versions of very long trampolines set into the floor. The fast track was the first generation of the same equipment. The power track took it one step further. But that, according to Aubertin, is the general rule of how work is done in the Montreal studio.

Each new production starts from point zero. Each time the complexity is increased because the company must try to top what it has already done with something that is bigger, more complex, more involved. So there are always challenges. It's a very dynamic environment because the work in the studio never repeats itself.

But innovation alone is not the ultimate goal. The studio's role is to push the artists into creating what the conceptors want, knowing it must be something that can be performed ten times a week. So in addition to pushing the boundaries, at the same time the individuals the trainers are working with must be respected, remembering that they are human and that the company wants to keep them for as long as possible.[3]

There is one other consideration the trainers must keep in mind at this time. The artists must be given adequate physical training to develop their strength and flexibility, but the workload must be carefully monitored so that it is conducive to their being able to do the show.

In addition to maintaining the performance physically, there is the problem of maintaining the artistic standards. Occasionally new acts or replacements for prominent company members must be integrated into the company, and that requires other rehearsals, as it did for instance when Slava Polunin, the Russian who created the clown routines that are a vital element of the fabric of *Alegría*, left the show. He left his creations behind to be performed by others. Such rehearsals had to be handled differently than those when it was an acrobat being replaced.[4]

Another significant change involved the flying act in *Mystère*. Several years into that show's run, this major element was changed to a high bar act, necessitating first recasting and retraining and then rehearsals to integrate the technical changes the new equipment required.

Approximately every two years every element of a performance is reconsidered. Some cast members may be let go altogether or shifted to other Cirque du Soleil productions when a change of context is deemed advantageous.

Once a production of Cirque du Soleil has opened, maintaining the integrity of the director's vision becomes the responsibility of the artistic director. His work is really akin to resident director. At the Bellagio in Las Vegas where *O* is holding forth, that job first belonged to Pavel Brun.[5]

There is no exact equivalent to this role in either the theatre or other circuses. The closest anyone comes to performing such duties in another troupe would be the company stage manager. But in the Cirque du Soleil scheme of things the artistic director is much more than that. The difference is that a Cirque du Soleil production is never regarded as a finished product. It is always a work in progress that continues to evolve from the day it opens until the day it closes. According to Brun, *O*, or any of the company's productions for that matter, contains a lot of room for "improvisation and individual expressiveness. It is very, very flexible. Since the work is not fixed or 'frozen,' it is not something a stage manager could reproduce at any given point or place."[6]

The role of artistic director, therefore, entails more than just being the director's eyes and ears. He is the director's artistic heir, so to speak, and is, therefore, responsible for the artistic and creative well-being of the show. In order to assume such a role, the artistic director shadows the director from the very beginning of the creative process. He attends every meeting with the conceptors, listening and taking notes. "I wrote down every word Dragone said and every emotion he felt," Brun reveals.

Of course he must be in total sync with the director. It will be his responsibility to decide what "improvements" the cast has discovered should be retained and which should be excised.

One should not infer from this that the artistic director is merely a watchdog or policeman. The artistic director's responsibility extends beyond the people on stage to the entire crew backstage. To maintain a consistent level of artistry in each performance, the artistic director's role amounts to ensuring the "happiness of every creative human being involved in it."

One aspect of *O* that almost guaranteed that it would be changing is the age of the cast. At its opening the cast was very young. Most were in the age range of seventeen to twenty-one years. The fact that many people in the cast would literally be growing up in the show meant that there was bound to be a drastic change in a few years. So in "looking after the long-term development of the show," there must be a certain amount of flexibility in what happens on stage. "The seventeen-year-old will be nineteen in two years," Brun says pointing out the inevitable and obvious. "They cannot fake being seventeen. The show will grow up with them."

Brun knows from whence he speaks. Before assuming his position with *O* he was the artistic director of the company's first permanently based production, *Mystère*. "That was the case with *Mystère* as well. I spent three years of my life watching it grow."

That nurturing process, which is more or less the same in all Cirque du Soleil productions, involves two staging sessions each week in which routine cleanup work is intended to eliminate any problems that may have crept into the performance and, as was the case with *O*, adding certain elements that were not ready to become part of the performance at the time of its premiere. A weekly training session is standard practice in all Cirque du Soleil productions. These are intended to help the artists maintain the physical aspect of their performances.[7]

Sometimes the artistic director will initiate changes. Fourteen months after *La Nouba* opened in Orlando, Florida, the introduction to one of the featured acts was being rethought. The artists involved were told to work on this segment of the performance by themselves. When they had solved the problem, their ideas were discussed with the artistic director, who, working on his knowledge of the original conception, then decided what and how much of what the artists had shown him he wanted to use.

So that the routine of doing ten shows a week does not cause a performance to devolve into a rote rendering, various workshops are randomly scheduled to stimulate the creative spirit. In the case of *O*, for instance, most of the cast had little or no theatrical background, so Brun taught them about the environment of the theatre and the significance of certain theatrical conventions. He also offered workshops in movement, acting, and improvisation. Occasionally experts in related fields are brought in to offer classes in stage fighting or mime. Even though such techniques may not be used in the performance, Brun believes they give the artists "a better understanding of their biomechanical coordination."[8]

And to keep everyone on his or her toes, one of the coaches or the artistic director watches at least one of the two daily performances every day and either delivers his notes to various artists individually or in one of the weekly company meetings, if the matter involves several people.

"We have to keep it interesting," *La Nouba*'s Witek Biegaj insists. "And keep everyone happy." That involves keeping everyone physically fit and comfortable on the road and at the permanent installations as well as in the studio. To help achieve that, Cirque du Soleil has two physiotherapists stationed at each of its productions. These people provide more than therapy for the injured. They also give massages to any of the artists who wish them. Facilities backstage include a gym stocked with various exercise equipment, a whirlpool, weights, ballet barre at a mirrored wall, and a personal computer.[9]

The quality of life for the *La Nouba* company is further enhanced by a dining room and a kitchen that offers a choice of several healthful and gourmet meals on performance days. A lounge area provides various recreational facilities for relaxation between performances and after company meetings. An in-house costume shop keeps the artist's wardrobe in pristine fashion (and when it can no longer provide that service, the costume is replaced with a new one built back in Montreal) and the prop shop keeps everything the performers will need in perfect working order. "When you do 476 performances a year, you must work to keep it fresh," Brun concludes.[10]

The first Cirque du Soleil show to do that many performances was *Mystère*. Prior to its opening in Las Vegas, each of the touring productions gave approximately 262 performances a year. The impact of doing so many more performances and in a sedentary situation also had to be addressed by the company. "The toll is very different," Heward observes. "The artists work intensively for a slightly shorter time, and people used to touring may grow to hate or love where they are." All that has to be taken into consideration if a production is to thrive.

Mystère has established many firsts for the company and has been the proving ground for the kind of management policies, both administrative and artistic, that have kept the company in the foreground of innovative performance art. It was the company's first production to be installed in a theatre built especially for it. As such it was the first to remain in one location rather than moving from venue to venue, creating a number of unique problems that involved integrating the performers not only into a new style of performance, but a new style of living. The monotony of repetitive performance could not be broken by changes in location and scenery. This was especially true for what has become the signature element of all Cirque du Soleil productions, the house troupe, or as the French Canadians prefer to put it, the *troupe maison*.

A complex hierarchy of administrative and artistic support is now firmly in place at *Mystère*. Its purpose is to keep every one of the 75 artists and 68 technicians happy, involved, and enthusiastic, and to create a kind of partnership in excellence that strives not only to maintain the show's level of artistry, but keep it perpetually striving to outdo itself.

Karen Gay, who was *Mystère's* company manager, explains that from the French, the title translates as director of operations. It is her job to oversee or manage the financial and human resources of *Mystère*. "My role," she says simply, "is to see that all the humans are happy in an environment that enables them to do their show well. Every group has a different dynamic. This group has a multicultural dynamic."[11]

Gay came to *Mystère* in February of 1998, at a time when Cirque du Soleil was hiring a company manager for the first time. "They knew," she explains, "that *O* was going to come on, and they needed a company manager. They always had someone, but they never called it a company manager." At that time the top administrative staff in Montreal had decided they needed a general manager to preside over both of their shows in Las Vegas. That person is Gay's supervisor.

"What is unique is that as company manager, usually you're it," she says, attempting to explain Cirque's unique approach to management. "Here I have a staff of fifteen managing the show. For me on the road, prior to coming to Las Vegas, that meant [booking] hotels, [finding] a mall to stop at halfway through the day and [providing] a smoke break. That kind of thing. Here it's a little different because they have their personal family lives. I don't necessarily have to manage their mortgages and day-to-day living and things like that, except during the first couple of weeks until they get situated."[12]

In all, there are 167 people involved in operating *Mystère*, including artists, technicians, and staff in office. Fifteen of those people meet each week to steer the company's operations. "What's great about the company is that they really give you the financial resources, and the freedom to figure out how best to do that. It could be anything from knowing when somebody needs a pizza instead of what we get down in the employee dining room, which is not like the Cirque du Soleil kitchens on the road. This is hotel driven. When Cirque does a kitchen, they do it right, because they know all the needs of the artists. Here the artists are left more to their own devices. So it might be [a pizza] or it might be an after-hours get-together, or a party or two, but also it's making sure that you know what somebody is going through with an injury.

"When I budget for the quality of life, I include things like cultural reimbursement so that when *West Side Story* comes into town, I can put some money towards some tickets that people will actually go out and see things other than what they see all the time. A long time before I got here, the company started taking trips to see the other Cirque shows when they visited San Diego, and they went to the Laguna Festival, the Pageant of the Masters, an arts festival, so that they can walk along and see some visual arts. Sometimes we throw in museums, so they're not just punching the time clock, which would be very easy to do in this kind of town. It's a really interesting challenge to keep that from happening."

Sometimes some of the other shows in town invite company members to join their audience, and *Mystère* has done the same, most recently right after 9/11, when the entire city was experiencing a dramatic drop-off in attendance.

Visiting the competition is a good way of keeping up with what is happening in town and doing a little scouting as well. "We might find one or two artists whom we would really like to have some day," the company manager notes. "It's nice to see where they're coming from, from an artistic standpoint. There's a lot of research that can be done by knowing the other shows in town."

Very few who arrive fresh from sports venues, it turns out, decide Cirque du Soleil is not for them. "It either clicks or it doesn't." For those for whom it clicks, "When they feel that artistry building inside of themselves they may begin to see something in a new way for themselves. It may be five or six years before they get there, but they do get there." And that's where the artistic team takes over. "Artistic rules here," Gay says simply. "That's why we have an artistic coordinator; that's why we have three coaches; that's why we have the physiotherapy department. There's no skimping on the costs for the artistic integrity of the show."

"What's great is that Cirque is always evolving," she says. "You don't have to be the same as the person before you because everybody is bringing in their own background to it. Cirque allows you to move that character to wherever you want to go within the confines of whoever is looking after the show at that point. The show was created through workshops with Franco [Dragone], which means that the artists helped create it. Their physical makeup at that time dictated what this or that character became and so through its life, unlike a book show, this life keeps evolving. We feed it, keep it alive, and give it new artists, and it has a new and different look now than it did three years ago."

For instance, for a long time, since its creation, a male always played the character of the red bird, but at one point it turned into a woman dancer. One of the women in the company said, "I want to try that character." She was given the opportunity to try, and she held the role for a time before it reverted back to a male character.[13] Those changes had to be approved by the artistic coordinator.

Mystère's former artistic coordinator, Eric Heppell, says that titles "tend to change and, depending on who holds the title, they tend to do things differently. The company is changing so much and so fast, it's hard for me to keep up, but in general, the artistic directors are in charge of two shows and mostly have to deal with a lot of administrative details, and once in a while they come and work on the show and that's their little treat, but mostly they deal with the things that are not so much fun, while the artistic coordinators [like me] are based on the show. So on the touring shows, for example, the coordinator is always there touring with the show. The director, in general, would be based in Montreal and will cover two shows."[14]

Heppell started his association with *Mystère* as a coach, and also worked as troupe maison coach at the creation of *La Nouba*. Not every coordinator has done the creation. "Most artistic directors in general will have because there are not that many directors," he says. "I think there are five and most have been with the company for a very long time. With more and more shows coming on, however, they are going to have to start looking outside the company to hire people. We are trying to encourage people to grow within the company, which is better because it is such a strange animal that it is usually difficult for someone from the outside to understand exactly how Cirque du Soleil works."

The "fun stuff" to which Heppell refers involves working directly with the show, doing "things that impact the show in a positive way. So staging helps and giving notes and corrections helps, but it goes further than that. It goes into planning and trying to create a good working environment with your artistic team, which includes the coaches, stage management, and also the physiotherapy department. We have to work hand in hand with them because we have to know what we can and cannot do.

"So when you create a good ambiance within that team it usually spills out onto the artists and then you just have a show like *Mystère*, which is running very well. We are one big, happy family. It's not always like that, quite frankly."

Heppell says that he does not watch every single performance. "I would go insane," he admits. "I have a pattern. I have been with the company for nine years now. I was a coach on *Mystère* for five years, went to *La Nouba*, and then to *Saltimbanco*, and came back to *Mystère* before moving on to *Kà as* artistic coordinator. So it's a long time, and I know that if I force myself to look at ten shows a week, I would go crazy. If I were just starting on the job I would do ten shows a week, but I've been here for a very long time, so I try to watch probably three shows completely, the very first show of the week and then for sure the last day and then somewhere in the middle, but other than that I will watch parts, parts that I'd like to modify or correct, and one thing the artists appreciate is, if I give them notes after the first show, they want to know if they have corrected it or not in the next show. Actually I have to tell them by the next show because if I wait for the next day it might be completely different people doing the cues, because we have quite a bit of rotation. So what I will do is watch the first show and then, at the second show, I'll watch the parts I've given notes on to make sure that they were corrected, and then I will let the artists know how they did.

"We try to encourage growing through the company. Some artists are quite content doing whatever they're doing in the troupe maison, but others start as troupe members and want to grow more. We had one guy in the high bar act, which is a troupe maison act, who said, 'I would like to learn the flying man act,' and at that point it was good timing because we had just lost our backup. So we allowed this guy to train and to learn, and then unfortunately we lost our main guy, and now this young guy who had no experience of being alone on stage is performing every night and holding the show quite well on his shoulders.

"I saw *Mystère* being built. There were some really ambitious ideas that didn't make it into the show, and there were very ambitious ideas that appeared through the creation but were not there right off the bat and became part of the show only during the run. Quite a bit of that happens, especially with Franco Dragone, because he is very open, and if he has a cast that is incredibly generous to offer him suggestions and propositions he will integrate these things into the show."[15]

The idea of a company troupe was a well-established principle by the time Heppell joined the company in 1993. "Basically it is a core of people that are the heart and soul of the show. They thread the show together, because they not only appear in one act, but they also appear in multiple acts, and then they do cues between the acts throughout the show, so basically they are busy throughout the whole show and that gives the Cirque du Soleil performances this nice homogeneity.

"The background of most of these guys and girls is sports. Sports acrobatics, trampoline, and gymnastics. These disciplines are basically the building blocks of circus disciplines, and although they are not circus performers [when they come to us], they can be transformed into circus performers with this background."

Discussing his personal management style, Heppell says, "I strongly believe that just doing your job is never enough. I have total respect for the fact that they have a very heavy schedule of shows, 400 performances a year. It's unheard of. I don't think there are many performers who do that many shows, but that being said, you still must always find a little something that you can improve on, be it acrobatics, be it artistically, or be it looking in a new direction, like someone becoming a character or developing his or her own solo act. So I try to set goals for each and every one of them. I have meetings with each of the artists in January, and we sit down (individually), and I ask them what they see in the future, what they would like to do. Some of them are very new here, and they say they just want to learn to do their job here, and I say that's good enough for this year, or they say they would like to learn to speak English. Okay, that's a goal. Most of them are quite young, so they pick up the language quite fast."

On the first day of a new performance week the troupe has its weekly meeting. "We couldn't start the week without having one big training session when we say, 'Okay this week, this is what's going to happen. You're going to be there, you're going to be here, you're going to be there,'" Heppell says, explaining the policy of rotating roles. "It would be asking for trouble to just say, 'Okay, we've changed everybody's position. Just read the paper, and make sure you're in the right spot.' That's really asking for an accident."[16]

Part of the training simply involves everyone getting his or her head back into the show. It also involves giving everyone a chance to practice the role or roles he or she will be playing in a week's rotation. "Maybe [the performer] hasn't done this image in several weeks, so if he's going to be in tonight, he definitely needs to train it," Heppell points out.

"At first, when we started, we had no rotation. All the positions were determined, and that was it. Suddenly someone rolled his or her ankle, so what could we do? We would have emergency meetings backstage, in the training room. 'You're going to do that, and I'm going to do this,' and somebody would say, 'No, I can't, because . . .' At one point we finally realized we had to do rotation. The funny thing about it was the artists in the beginning took it very personally and said, 'No, that's my image. I want to be the only one to do it. I don't want to share it.' 'Okay, [we argued], but when you're injured we're screwed,' so over the years we've learned to accept that we have to live with rotation. And we try not to do it too much. If we start it for the week, we keep it for the week. And the next week we might change. It is to protect us in case of sickness or injury. We can always cover everything, and right now the cast is very healthy, and you can see the show any night and you couldn't tell the difference between this version and another version.

"Last week I went to see an older show here in Las Vegas," he says, recalling the company manger's policy of visiting other shows in town. "I saw many problems that could happen here. I saw artists who had lost their motivation on stage. I saw artists that were not paying attention any more to what they were doing. I saw artists who talked to each other on stage, out of the corner of the mouth. I also saw the mistake of a show that is getting older and trying to stay current by copying what is working at this point [in other shows]. They have some Cirque du Soleil-type acts, and they don't fit in, and it looks bad. The best thing to do is to stay true to yourself and just say, '*Mystère* is a classic Vegas production that represents an era of Cirque du Soleil,' and I think there is no shame with a classic, so we're going to keep it very fresh and tight."

There are some aspects of his job, the 39-year-old Heppell admits, that are not too much fun. "Some aspects really stress me out. My [artistic] director is not here very often and basically she backs me up, but I'm the one who sees everything every day, and if someone does something extremely awful, I have to go in there and [reprimand or let go], so that aspect is not my favorite, but it is necessary. Usually when someone is not working well in a group environment, the other members of the group expect me to do something, because this person is not contributing. But sometimes it's hard to, because there are heavy consequences in their personal lives. But when it produces good effects, and you see that you have a happy cast, I guess it is all worth it."

Heppell, too, has goals of his own, which include taking *Mystère* to a level that it's never been to before. "The show is strong, but I really have ideas and goals that we are going to achieve. They are small goals, but one thing I've learned from Cirque du Soleil is that in small things you find greatness. Here we put so much attention into silly little details that 99 percent of the audience will never pick up on.

"What I really respect in this company," he says in conclusion, "is that there is always the ambition to surprise."[17]

★ ★ ★

For Nancy Mallette, *Mystère*'s former operations production manager who is now working on *Zumanity*, it has been the public demand for tickets that drives everyone in the company to ensure that the quality stays very high. "Over time," she says, "we've learned to take a good hard look at what it means to be a high-quality production and to continue to drive that point and improve on it. Cirque, I find, is one company that does not rest on its laurels. They continue to improve, make refinements. The triple-bedded trampoline [a feature in one of the company acts], for instance, is now in its fourth iteration technically. The crew here just redesigned it."[18]

As operations production manager, Mallette oversees the seven technical departments: carpentry, props, sound, rigging, lighting, automations, and wardrobe. "Our focus," she says, "is on having everything looking pristine.

The set is cleaned two and three times a week. Any blemishes or marks are worked on, on a regular basis."

There are sixty-eight people on the crew list, including those on call. It takes approximately forty-four technicians to operate the show in the evening. "We have a really small turn over, and I chalk that up to a really positive work environment."

To keep her crews from going stale, a distinct possibility among technicians, they are asked to learn the cues for all the tracks in their department so, like the artists, they can also rotate. "And what is nice about that is that it offers you some variety. You see different people. You have interaction with different artists," Mallette points out.

Mallette sums up the prevailing attitude by observing a certain pressure about being involved with Cirque du Soleil. "I don't hear people say, 'Oh, that's good enough.' They are always looking for ways to improve, and it's a nice feeling."[19]

★ ★ ★

Ringling Bros. and Barnum & Bailey maintains its production studio, which operates under the title Hagenbeck-Wallace, in Palmetto, Florida. Like Cirque du Soleil's scene shop in Montreal, it is a self-contained facility capable of producing all the scenery, props, and décor, not only for the circus, but also the Disney ice shows produced by Feld Entertainment.

The production schedule is managed so that the shops never have to build more than one show at a time. Normally they build two new productions a year, each requiring about three months to complete. Its busiest time was when *Barnum's Kaleidoscape* was added to the schedule. For the circus, construction begins immediately following the white model meeting.

In addition to facilities for drafting, welding, creating soft sculpture (which has replaced fiberglass in most of the construction), there is a specially designed chamber where acrylic paints are sprayed onto the floats and props, as well as storage for props and vehicles used in previous productions. The philosophy here is that nothing is ever thrown away because it may prove useful in the future.

During the peak of production, September through November, thirty to thirty-two people work in the studio, some full-time; others are jobbed in, particularly painters recruited from the nearby Ringling School of Art.

Although the spec pieces built here will have a relatively short life span, the two years of each tour, everything is built to last. All of the equipment undergoes an enormous amount of stress related to travel and the peculiarities of each building. Should anything break down and need repair, the full-time staff is able to troubleshoot support over the phone or, if necessary, go out to the unit in need of help. The details of every piece of equipment are kept on computerized files. Hagenbeck-Wallace also keeps files on the parameters of every building the show plays.

Although almost all of the circus's creative people refer to Hagenbeck-Wallace in terms suggestive of magicians, the studio's staff prefers to think of itself as the people who keep things on "the level of reality."[20]

★ ★ ★

The Big Apple Circus's Creative Center is located in Walden, New York. It is far less sophisticated technically than either the Ringling or Cirque du Soleil facilities. That is because its physical productions are not as technically elaborate. As a one-ring circus, its one scenic element is the performers' entrance and bandstand.

The Center does, however, provide ample room for training and rehearsing new acts, comfortable quarters for the animals and an area where campers, caravans, and mobile homes and the people who inhabit them can have all their needs met. The entire production and creative staff, along with the artists, reside here during most of August when each new show is put together.

★ ★ ★

But the new circus must do more than nurture its artists. It must first find and train them. Prior to the last quarter of the twentieth century, circus artists were born, not made. Their training was provided by their parents, or they were apprenticed to another family to be taught a specific skill. All that changed with the new circus. Many of the contemporary circus's artists come from non-traditional backgrounds, recruited from competitive sports. Others, training specifically for a career in the circus, are products of one of the circus schools that have been founded around the world in the past quarter of a century.

For many years under the now deposed Soviet system of government, Russian circus performers, products of what came to be known as the Moscow Circus School, were considered to be the best trained in the world. While their graduates often lack the extraordinary level of skills achieved by the Russians, the system of schools supported by the French government has in recent years supplanted the Soviet schools as the most extensive in the world.

Studies conducted in France have found that young students are often involved in leisure-time circus programs for as many as ten years before becoming involved in a professional training program aimed at a career in the circus arts. As a result, France's national circus school, Centre des Arts du Cirque, located in Châlon en Champagne, is able to enroll students who may have had as much as fifteen years training in circus skills and tutoring in circus history before they get there.

The program in Châlon was put into place in 1984. What the government did at that time was to put the top of a proposed pyramid of instruction into place first. It consisted of a four-year program of study and training. Underneath it was anarchy.

Then in 1990, the programs that made up the first two of the school's four years were moved to Remy, a suburb of Paris. At that point students were provided two years of training in acting, dance, acrobatics, and a specific circus discipline in preparation to moving on to Châlon, where they would then take three more years of intensive study. The resulting five-year program thus consisted of a two-year prep school and three years of professional training.

Over the past several years, however, there has been an explosion in the popularity of circus arts among young people. As a result, seven new schools have been put into place to train people to pass the entrance exam of the two-year program that precedes the work at the school in Châlon, which can only take fifteen to eighteen new students a year. There are, however, 105 people in training programs (aside from the people who are not in formal programs) preparing to take the entrance exam.

But even that is just the tip of the circus iceberg in France. As of 2004, there were more than 500 circus schools in France. More than a hundred of these schools come under the French Federation of Circus Schools. Another 300–400 have elected not to enter the federation, which oversees such matters as the quality of hygiene and safety in the schools.

The school at Châlon is housed in a historic circus building that was first erected in 1898, one of six hard (i.e., permanent) circus buildings left in France. It was renovated especially for the school between 1983 and 1985. In addition to renovating its building, the school's program has gone through several ideological transmutations. When it first opened, the teaching staff consisted of famous circus artists, and, as a result, the school ended up being a cluster of tiny schools within the larger one. Each discipline built a school around its guru, without any real cohesion in the school's ideology. At the end of the school year, the students presented their numbers.

The annual end-of-the-year shows became what are known in the theatre world as cattle markets. All the circus producers and casting directors came to see what new talent was available. The last six months of the school year, therefore, were devoted to getting an act ready, and if anyone did not accomplish that, he tended to think his life was over, believing he would never find work in the profession.

"No one, at age twenty-two when his schooling is finished, should think that his life is over or that his creative life is going to stop there," an ex-official of the school, Tim Roberts, insists.[21]

Another problem with that practice was that the student numbers tended to be exact reproductions of those of their teachers, because the teachers only taught what they knew how to do. So the school saw the same balancing act three years in a row, because it was the same teacher. They were technically well done, but ultimately imitative.

Then, in 1990, Bernard Turin came to the school and "shook everything up." Under his leadership the mission of the school was no longer to produce circus artists who would continue a traditional art. The school's new goal was to help young people become the circus artists of tomorrow. A lot of the teachers were not in agreement with that, but the students starting bringing new ideas to their teachers.

"But," Roberts observes, "you can't get away from tradition entirely. If you were a musician you'd still have to know how to read music, play your instrument, and understand the history of music. But how you interpret these things is going to be contemporary, considering the person doing it." The same is true of the circus arts.

It took several years for everyone to accept this new attitude that Turin installed. The most significant attitude change involved the idea that the students were not artists while they were in school and were only going to start being artists when they left. So the job of the school was to give them the tools to help them become successful artists. "In an art school," Roberts points out, "you're not expected to have an exhibition the day you get your diploma, or to hang it up in an art gallery until the day you die. You leave school to become an artist, to begin your own artistic life when you get out of school, influenced by what you learned there."[22]

Instead of producing the traditional end-of-the-year show, the school began hiring a director or choreographer with a reputation for innovation, who was asked to create a new circus experience. The school does not tell this person what the show should be. The only stipulation is that the entire class must be used. Besides that, he or she is given a budget of approximately $75,000 and the keys to the building.

For three months the director and students live in a creative environment outside the bubble of the school. As long as they stay within the budget there is no interference, no spying, and no worried updates. It's a big risk for a national school, but it seems to be working, if anything too successfully, according to critics.

In the second year of this approach to producing the end-of-the-year show, the choreographer Josef Nadj was imported to create a show, which he called *Le Cri du Caméléon*. That year a producer came and said, "I'll take the whole show." Not just the individual cast members, the entire show: the concept, the cast, the physical trappings, and the staging. It toured professionally for two years, appearing in dance circles and contemporary art venues as well as before circus fans, playing more than 600 performances. That's when some people started saying, "All they are interested in doing is using government money to produce shows."[23]

Speaking of money, the French government allocates approximately $5 million a year in support of the circus. Half of that goes to the national circus schools in Châlon and Paris and the seven preparatory schools. The other half is split among all the contemporary circus companies, some of which are traditional in nature. In so doing, France became the first country in the free world that specifically allocated money to circus.[24]

Despite the welcome gesture, it is not a great deal of money, especially in comparison to other art institutions. The opera, for instance, received 800 million francs. The school's budget is roughly equivalent to what is allocated to the cleaning ladies at the Louvre. With so little money having to be divided amongst so many, turf wars tend to spring up. That, according to Roberts, accounts for the criticism leveled against the school's productions. The school, on the other hand, feels the practice is well worth the expense because the students gain a high quality, creative experience.[25]

And the school does get a lot for its money; Josef Nadj would certainly not accept work elsewhere for what the school pays him. He comes because he knows he will have a high quality, creative experience, himself. He and other choreographers are anxious to work with the school's students because the young artists bring so many more diverse talents to their work other than just dance. And they are physically capable of responding to many different demands and material.

What has been happening of late is that because of the reputation of the school's shows, creative people are vying for the opportunity to work with the students. The school is able to attract top choreographers and directors to do workshops, despite the rather low pay, because of the quality of the students with whom they can work.

Because of the grumbling from the country's professional circuses directed at the school's productions, a negotiated agreement was reached under which none of the school's productions would be allowed to play more than fifty times outside the venue of the school: three weeks in Paris, a week in Avignon, and performances in four other major cities. While they are appearing in the school show, the students still have access to its facilities if they wish to work on a résumé, take a dance class, or participate in a week's workshop. They can also come and practice between shows.

The most significant change for the students in all this is that while at the school they are no longer actively engaged in creating a number or an act. "We feel that is the student's responsibility," Roberts says. The school is there only to prepare them to take up that responsibility. "For us, even putting on the show is a training experience like everything else," he says.

"We never talk about getting a number, because it tends to make the kids flip out, as if their life depended upon having a number together by the time they graduate. So what we do is work on technical routines and do exercises in style. We might try forty-eight different ways of doing the same routine. We pick out various styles from videotapes. That way they don't get stuck in a routine. The skills will have been in place for months by the time they graduate; the form they choose to cast them will take just a few weeks to take shape. All the styles are in their bag of tricks if they want to use any of them."

This really amounts to looking at circus artists in an entirely new way. Can circus performers be considered true artists if they develop one act and then never change it for the rest of their professional lives? According to the French, the creative process should be ongoing. "We want them to be able to create," Roberts says. "We don't want them to repeat or be trapped at all."[26]

Obviously a show created by someone outside the school makes it difficult to evaluate each of the students fully, fairly, and accurately. As a result, the students are required, in addition to their participation in the end-of-the-year show, to perform a presentation of their own devising, which is judged by the entire teaching staff and several invited experts. These presentations are evaluated on both their technical and artistic merits, in much the same way that Olympic athletes are scored in certain sports. If one fails to live up to certain standards, he or she will be given a certificate of attendance rather than a diploma. This happens less and less often because of an ongoing winnowing process at each level of development.

Each performance discipline has two people on its jury, one of whom is known for his or her artistry, the other for technical merit. So there will be one sports person and one circus person watching the same family of disciplines. "We're trying to avoid having someone cover up technical deficiency with artistic ability," Roberts explains.

"The diploma, therefore, is awarded in two phases. In July the students must demonstrate their technical ability. There is more emphasis on the technical ability than the artistic at that time because the students make up the presentations themselves. Then in December they present the show they have been preparing with a guest director. That way if the director pushes the technical aspects to the side we still have a way of judging it." Although students may fail to receive a diploma if they are judged to be technically deficient, they are not excluded from the final show, where they may stand out artistically.

Getting to the final point of evaluation is a rigorous process in itself. Along with their chosen discipline the students study dance, music (all must play at least one musical instrument), and even take thirty-five hours a year in the study of English. Each morning is spent working on the various aspects of the students' specialties. In the afternoon, they have acting and dance workshops, and they are constantly evaluated in order to give the staff an overall insight into what each student is about and his or her capacity to perform a particular discipline creatively. That goes on for five days a week.

The school's goal is to train people to be able to work with contemporary creators, or, if they choose, create their own shows. That doesn't mean the door is closed to tradition. "We don't train people to do traditional acts," Roberts explains. "We train them so they can do whatever kind of circus they want. We want to produce highly trained people who could work in any style."[27]

With the retirement of Bernard Turin in 2002, however, the Châlon school has faced a somewhat uncertain future, insofar as its artistic philosophy is concerned, and possibly its place in the hierarchy of French circus schools. The first of these questions is, of course, a result of a change in leadership; the second because of the opening in 2003 of the Fratellini school. Unlike the Châlon center, the Fratellini installation has a dual vocation, mostly because of financing. Part of it is recreational, and the other, the smaller segment, is purely professional.

Established in 1971 by Annie Fratellini, the granddaughter of Paul Fratellini, the school, by virtue of its founder's roots in traditional circus (she is the fourth generation of one of Europe's most illustrious circus families), has always been more mindful of tradition than are the people at Châlon. Paul Fratellini, Annie's brother, is the current president of the organization that administers the school. Its professional program is completely endorsed by the government, putting it into the extraordinary position of being able to pay its students, since they are considered to be in an apprenticeship, and French law requires that apprentices be paid. Imagine such a system in the United States.

The recreational students, on the other hand, must pay for their instruction, and this amounts to the largest source of independently realized revenue.

The new building is most extraordinary, constructed entirely of wood, most of which came from the trees destroyed at Versailles by the tornado of 2001. The facility boasts three big gymnasiums, any one of which is capable of supporting a flying trapeze rig, which, of all aerial acts, requires the most space. Most amazing of all is a performance space formed in the traditional circle, but outfitted with the most sophisticated contemporary technical equipment. Dance studios, a sauna room, gymnastic apparatus room, three workshops for metal and woodworking and costumes, offices, and stables complete this amazing structure dedicated to training circus artists. But it is unique in other ways, beyond its design. The heating system, which, instead of heating the room, heats the bodies in it, is very economical, and much of the power is generated by solar energy.

The finances for the new building were raised by the Fratellini organization itself, which is why they built it so efficiently and so economically. The operating budget, however, is heavily subsidized, with government money. "You don't do anything in France without government subsidy."[28]

Another approach to training is found in Canada's École Nationale de Cirque (ENC), founded in 1980. In 2000, Marc Lalonde became the director of the Canadian school, coming to the circus from the worlds of dance and music. Trained as a classical dancer, he performed professionally with both classical and contemporary dance companies and eventually earned an MBA from the University of Montreal in arts administration. His studies included the evolution of cultural policies in Canada and abroad and research on trends in cultural management.

At the time Lalonde came aboard, the ENC was at a point in its own development where it knew it needed to grow, both in the number of students it serves and in the diversity of programs it can offer. To do that, it had to find new sources of funding.

Currently it is funded by both the federal government and, to a greater extent, the provincial government, receiving funds from both the province's educational and cultural departments. In the past there have been few to no contributions from private sources. To increase its projects, many of which were already planned by the past director, extra funding was essential. Hence, Lalonde's appointment. He is notably experienced in the art of fund-raising.

The school moved into its new facility, directly across the street from Cirque du Soleil's international headquarters and in the heart of what has come to be known (in English) as Circus City, in November of 2003. This multilevel structure occupies 77,000 sq. feet, which is about three times larger than its previous quarters, where it had been from its inauguration almost fourteen years earlier.

In addition to the professional level of training offered, the school also has a preparatory program and a recreational program. Admission to all programs, but for the recreational, is by audition. The recreational program, however, will soon provide a service to another of the school's offerings, a training program for instructors in training. The goal of this program is to train the future trainers who can safely teach circus skills in a variety of situations, thereby filling a great need in the circus industry, because very few performers who retire become trainers and very few of these people are trained pedagogically to become effective teachers.

This year-long program will have two levels, the first aimed at training those who will teach circus arts to kids in a recreational context or in a social intervention program. The second level is intended to train those who will work in professional preparatory and superior schools. "Hopefully we will increase the quality and qualifications of trainers who are already working in circus schools, as well as the number of trainers that are available so that circus schools could be set up in cities where now there are none," says Lalonde. "For us this program is very much strategic because in order to attract good applicants who are well-prepared, we need for those applicants to be well-trained in preparatory schools."[29]

In addition to this new program, the school is hoping to attract and accommodate more students without lowering the level of entrance. Current enrollment is about ninety students, exclusive of the recreational program. That number was expected to rise to 110 within a year of opening the new facility. Twenty-five applicants are accepted in the first year and, on average, seventeen to twenty graduate from the three-year program. "No other circus school in the world that we know of graduates that many," boasts Lalonde. Even France's national school graduates fewer, about thirteen a year. In 2004, there were sixty-seven young artists enrolled in the highest level, or professional, program.

For those enrolled in the high school program (also a preparatory program), the school must provide, as mandated by the provincial education department, the entire secondary school curriculum. The number of students in this program is small because teenagers are not yet ready to make the necessary commitment.

A new program planned for the graduates of the professional program is a three-month workshop in which the participants will be involved in the process of creating a new show with a director or choreographer. They will have created their own acts by this time, and these may or may not be used, or not used in their entirety in this new work, "so it's another type of experience in which they will work as both creator and interpreter," Lalonde adds.[30]

A part of the program that had to be curtailed in the school's former home, because of space limitations, was the professional advancement program wherein graduates and other professionals were able to return and work on enhancing a particular skill or refining their act under the tutelage of several specialists. Within the new building there are now several studios that will be devoted exclusively to such work.

In addition, a studio on the fourth level of the building has been designed to be available to any professionals. It is reserved for individuals who wish to work by themselves without a trainer or for creative residencies. It has been designed mainly for acrobatic work, but it is possible to do almost anything here, including aerials. The use fee is just one dollar per hour.

"For us it's an advantage," Lalonde says, "because our students will always be connected to professionals. They can see them through the studio's window. It's a way for us to inspire our former students to come back here and perhaps teach or give workshops."[31]

Other facilities include the main training studio, which includes a foam pit and a fast track. Clustered about it are a number of smaller studios for acting, dance, clowning, and physical conditioning. On the same level there is ample space for costume storage and workshops for students who wish to design and/or build a prototype for an accessory or a prop. A library, open to the public as well as students, is located on the sixth level.

At its opening in 2003, the school employed ten full-time instructors, whose expertise is supplemented by many other specialists who work on a part-time basis. Most of those who teach circus techniques are full-time.

Students are expected to arrive at a professional level in their chosen skill area, as well as display a high level of accomplishment in all five skill families: acrobatics, aerials, balance techniques, clowning, and manipulation.

In addition to preparing its students to work professionally in the international circus, the school also provides them with the expertise to be successful in finding funding for any creative project they would like to pursue. Realizing that its students will be competing for such funding with dance and theatre students who have studied at universities, and because the school is anxious to have the circus arts recognized as a real form of art as noble as all other forms, "we are trying to give them the tools to defend their projects," Lalonde says.[32]

Since a circus artist can expect to work anywhere in the world, information on the school's application forms is presented in both French and English, as are its website and brochures. "There is no reason why language should put anyone off," Lalonde insists. "We offer foreign students immersion classes in French so they can understand the instruction, and we encourage them in the last summer before coming here to take a French course. The good thing is they come out of the school with a second language. It's a test for them. Are they ready to travel? Are they ready for an international profession? If you are not ready to learn another language, to leave your hometown and family, then perhaps the circus is not for you."

One final consideration: Montreal, Lalonde points out, is a relatively inexpensive city and the affordable apartments are passed along, like a legacy, from one generation of students to the next.[33]

★ ★ ★

Although there has been a growing tradition of circus training at the grassroots level in America, until recently there has been little effort to encourage the participants of these programs to become professional circus artists. It is generally thought that the reason for that is the low esteem with which the circus profession has previously been held in this country. But there are other problems, practical concerns that have little to do with perceptions. The physical size of America makes it very difficult for one school to draw students from all areas of the country. The travel and subsequent living expenses for such students would be prohibitive. As a result, in contrast to the French model of putting the top of the pyramid in place before the base, America has only a base. And it is diffuse, disorganized, undirected, and truncated.

This is certainly not intended as a criticism of the grassroots programs; it is simply to say that there has been, for a very long time, almost nothing at the top of the pyramid, nationally, toward which the most talented participants can direct their work. America's first thought of a national circus school came from the founders of the Big Apple Circus. Part of their original vision was the goal of establishing a conservatory, much like that of the New York Ballet, to work in conjunction with the performance unit. The costs of creating such a program were such that the circus's founders never even came close to finding adequate funding for this part of their dream.

Is it any wonder then that an enterprise that started out calling itself the National Circus School of Performing Arts eventually changed its name to Circus Sarasota? Although a professional training program is still a long-range goal, its cofounders, Dolly Jacobs and Pedro Reis, have discovered (as have the Canadians) that a talent for fund-raising is at least equally as important as a talent for the circus arts. Like the founders of the Big Apple Circus, Reis and Jacobs have had far more success in producing circus performances than they have had in finding students for a projected national school.

The closest America has come to offering a professional program with a national constituency is San Francisco's Circus Center and its training program, the San Francisco School of Circus Arts. The vision for the school was set down in 1985 by Judy Finelli and Wendy Parkman. It was their goal to create a professional training program feeding talent into a professional performing troupe. Finelli is still very closely involved. She works with the clowns in Jeff Raz's Clown Conservatory, and Parkman directs here occasionally, providing a rare sense of continuity and commitment as the school moves closer to achieving its original mission.

What has distinguished the program from the beginning and proven to be its major magnet is that its training and instruction are headed by a world-class artist, Lu Yi, who is capable of guiding students in many different acrobatic disciplines. In addition to Lu Yi, the school can also boast of "four of the best Chinese acrobatics teachers outside of China" and its contortionist instructor, Sirchmaa Byamba from Mongolia.[34] And with its newly negotiated partnership with the New Pickle Circus, the San Francisco school may become the first program in America to realize the ambition of having a conservatory program feeding talent directly into a professional circus company.

The executive director of the San Francisco School of Circus Arts, which is the principal constituent of the Circus Center, is Pat Osbon. He comes to the circus through a rather circuitous route. His first job was as an administrative aide in the United States Senate. Tiring of that, but still interested in what he calls "lefty" politics, he was drawn to political theatre, and inevitably the San Francisco Mime Troupe, which he served as executive director until Tandy Beal, then artistic director of the Pickle Family Circus, asked him to come work for her. It was through that association that he became familiar with the San Francisco School of Circus Arts.

As it happened people connected with both organizations were, at the time, beginning to talk of a merger, and Osbon was instrumental in helping to raise the money to make that happen. When it did, in 1999, he took up his present position.

By 2003, the school's annual budget was $1.8 million, having quadrupled in the four years since the merger. About a third of that money comes from tuition. Another 20 percent is earned from other sources such as student fees, corporate performances, and individual user fees. The remainder is contributed.

Tuition, at that time, was $17 an hour. Students could earn discounts for multiple classes that maxed out at 20 percent, allowing a student to take three classes for about $13.50 an hour. The number of hours a student might elect to spend in training depended upon his or her goals. If these were merely recreational, the student might only be in attendance for an hour or an hour and a half a week. Professionally oriented students would take twenty hours of classes a week. Those enrolled in the Clown Conservatory must spend thirty-nine weeks at the school and, as a result, are eligible for the school's very generous scholarship/work study program. Very few clowns have been able to afford the $4,000 to $4,500 tuition.

The students who work with Lu Yi, the school's renowned master teacher of Chinese acrobatics, average six to eight hours a week of training directly under his supervision. They do not pay for the time they spend at the school training on their own, but they are required to pay for their insurance and an individual user fee. With the students creating their own schedules, coming and going as they choose, the structure is obviously rather loose.

In 2004, the school's training was augmented by theatre classes given by Dan Chumley, who used to be the director of the Mime Troupe. Despite such opportunities for further study, the school does not currently provide a training program that corresponds with what would be done in Moscow, or even

Montreal. The closest it comes to that is with its Clown Conservatory, a two-year program that, for the 2004–2005 session, drew seventeen students from eight states, France, the Czech Republic, and Switzerland.

In 2003, Dominque Jando left his position as associate artistic director of the Big Apple Circus and was brought to San Francisco to establish a full-fledged professional program. A year later he had developed the curriculum and syllabus for the program and contacted several internationally known trainers to become instructors. Unfortunately the presumed funding never materialized and the program's timetable, according to Osbon, was moved back, and Jando departed.[35]

When he first arrived in San Francisco, the French circus historian saw the professional program and the Pickle Circus working hand in glove. "Another project is to revive the Pickles as a tenting show, a real circus, not one on stage," he insisted at that time. According to Jando, providing the physical facility required to accomplish that goal needed to become another of the Center's future priorities.[36]

Obviously, a major hurdle in all this was funding. In the matter of attracting qualified and talented students, an ongoing concern is the cost of housing. Everyone acknowledges the difficulty for students in having to come to San Francisco and paying tuition as well as rent, especially when they can currently go to Montreal or some place in Europe where there is heavy government subsidy to help ease the financial burden. To combat that, Osbon says, "One of the things that we have got to do is raise an endowment so we can offer scholarships to draw students here. We are never going to have government subsidy to the extent Montreal or Europe does," he acknowledges, "but we do have an opportunity here to raise money for an endowment. Being a unique circus organization in the United States with Lu Yi here and the professional training programs that we want to establish and offer here, I think we can raise money nationwide to support scholarships for special students."

To do that, a development person was hired in 2004 to work with the staff in raising funds on the local level. Before taking any fund-raising campaign to a national level, however, the school and Center acknowledge that they must first burnish their reputation at home. "We're just now starting to gain local recognition for the quality of the programs we offer," Osbon believes. "People have been aware of the Pickles for many years. It was thirty years old in 2003. The local population hasn't put the Pickles and the school or the Circus Center together, but as we continue to do more performances, more community outreach, we are beginning to draw the attention of funders and people here in San Francisco and the Greater Bay area."[37]

At the present time the Pickles present an annual performance during the holiday season. "Our plans," Osbon says, "are to reestablish the Pickles here on the West Coast, touring from Seattle to San Diego. That is a long-range plan. We don't have the staffing, the infrastructure to support that kind of tour yet, so we're doing what the Pickles have done for most of the past six or seven years, which is to do a Bay area holiday show and a brief tour."

The Center's community outreach includes working with many groups in the community to teach circus arts to at-risk youth, teenaged girls abused in their relationships with boyfriends, and to battered women and their kids. "It's amazing to see how learning circus skills helps critical thinking skills by building self-confidence, and self esteem," Peggy Ford, the Center's program director, points out. "There are also plans for a new program in partnership with the Summerbridge Program in San Francisco to teach circus skills to exceptionally talented students whose public schools are failing them because of cuts in their own arts programs."

A graduate of Ringling's Clown College, Ford came to the school from Make-a-Circus, where she was the artistic director, directing and writing shows and inaugurating the teen apprentice program. "We got into the building here," she recalls, "because we were good friends with Wendy [Parkman, the school's cofounder] and Lu Yi at a time when Make-A-Circus needed a place, and the school let us move in." Since her programs are separate from the instruction, "There's lots of variety." Her other areas of concern are the various scholarships and work/study programs. "I want to make sure it's not about the money," she concludes. Many of the younger students work off the cost of their training by appearing with the Circus Center's Youth Circus.

"We just want to see good circus people get the training they need. At a certain point it becomes a question of being able to afford the training. The better you get, the more training you need, and the longer you can train, the harder the tricks you can do, and the more you need of Lu Yi."[38]

In addition to building an endowment, the school and Circus Center are preparing to undertake a campaign to raise capital for a new facility. "But this is all down the road a ways," Osbon admits, "but we've got the time. Look at the rapid growth we've had over the last four years, and [the fact that] we've never incurred a deficit here. Our fund balance has gone from $64K to over $400K." That, he believes, demonstrates sustained, responsible growth. "And if we continue to project that into the future I have no doubt we will be able to [reach our goals]."[39]

In 2004, there were approximately 900 students involved in the school's various programs. That included close to 400 students in the summer circus camp, which runs weekly camps for ten weeks. The vast majority of the students are, therefore, recreational. Including the clowns, there are between fifty and sixty professionally oriented students. That number, it should be pointed out, is comparable to any of the major circus schools in the world.

The school had a roster of about forty instructors in 2004, including half a dozen flying trapeze instructors and those who offer training in trampoline, clowning, and contortion. The instructors' time at the school varies. Some instructors will only be there for two or three hours a week, but these people teach highly specific skills, as for instance the Mongolian contortionist who has no more than a dozen students. Lu Yi and his staff are at the school full-time. Additional Chinese instructors, identified by Lu Yi, were scheduled to join the faculty before the end of 2005.[40]

Another significant step the school and Circus Center have taken toward the realization of their goals of a new building and a professional program is the revitalization of their Board of Directors. For many years, in lieu of a professional staff, the board had been made up of students who were involved in the school's day-to-day management. In the past few years, however, the board has come to be made up of new people from outside the organization who have connections to new communities and funding sources. The financial requirement for board membership is a minimum contribution of $1,000 along with a commitment to raise another $5,000. This has not proven to be a stumbling block.

In an effort to move forward, the school has also begun seeking accreditation through the National Association of Schools of Theatre. This, of course, would give its programs greater legitimacy and some degree of official status within the educational community. "It's a long process," Osbon points outs, "but when we have the professional program established, the students enrolled in it will have the ability to get low-cost government student loans. It will also help with immigration issues for both students and guest teachers." Accreditation will also help in getting funding from the National Endowment for the Arts. Osbon is proud of the fact that his first proposal submitted to the NEA was successful. It helped fund the Clown Conservatory and has continued to provide support ever since.[41]

★ ★ ★

Meanwhile, on the other side of the world, Jane Mullett, the past director of training for Australia's renowned youth program, the Flying Fruit Fly Circus, spent three months of 1992 touring China, Russia, and Europe, looking at circus schools, a Winston Churchill scholarship as her benefactor. What she saw, she says, "was absolutely eye opening," especially in comparison to what there was in Australia at that time.

"I came back convinced that we needed to start a school," and to make her resolve even more firm Cirque du Soleil stepped in, somewhat surprisingly, to provide further inspiration. Following a visit from Guy Laliberté, an offer came, out of the blue, to fly Mullett and one of the other members of the Flying Fruit Flies, courtesy of Cirque du Soleil, to Santa Monica to see the company's new production, *Saltimbanco*. From there it was off to Las Vegas to see *Nouvelle Experience* and then to Montreal to see what was happening there.[42]

Back home in 1993, Mullett, with the help of fellow Fruit Flies staffers Elizabeth Walsh and John Paxinos, convened a national conference "to ask everybody how they felt about my going about getting a circus school started," she says with a laugh, as amused with her own audacity as she was sure her audience was as well. That anyone came at all is a testament to the reputation she had built within the Australian circus community, among both the traditional and the new circuses. "There has always been a very strong sense in Australia, even though the links at times have been difficult, that the new circus movement would not have started without the traditional circus sharing skills. There has always been, in spite of differences in ideas and a whole lot of other differences, an understanding of the similarities of what we have in common. So we've always invited each other to our shows. We're all different parts of the same life. We just have different ways of expressing it."

The consensus of that exploratory meeting, Mullett says, with the same air of amusement at the slightly patronizing pat-on-the-head tone of it all, was, "Well, Jane, if you want it, if you really think we should start a circus school, go right ahead." But that was enough of a mandate for her to spend the next six years working on making it happen.

She began by ringing up the Australia Arts Council and asking for the funding needed to do a feasibility study. They advised her that she really needed to find an educational outlet with which to affiliate herself, which she immediately did by taking a job running Swinburne University's fee-for-service program for the arts.

But even from this position, "it took a long time to get people to understand what was involved, even though I had videos." She argued that the program should be a three-year degree course. There was to be an academic component, but mostly it was hands-on technical. "It seemed to me that if people like Mel Gibson were coming out of courses like NIDA [The National Institute of Dramatic Arts], we needed to produce as high a level of circus. It also seemed to me that we already had enough community circus, and if we had the top level [following the French thinking], the middle level would fill itself out."

The rest of the world had already set up massive circus schools, and Mullett believed "we had a window of opportunity to make sure that Australians were able to compete on a technical level as well as a cultural level in the world. That was really the push behind NICA [National Institute of Circus Arts], to make sure that Australia and its long circus tradition was not left behind."[43]

There was, obviously, a method to Mullett's having dubbed the proposed school with a name that sounded like and formed an anagram not unlike the prestigious dramatic arts academy. She wanted to put the two into the same category and borrow a bit of the older school's cachet. "The argument," she continues, "was that circus in Australia was as important culturally as dance and theatre, and if we could get it funded through the federal arts body, it would do a number of things. It would signal that the Australian cultural landscape considered circus an important art form. It would give it a prestigious stream of funding (not without its problems), and it would keep the school from being completely subsumed within the university. The university contributes a great deal of its resources, but the school has its own board of directors, the majority of which are associated with Swinburne University."[44]

Those six years, between the time of Mullett's national circus convocation and the funding of the school, were spent knocking on government doors and lobbying. Finally it took Cirque du Soleil's coming to town to provide the final push. "When Cirque du Soleil came through," she says, "people saw what was possible."

But of course the university's efforts cannot be discounted. The idea was taken to the university's vice chancellor, Iain Wallace by Pam Creed. "They really backed it; they backed me to go up to the capital, Canberra, to lobby," Mullett says. "They provided a consultant to help me scope the Australian industry and put together a five-year budget. The university also set up an advisory group to oversee the development of the project. Creed was on that advisory board and acted as manager at various stages of the project until she took it over as director. The school is still connected to the university, but it is a stand-alone unit, funded directly by the federal government through the Department of Communications, Information Technology and the Arts, just as is NIDA.

"So it was my vision and Pam's tenacity and know-how on the ground, particularly with Technical and Further Education (TAFE), since NICA straddled both higher education and TAFE. And besides all that, there were many members of the circus and theatre industry who wrote letters that Mullett characterizes as 'amazingly supportive.'"[45]

The school was officially incorporated in 1999, delivering Australia's first Bachelor of Circus Arts. It also provides preparatory programs for people who wish to audition for the degree program, as well as training for those already in the profession, all in a new, especially designed facility.[46]

"Once people picked up the idea, once other people armed the project, it didn't need my vision anymore. I passed my vision on. I got to a point where my vision had been taken up by a whole lot of other people who then went about the practicalities of actually setting it up," Mullett says with a mixture of satisfaction and disappointment.

NICA graduated its first class of circus artists in 2003.

★ ★ ★

The existence of these and other circus schools and training programs in the United States and around the world, The Circus Space in London, for instance, guarantee that the contemporary circus will always be well stocked with innovative artists and an inexhaustible creative energy, and the concepts that the new circus movement has brought to the contemporary circus will prevail.

NOTES

1. The author's personal tour of Cirque du Soleil international headquarters, Montreal, Canada, August 20, 1998.

2. Patrice Aubertin, personal interview with the author, Montreal, Canada, August 20, 1998.

3. Aubertin interview.

4. Lyn Heward, personal interview with the author, Montreal, Canada, August 20, 1998.

5. Pavel Brun, personal interview with the author, Las Vegas, October 21, 1998.

6. Brun interview.

7. Brun interview.

8. Brun interview.

9. Witek Biegaj, personal interview with the author, Orlando, Fla., July 20, 2000.

10. Brun interview.

11. Karen Gay, personal interview with the author, Las Vegas, June 26, 2002.

12. Gay interview.

13. Gay interview.

14. Eric Heppell, personal interview with the author, Las Vegas, 26 June 2002.

15. Heppell interview.

16. Heppell interview.

17. Heppell interview.

18. Nancy Mallette, personal interview with the author, Las Vegas, June 26, 2002.

19. Mallette interview.

20. The author's personal tour of the Hagenbeck-Wallace studio, Palmetto, Fla., January 25, 2001.

21. Tim Roberts, personal interview with the author, Châlon en Champagne, France, July 7, 1999.

22. Roberts interview.

23. Roberts interview.

24. Belgium and Great Britain have recently joined the ranks of those nations providing support for the circus arts. In both cases this has been accomplished by funding college-degree programs as part of the national university curriculum. L'Ecole

Superior des Arts du Cirque in Brussels and the Circus Space in London both receive considerable financial support for their advanced degree programs.

25. Roberts interview.

26. Roberts interview.

27. Roberts interview.

28. Dominique Jando, personal interview with the author, San Francisco, June 13, 2003.

29. Marc Lalonde, personal interview with the author, Montreal, Canada, June 3, 2004.

30. Lalonde interview.

31. Lalonde interview.

32. Lalonde interview.

33. Lalonde interview.

34. Pat Osbon, personal interview with the author, San Francisco, June 13, 2003.

35. Osbon interview.

36. Jando interview.

37. Osbon interview.

38. Peggy Ford, personal interview with the author, San Francisco, June 13, 2003.

39. Osbon interview.

40. Osbon interview.

41. Osbon interview.

42. Jane Mullett, personal interview with the author, New York, July 30, 2003.

43. Mullett interview.

44. Mullett interview.

45. Mullett interview.

46. Bob Burton. "An Australian Circus Dream Comes True," *Spectacle* (Spring 2001): 49–50.

Bibliography

PUBLISHED SOURCES

Albrecht. Ernest. "Splashy Circus Spectacular a Treat for One, All," *Home News*, April 2, 1969, 23.

———. "Gebel-Williams Makes a Circus a CIRCUS," *Home News*, March 27, 1975, 16.

———. "Cirque du Soleil Builds a Spectacular Shangi-La," *Spectacle*, Fall 1998, 22–26.

———. "Can an All-Aerial Circus Fly?" *Spectacle*, Summer 1999, 34–35.

———. "Bartabas, Listening to Horses," *Spectacle*, Winter 1999.

———. "A Bunch of Clowns Get Serious," *Spectacle*, Summer 2001, 8.

Beal, Tandy. "Weaving It all Together," *Spectacle*, Spring 1999, 17.

Burton, Bob. "An Australian Circus Dream Comes True," *Spectacle*, Spring 2001, 49–50.

Cirque du Soleil. *O* press packet.

Conrad, Charles P. "The Sawdust Music Man," *Spectacle*, Spring 2000, 7–9.

Gladstone, Valerie. "Everything Is Danceable?" *New York Times*, March 21, 2001, AR 12.

Holland, Bernard. "Taking a Cue from Pictures to Modern Dance and the Circus," *New York Times*, December 30, 2004, E5.

Jando, Dominique. "The Master Builder of Circus Acts," *Spectacle*, Spring 1998, 16–17.

———. Production Notes, Big Apple Circus, August 4, 1999, to July 16, 2000.

Jecko, Timothy. "Brigitte Larochelle Brings a New Brand of Music to the Big Apple," *Spectacle*, Spring 2000, 12–13.

Kelly, Emmett. *Clown*. New York: Prentice Hall, 1954.

LaBalme, Corrine. "The Dancing Horses of Versailles," *New York Times*, March 2, 2003, TR 3.

Lorant, Terry, and Jon Carroll. *The Pickle Family Circus*. San Francisco: The Pickle Press, 1986.

MacKinnon, Cecil. "Collaboration is the Name of the Game," *Spectacle*, Spring 1999, 15.

McGill, Stewart. "Introducing the Alchemist," *Spectacle*, Fall 2002, 49.

————. "When East Meets West It Is to the Music of Violaine Corradi," *Spectacle*, Spring 2000, 14–15.

O Press conference, Las Vegas, October 21, 1998.

Pogrebin, Robin. "How Cowboys and Cowgirls Get Into Step," *New York Times*, March 1, 2002, E1, E8.

Riding, Alan. "Using the Horse to Hold a Mirror to the Human," *New York Times*, September 6, 1998, 20.

Schechter, Joel. "Training Clowns for a New Circus," *Spectacle*, Summer 2001, 38–39.

Schiffman, Jean. "Spotlight on Tandy Beal," *Dance Teacher Now*, October 1994, 36–45.

Seldes, Gilbert. *The Seven Lively Arts*. New York: Harper and Brothers, 1924.

Severo, Richard. "Gunther Gebel-Williams, Circus Animal Trainer, Dies at 66," *New York Times*, July 20, 2001, B7.

Sugarman, Robert. "Alla Youdina, Weaving New Webs," *Spectacle*, Fall 2000, 26–28.

Third World Convention of Circus Directors. *Music and Circus Directing*. Paris, France: January 16, 1995.

Wadler, Joyce. "Still Bringing Out the Animal, and Animals," *New York Times*, April 9, 1999, B2.

PERSONAL INTERVIEWS

Antoine, Didier. April 19, 2003, Las Vegas, Nev.

Aubertin, Patrice. August 2, 1998, Montreal, Canada.

Bennett, LeRoy. September 15, 2003, Atlantic City, N.J.

Biegaj, Witek. 1. August 20, 1998, Montreal, Canada. 2. July 20, 2000, Orlando, Fla.

Brown, Debra. May 14, 2003. Montreal, Canada.

Brun, Pavel. October 21, 1998, Las Vegas, Nev.

Caron, Guy. August 28, 1997, Walden, N.Y.

Christensen, Michael. March 9, 1999, New York, N.Y.

Cutler, Miriam. May 21, 2000, St. Louis, Mo.

DeRitis, Raffaele. 1. March 6, 1999, Sarasota, Fla. 2. March 7, 1999, Sarasota, Fla. 3. May 1, 1999, Los Angeles, Calif. 4. June 4, 1999 (e-mail).

DeSanto, Greg and Karen. July 9, 2001, Baraboo, Wis.

Dragone, Franco. April 1, 1999 (telephone).

Feld, Kenneth. May 10, 1999 (telephone). 2. April 5, 2000 (telephone). 3. March 31, 2001, New York, N.Y. 4. September 17, 2001, Vienna, Va.

Ford, Peggy. June 13, 2003, San Francisco, Calif.

Gay, Karen. June 26, 2002, Las Vegas, Nev.

Gebel, Sigrid. September 21, 2001 (telephone).

Gillett, Eric Michael. October 4, 1998, New York, N.Y.

Gneushev, Valentin. March 15, 2001, New York, N.Y., translator Elena Panova.

Golovko, Vilen. November 14, 1998, Reno, Nev.

Greenberg, Julie. January 26, 1999, Chicago, Ill.

Gruss, Stephan. July 8, 1999, Orange, France.

Heiden, Aurelie. July 20, 2000, Orlando, Fla.

Heppell, Eric. June 26, 2002, Las Vegas, Nev.

Heward, Lyn. Montreal, Canada. 1. August 20, 1998. 2. May 15, 2001.

Holst, Tim. 1. May 1, 1999, Los Angeles, Calif. 2. April 1, 2001, New York, N.Y.

Hudes, Linda. March 16, 2000 (telephone).

Jacob, Pascal. 1. May 2, 1999, Los Angeles, Calif. 2. July 13, 2002, Milwaukee, Wis.

Jacobs, Dolly. 1. August 5, 2000, Sarasota, Fla. 2. August 7, 2000 (telephone).

Jacobs, Lou. April 27, 1983, New York, N.Y.

Jando, Dominique. June 13, 2003, San Francisco, Calif.

Jenkins, Jeff. January 26, 1999, Chicago, Ill.

Lafortune, Luc. May 14, 2003, Montreal, Canada.

Lalonde, Marc. December 13, 1999 (telephone).

Larible, David. March 7, 2002, East Rutherford, N.J.

Lubin, Barry. 1. November 8, 1998, New York, N.Y. 2. December 11, 1998, New York, N.Y.

MacKinnon, Cecil. May 21, 2000, St. Louis, Mo.

Mallette, Nancy. June 26, 2002, Las Vegas, Nev.

McKinley, Philip. April 9, 2001, Edison, N.J.

Mullett, Jane. July 30, 2003, New York, N.Y.

Nock, Bello. April 1, 2001, New York, N.Y.

Osbon, Patrick. June 14, 2003, San Francisco, Calif.

Pisoni, Larry. June 2, 1995, Charleston, S.C.

Polunin, Slava. April 12, 1995, New York, N.Y.

Ragatz, Steve. January 4, 2003 (telephone).

Raz, Jeff. March 12, 2001, San Francisco, Calif.

Ricotta, Anthony G. April 19, 2003, Las Vegas, Nev.

Roberts, Tim. July 7, 1999, Chalon, France.

Shiner, David. December 6, 2000, New York, N.Y.

Slater, Glenn. March 20, 2000 (telephone).

Smith, Craig Paul. April 19, 2003, Las Vegas, Nev.

Smith, Steve. 1. January 27, 2001, Sarasota, Fla. 2. March 29, 2001, New York, N.Y.

Starobin, Michael. March 20, 2000 (telephone).

Youdina, Alla. 1. April 7, 1998, New York, N.Y. 2. April 1, 2001, New York, N.Y.

Zerbini, Sylvia. 1. March 6, 1999, Sarasota, Fla. 2. September 29, 2001, West Springfield, Mass. 3. November 12, 2001, Williston, Fla.

Index

About the Author

Ernest Albrecht is the founder of *Spectacle*, a quarterly journal devoted to the circus arts, which he now serves as editor/publisher. This unique publication enjoys an international subscription base that includes all the major circus schools, libraries, and museums around the world, including the libraries of major American universities, New York City, and Bibliotheque Nationale de France.

For twenty-eight years he was the theatre critic for the New Brunswick (N.J.) *Home News*. During that time he published more than 3,500 reviews of New York, London, and regional theatres and interviewed numerous personalities ranging from Judy Garland to Liza Minnelli and Pablo Casals to Gunther Gebel-Williams.

He has published articles in *Time, Variety, Theatre Crafts, Bandwagon, Grit, Circus Report, Le Cirque dans l'Univers, Planet Circus,* and *Circus Zeitung.* He has also contributed several biographies of circus artists to Oxford University Press's *American Biography,* the entry devoted to circus in *The Encyclopedia of American Folk Art,* and *L'Annuaire Théâtral 32: Cirque et théâtralité nouvelles pistes.*

His previous book, *The New American Circus,* published by the University Press of Florida, has won worldwide recognition and is considered to be one of the most important books on the American circus published in the past twenty-five years. His first book, *A Ringling by Any Other Name—The Story of John Ringling North and His Circus,* published by Scarecrow Press, was hailed as "a major contribution to the scholarship of the modern American circus."

He has lectured on various aspects of the circus at the Circus World Museum and the Ringling Museum of Art.

For fifteen years, from 1973 to 1985, he was producing director of Plays-in-the-Park, an outdoor musical theatre that was the springboard for many performers, designers, and directors.

Albrecht earned his BS degree from Rutgers University in 1959, winning the award for outstanding contribution to university dramatics in his senior year. His MA in theatre is from Northwestern University in 1960, where he also completed postgraduate work in theatre under a University Fellowship in 1964.

He taught composition at Middlesex County College from 1967 to 2005. He has also taught dramatic criticism at Rutgers and Princeton Universities.